Corporate Sustainability

Founded in 1807, John Wiley & Sons is the oldest independent publishing company in the United States. With offices in North America, Europe, Asia, and Australia, Wiley is globally committed to developing and marketing print and electronic products and services for our customers' professional and personal knowledge and understanding.

The Wiley Corporate F&A series provides information, tools, and insights to corporate professionals responsible for issues affecting the profitability of their company, from accounting and finance to internal controls and performance management.

Corporate Sustainability

Integrating Performance and Reporting

ANN M. BROCKETT

ZABIHOLLAH REZAEE

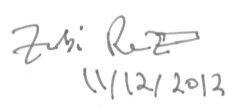

To: David Feit

Zubi Rez

11/12/2013

WILEY

John Wiley & Sons, Inc.

Library of Congress Cataloging-in-Publication Data:
Brockett, Anne.
    Corporate sustainability : integrating performance and reporting / Anne Brockett, Zabihollah Rezaee.
        p. cm. — (The Wiley corporate F&A series)
    Includes bibliographical references and index.
    ISBN 978-1-118-12236-5 (cloth); ISBN 978-1-118-22471-7 (ebk);
    ISBN 978-1-118-23806-6 (ebk); ISBN 978-1-118-26279-5 (ebk)
  1. Sustainable development reporting. 2. Sustainable development—Economic aspects.
  3. Sustainable development—Accounting. I. Rezaee, Zabihollah, 1953- II. Title.
    HD60.3.B76 2013
    658.15'12—dc23   2012022658

This book is dedicated to Mrs. Brockett's family, Mike, Zachary, Noah, and Jacob and the loving memory of Dr. Rezaee's parents, Fazlollah and Fatemeh Rezaee.

Contents

Preface

ORPORATE FAILURE IS TYPICALLY a reflection of ineffective corporate governance and the lack of focus on sustainability performance. Events significant enough to bring down high-profile companies (AIG, Bear Stern, Societe Generale, and Olympus) do not happen overnight and often relate to lack of sustainability performance. In a message to shareholders in the 2012 Annual meeting, the president and CEO of Starbucks underscores the importance of business sustainability in creating value for all stakeholders including shareholders, customers, and communities. This book presents recent developments in sustainability performance and sustainability reporting and assurance. Business organizations are key contributors to sustainability performance to ensure long-term sustainable development of the economy and society. In this context, sustainability reporting and the assurance process in collecting, analyzing, and disclosing sustainability performance is important. The concept of business sustainability and corporate accountability has become an overriding factor in successful strategic planning for many organizations worldwide. Business sustainability is a process of increasing the positive impacts and reducing negative effects of operations on sustainable economic, social and environmental performance. The idea is that an organization must extend its focus beyond making profit by considering the impact of its operation on the community, society, and the environment. The concept of the "triple bottom line" is often used to assess an organization's success from three perspectives—profit, people, and the planet. This expansion of determining an organization's sustainable performance and long-term value-adding strategies has driven a need for new reporting and accountability structures which extend beyond financial statements into nonfinancial key performance indicators based on environmental impact and social responsibility.

This book provides an introduction to the importance, relevance, and benefits of business sustainability and accountability reporting in all areas of economic, governance, social, ethical, and environmental performance (EGSEE). The book identifies financial and nonfinancial key performance indicators (KPIs) for each of the five areas of EGSEE and their integration into the organization's strategic mission, goals, operations, and culture. Traditionally, business enterprises have focused on earnings as the "bottom line" and the major financial KPIs for measuring sustainable performance. As businesses evolved and their role in society as a good citizen was developed and their impacts and possible external costs became more noticeable, the refocus on a multiple-bottom-line was inevitable. The "multiple-bottom-line" does not replace but rather supplement the conventional bottom-line by measuring performance in all areas of EGSEE. Many companies issue sustainability reports to communicate with a variety of stakeholders on their EGSEE performance. Auditors in providing assurance on sustainability reports play an important role in identifying both strengths and concerns of sustainability performance and lend credibility to sustainability reports.

Globalization, technological advances and a move toward stakeholder theory of corporations have given impetus to the sustainability reporting movement. The overriding principles of sustainability are responsibility and accountability to all stakeholders and effective disclosures of EGSEE sustainability performance to such stakeholders. It appears that research and books in business sustainability are fragmented with a lack of an integrated approach covering all EGSEE. Moreover, different authors address one or more components of business sustainability without a comprehensive framework for interdisciplinary integration. Business sustainability practices required integrated approach of systematically addressing EGSEE.

Sustainability performance and accountability reporting have gained a new interest during the recent financial crises and resulted global economic meltdown. The ever-increasing erosion of public trust and investor confidence in sustainability of large businesses, the widening concern about social responsibility and environmental matters, overconsumption of natural resources, the global government bailout of big businesses and the perception that government cannot solve all problems of businesses underscore the importance of keen focus on sustainability performance and accountability reporting. The true measure of success for corporations should not only be determined by reported earnings, but their governance, social responsibility, ethical behavior, and environmental initiatives. Business sustainability education demands knowledge-based in business sustainability. Wouldn't you want to leave more resources for the next generation? Wouldn't you want your business to grow continuously? Wouldn't you want to govern your business effectively? Wouldn't you want to have an ethical and competent organization culture? Wouldn't you care about your corporate social responsibility, customers' and employees' satisfaction and ethical workplace? Wouldn't you care about green and lush environment? Wouldn't you care about profit, planet, and people? If you answer yes to any of the above questions, this book will be of interest to you.

PURPOSE OF THE BOOK

This book offers guidance to organizations that focus on sustainability performance and accountability reporting in reflecting their key performance indicators (KPIs) in all areas of EGSEE business affairs. For the purpose of this book, sustainability reporting refers to the ongoing process of identifying, measuring, recognizing, disclosing, and auditing sustainability performance in the five areas of EGSEE. Traditionally, organizations have reported their performance on economic affairs. Their focus only on financial results has become complicated and irrelevant to the extent that many corporate stakeholders find conventional financial reports less value-relevant. Furthermore, investor activisms, stakeholders, global organizations, and the public have increasingly demanded information on both financial and nonfinancial KPIs in this platform of accountability and sustainability reporting. This book examines the development of sustainability performance initiatives and strategies as well as sustainability reporting and assurance.

The primary theme of this book will be on the examination of sustainability performance and accountability reporting and their integration into strategy, governance, risk assessment, performance management, and the reporting process of disclosing governance, ethics, social, environmental, and economic sustainable performance. This book also highlights how people, business, and resources collaborate in a business sustainability and accountability model.

The emerging issues of sustainability performance, reporting, and assurance are integrated into all chapters. This book includes features, practical examples, and refinements valuable to professionals of all levels, corporate leaders, directors, and executives, as well as auditors, practitioners, and educators. This book is helpful to the following:

Auditors: External and internal auditors should find the chapter materials on sustainability EGSEE performance and reporting relevant, useful, and suitable to their audit functions, gearing their audit procedures toward providing sustainability assurance services. External auditors should expand their audit services beyond conventional audit of financial reports and provide assurance services on all five EGSEE dimensions of sustainability performance reporting.

Corporations, their board of directors, audit committees, executives, legal counsel, managers, supervisors, and employees: Business sustainability and sustainability performance, reporting, and assurance is becoming the theme of the 21st century, and corporate stakeholders have shown interest in and demand for sustainability EGSEE performance disclosures. Best practices of sustainability initiatives and strategies as well as sustainability reporting and assurance discussed throughout the book should help public companies and their board of directors, executives, financial advisors, and legal counsel effectively discharge their responsibilities and assume accountability for achieving sustainability performance.

Business schools and training programs: The book can also be utilized in educational and training programs of business schools, accounting programs, and professional organizations. Other professionals, such as compliance officers, management accountants, environmental activists, ethics and compliance officers, socially responsible activists, and financial institutions, who provide sustainability training services to corporations, will find this book useful to their professional services and activities.

Global sustainability professionals: Promotion of global sustainability performance, reporting, and assurance by high-profile organizations such as the Global Reporting Initiative (GRI) and International Integrated Reporting Council (IIRC) makes the book attractive to corporations, business schools, and professionals worldwide.

HIGHLIGHTS OF THE BOOK

Obviously, much is needed to be done in this emerging area of business sustainability performance, reporting, and assurance including a book covering the following important topics:

- Introduction to business sustainability performance.
- EGSEE dimensions of sustainability/accountability reporting.
- Sustainability assurance services.
- Roles and responsibilities of key players in sustainability reporting.

- Laws, regulations, rules, standards, and best practices governing sustainability reporting and assurance.
- Designing green business cutting-edge facilities and green accounting and reporting.
- Development, adoption, and implementation of sustainable technologies.
- Preparation of business sustainability and accountability reporting and assurance education.
- Regulatory reforms and best practices in the post-SOX and Dodd-Frank (DOF) era are integrated into all eleven chapters.

ORGANIZATION OF THE BOOK

The focus of this book is on sustainability performance, reporting, and assurance. The organization of the book provides the maximum flexibility in choosing the amount and order of materials on sustainability. This book is organized into three parts, as follows:

Part	Subject	Chapters
I	An Introduction to Sustainability Performance, Reporting, and Assurance	1–3
II	Dimensions of Sustainability Performance	4–9
III	Emerging Issues in Sustainability Performance, Reporting, and Assurance	10–11

Each chapter starts with an executive summary, an examination of real-world sustainability, and each chapter closes with a list of action items which helps the reader further identify how to apply the chapter's materials to sustainability performance, reporting, and assurance. The eleven chapters of the book are organized into three parts. The first part contains three chapters, which describe the importance of sustainability performance, reporting, and assurance. These chapters also present initiatives, rules, regulations, standards, and best practices of sustainability performance, reporting, and assurance. Part II, presented in chapters 4 through 9, discusses each of the five economic, governance, social, ethical, and environmental (EGSEE) dimensions of sustainability performance and reporting. These chapters constitute the foundation of the book. Part III includes two chapters, which present emerging issues and best practices of sustainability performance, reporting, and assurance. These chapters also discuss future trends in sustainability performance, reporting, and assurance.

Acknowledgments

W E ACKNOWLEDGE THE PUBLIC Company Accounting Oversight Board, American Institute of Certified Public Accountants, Global Reporting Initiative, and the Prince of Wales's Accounting for Sustainability Project, the International Integrated Reporting Committee, and the International Federation of Accountants, Securities and Exchange Commission, the United Nations, Canadian Institute of Charter Accountants, and Big Four Accounting Firms for permission to quote and reference their professional standards and other publications.

The encouragement and support of our colleagues at Ernst & Young and the University of Memphis are also acknowledged. Specifically, we appreciate the invaluable advice and insights from several colleagues at Ernst & Young, including Steve Starbuck, Chris Walker, Robert Brand, Chuck Glazer, and Jim Gaynor. We thank the members of the John Wiley & Sons, Inc., team for their hard work and dedication, including Chris Gage for managing the book through the production process, Andrew Wheeler for his marketing efforts, and Stacey Rivera and Tim Burgard for their editorial guidance.

Our sincere thanks are due to our families, the Rezaee family, Soheila, Rose and Nick; and the Brockett family, Mike, Zachary, Noah and Jacob. Without their love, enthusiasm, and support, this book would not have come to fruition when it did.

Ann M. Brockett
Zabihollah Rezaee

PART ONE

An Introduction to Sustainability Performance, Reporting, and Assurance

CHAPTER ONE

Introduction to Business Sustainability and Accountability Reporting

EXECUTIVE**SUMMARY**

In this chapter, we introduce the concept of business sustainability and corporate accountability, its importance, relevance, and its various components. The wave of financial scandals in the early 2000s, the 2007–2009 global financial crisis, and subsequent regulatory responses have galvanized considerable interest in business sustainability, corporate governance, ethical, and corporate accountability. Businesses and professional organizations worldwide have also responded by developing a business sustainability framework consisting of five overriding dimensions of economic, governance, social, ethical, and environmental (EGSEE) performance.

The most important and commonly accepted dimension of EGSEE is economic performance, which is the cornerstone of business sustainability. Organizations survive and produce sustainable performance when they continue to be profitable and produce enduring performance that creates shareholder value. However, EGSEE dimensions are not mutually exclusive, they supplement each other and trade-offs can occur between them. On one hand, organizations that are run ethically, governed effectively, and are socially and environmentally responsible are expected to maintain sustainable performance, create shareholder value, and gain public trust and investor confidence. On the other hand, more economically profitable and viable organizations are in a better position to create jobs and wealth, which enables them to better fulfill their social and environmental responsibilities. Although the primary goal of many business entities will continue to be creating shareholder value through producing sustainable economic performance, organizations must also effectively deal with ethical, social, and environmental issues to ensure they are adding value to all stakeholders involved.

INTRODUCTION

For business, sustainability is defined in several ways. For example, the 2010 United Nations' (UN) publication "Corporate Governance in the Wake of the Financial Crisis" broadly describes business sustainability as "conducting operations in a manner that meets existing needs, without compromising the ability of future generations to meet their needs and has regard to the impacts that the business operations have on the life of the community in which it operates and includes environmental, social and governance issues."[1] The UN report further links business sustainability to corporate governance and suggests that sustainability information pertaining to social, governance, ethical, and environmental issues be incorporated with financial information in a single report that includes professional assurance on sustainability information.[2] The 2009 International Federation of Accountants' (IFAC) "Sustainability Framework" makes a similar recommendation. The IFAC suggests that sustainability be integrated into all aspects of business models from strategic decisions to operations, performance, and communication with stakeholders.[3] The IFAC's approach as described in "Sustainability Framework" addresses four different perspectives: "business strategy, internal management, investors, and other stakeholders."[4] Corporate sustainability can be summed up as conducting business to create value for present shareholders while protecting the rights of future shareholders and stakeholders.

Sustainability is a dynamic term that can be applied to various purposes and in a variety of settings. The modern use of the term *sustainability* was first developed in 1987 by the World Commission on Environment and Development (WCED)—also known as the Brundtland Commission—in a UN-sponsored study entitled *Our Common Future*. WCED described sustainability as an approach that "meets the need of the present without compromising the ability of future generations to meet their needs."[5] This captures a key component of sustainability—it is a process of establishing appropriate strategies, policies, and procedures that satisfy present needs without jeopardizing the future.

A program or an activity is considered sustainable if it meets all of the following criteria:

- Creates economic value.
- Increases public wealth with proper mechanisms for its distribution.
- Socially justified.
- Environmentally sound.
- Ethically conducted.
- Conforms to all applicable laws, rules, and regulations.

Several recent reports and publications, such as those by the United Nations Environment Programme Finance Initiative (UNEP FI) and the Canadian Institute of Charter Accountants (CICA), have discussed various aspects of sustainability performance in the areas of social, ethical, governance, and environmental sustainability.[6] In this book we add one more important dimension: making a sustainable profit through transparent economic performance.

THE CASE FOR SUSTAINABILITY

The 2007–2009 global financial crisis was caused by many factors, including inadequate risk assessment and management, ineffective corporate governance, and a strong focus on achieving short-term performance. Sustainable practices correct each of these failures and lead to long-term growth. Sustainability addresses all aspects of business and markets, from strategic decisions to operations, performance, and disclosures of sustainability information to investors and financial markets that could in turn prevent future economic, social, ethical, governance, and environmental crises. Integrated business practices and reporting are key factors in fostering sustainability.

Southwest's "One Report"

The first step to sustainability is transparency. Southwest Airlines annually issues the "Southwest Airlines One Report," which was initiated in 2009 to integrate the management report on financial statements with environmental disclosures and information on other aspects of operational sustainability. This integrated report focuses on meeting expectations regarding shareholders, customers, employees, and the environment by disclosing financial and nonfinancial key performance indicators (KPIs) on all aspects of sustainability.

Southwest examines the impact of business practices concerning financial decisions, suppliers, and employee training outcomes, as well as the company's environmental, social, and community impact. Southwest realizes benefits from integrated reporting through more effective and transparent communication with all stakeholders, which reflects the airline's commitment to high-quality service and good corporate citizenship beyond fulfilling its fiduciary responsibilities. It also establishes accountability, which is another key of corporate sustainability.

The 2010 "One Report" contains forward-looking information, disclosing the company's estimates, expectations, beliefs, intentions, and strategies for the future, though this cannot guarantee future performance. The report illustrates the continued steadfast focus on the triple bottom line—the performance (profit), the people, the planet—and conforms to the principles outlined by the Global Reporting Initiative (GRI).[7] Southwest Airlines intends to continue releasing its Southwest Airlines One Report on an annual basis.

CURRENT STATUS OF SUSTAINABILITY AND ACCOUNTABILITY

Several recent surveys have underscored the emergence of sustainability within the global business sustainability community. A study conducted by Ernst & Young in cooperation with GreenBiz Group in 2012 analyzed results from 272 executives and leaders of 24 business sectors in corporate environmental strategy and performance. The study revealed six key trends:

1. Sustainability reporting is growing, but the tools are still developing.
2. The CFO's role is increasing.
3. Employees emerged as a key stakeholder group for programs and reporting.
4. Despite regulatory uncertainty, greenhouse gas reporting remains strong along with growing interest in water.
5. Awareness is rising on the scarcity of business resources.
6. Sustainability performance rankings and ratings matter to company executives.[8]

This report sheds light on the profound shifts taking place in corporate sustainability as efforts move from purely voluntary programs that, while not mandated by laws or regulations, have become de facto requirements due to the expectations of customers, employees, shareholders, and other stakeholders.

These expectations are raising the bar for the quality of reporting and raising risks for companies whose disclosure and transparency do not hold up to scrutiny.

The Ernst & Young Survey reinforced findings from an earlier KPMG 2010 survey. The KPMG survey included 378 senior executives worldwide and revealed amongst its findings that about 62 percent of surveyed companies have a strategy for sustainability compared to 50 percent in 2008; roughly 5 percent have no plan for implementing corporate sustainability and the remaining companies were in the process of establishing such a plan. In addition, more than 42 percent of surveyed executives indicated that sustainability is a source of innovation, whereas 39 percent agreed that sustainability is a source of new business opportunities and growth.[9]

Organizations interested in producing reports to showcase their sustainability actions and commitments should address seven questions related to best practices, voluntariness, content, mechanisms, value relevance, and assurance of sustainability reports, as suggested by Ernst & Young (2010).[10] The questions are:

1. Who issues sustainability reports? (Best practices)
2. Why report on sustainability if you do not have to? (Voluntary)
3. What information should a sustainability report contain? (Content)
4. What governance systems and processes are needed to report on sustainability? (Mechanisms)
5. What are the challenges and risks of sustainability reporting? (Assessment)
6. Do sustainability reports have to be audited? (Assurance)
7. How can companies get the most value out of sustainability reporting? (Value relevance).

In June 2012, Brazil, Denmark, France, and South Africa formed a group to promote sustainability reporting in support of paragraph 47 of the UN Conference on Sustainable Development.[11] It is expected that other developed and developing countries join this group in requiring their listed companies to issue sustainability reports.

DRIVERS OF SUSTAINABILITY INITIATIVES AND PRACTICES

The Kyoto Protocol of the United Nations Framework Convention on Climate Change (UNFCCC) was a commitment by nations to reduce their Greenhouse Gas emissions to address global warming. The Protocol was adopted on

December 11, 1997, in Kyoto, Japan, and went into effect on February 16, 2005. The UNFCCC is an international environmental treaty with the specific objective of "stabilization of greenhouse gas concentrations in the atmosphere at a level to prevent dangerous anthropogenic interference with the climate system."[12] A detailed discussion of the Kyoto Protocol Framework and its implications for business sustainability is further discussed in Chapters 9 and 10.

The topic of sustainability is evolving and initiatives are growing around the world. With increasing pressure on energy and commodity prices and growing scarcity of raw materials, sustainable development is essential to ensuring the future viability of organizations. Also, increasing consumer demand and regulatory initiatives make sustainable development more attractive from a fiscal perspective. The 2010 United Nations Global Compact/Accenture study indicates that 93 percent of the 766 global CEOs reported sustainability as either an "important" or "very important" factor for the future success of their organizations and about 81 percent declared that sustainability issues are integrated into their organizations' strategy and operations.[13] Furthermore, consumer preferences drive organizations to seek sustainable development in order to remain competitive. As consumers become more educated about sustainable initiatives, they have come to expect changes in how products are produced and packaged. An increasing number of consumers are seeking out those organizations that demonstrate an awareness and concern about sustainability issues. Many consumers expect sustainable attributes to be an integral part of the products and services they buy.

Regulatory reforms and standards are also driving sustainability initiatives for organizations. With an increasing amount of pressure from the public, legislators have begun to mandate social responsibility and environmental sensitivity. As an example, the reduction of a company's carbon footprint, as part of the Kyoto Protocol, has driven companies worldwide to consider the climate change impact of their operations and develop strategies around reducing that impact over time.

A move toward the stakeholder theory implies that business organizations have obligations to a number of constituencies and thus should add value for all stakeholders including shareholders, creditors, suppliers, customers, employees, government, environment, and society. Conventional shareholder theory, however, implies that the primary goal of a corporation is to create shareholder value in a single objective function of maximizing financial performance. Business sustainability promotes application of stakeholder theory in protecting interests of all stakeholders and thus the main goal of value maximization for all stakeholders under business sustainability can be achieved when the interests of all stakeholders are considered. In the past two years, New York, New Jersey, and California have enacted laws creating a new hybrid type of corporation designed for businesses that want to simultaneously pursue profit and benefit society.[14] Benefit Corporations (BCs) are intended to fill a gap between traditional corporations and nonprofits by giving social entrepreneurs flexibility to achieve the dual objectives of doing well and doing good. The justification for BCs is that that existing law prevents boards of directors from considering the impact of corporate decisions on other stakeholders, the environment or society at large. Boards of directors of BCs are required to consider the impact of their decisions on specific corporate constituencies, including shareholders, employees, suppliers, the community, as well as on the local and global environment. The move toward the stakeholder theory and the more commonly accepted form of BCs is expected to promote business sustainability.

Sustainability reporting and assurance is still in its infant stage with many challenges and opportunities remaining before it will gain wide acceptance. Accounting and auditing standards are long-established for financial reporting and auditing. Standards also exist for measuring, recognizing, reporting, and auditing of governance, ethics, social responsibility, and environmental activities and performance, but these are fairly new by comparison. These include GRI and AA1000 issued in 2008 by AccountAbility (AA). There is an AA1000 assurance standard, as well as ISO standards and accounting profession standards for auditing sustainability metrics. Furthermore, organizations may be concerned about presenting unaudited key performance indicators (KPIs) on their ethical, social, governance, and environmental activities, which may create expectations and further accountability for them to improve their performance in these areas. Another challenge is to disclose concise, accurate, reliable, complete, comparable, and standardized sustainability reports that are relevant and useful to all stakeholders. PricewaterhouseCoopers's 2010 review identified several external drivers of sustainability reporting, including economic factors, competitive forces, trends in society, technology, environmental initiatives, and geopolitical factors. The majority of reviewed companies (74 percent) in 2010—compared to 49 percent in 2009—provided some forward-looking information on market drivers. Companies disclosed this information in response to either the emerging trend toward more relevant sustainability reporting or to mitigate investor perceptions about uncertain future economic prospects.[15]

A growing number of policymakers and regulators worldwide are responding to the demand for an interest in transparency and focusing on long-term and enduring performance through either requiring sustainability reporting (e.g., Sweden's guidelines for external reporting by state-owned companies and the Danish Financial Statements Act) or mandatory integrated reporting (e.g., the King Code III in South Africa and the Grenelle II Act in France). The Singapore Exchange, in July of 2011, released its "Sustainability Reporting Guide" for its listed companies, which requires disclosure of accountability for conducting business in a sustainable manner. A 2010 joint study suggests that regulatory requirements along with ever-increasing efforts to manage reputational risk and to identify cost cutting and efficiency savings continue to be the most common drivers of business sustainability initiatives and programs.[16] Recently, many organizations are advocating for increased sustainability reporting and driving the move toward disclosures, as described in Exhibit 1.1.[17]

BEST PRACTICES OF SUSTAINABILITY PROGRAMS

The Accenture and the UN Global Compact survey of CEOs suggests that while businesses view sustainability as essential to their future success, it is unclear exactly how they will go about making it an integral part of their strategic decision-making.[18] Multinational companies are ahead of the game, particularly in the utility and energy sectors. A survey of global CEOs reveals that 91 percent of CEOs in the energy industry report that their company will employ new technologies to address sustainability issues over the next five years.[19] For the utility sector, government regulation and resource scarcity appear to be the most significant drivers for change.

Even companies that have not fully embraced sustainability as a long-term strategic objective are finding ways to embed sustainable practices into everyday operational choices. In addition to directly influencing policy and procedure decisions, being green helps in recruiting and retaining employees. Moreover, successful companies are able to use sustainability to support their brand and generate a competitive advantage. In many cases, consumers are willing to pay a premium for products that directly support sustainable lifestyles or from companies that have embraced sustainability. Although the paths to integrating sustainability vary and the future is somewhat unclear, what is clear is that there is a significant amount to be gained from embracing sustainability as both a long- and near-term strategy. Exhibit 1.2 presents a

EXHIBIT 1.1 Organizations That Have Promoted Business Sustainability

Organization	Publications/Activities	Description	Year	Web Address
Asset Management Working Group of the United Nations Environment Programme Finance Initiative (UNEP FI AMWG)	*Fiduciary Responsibility: Legal and Practical Aspects of Integrating Environmental, Social and Governance Issues into Institutional Investment*	Makes recommendations to help institutional investors integrate ESG issues into investment decision-making.	2009	www.unepfi.org
UNEP FI AMWG & the World Business Council for Sustainable Development (WBCSD)	*Translating ESG into Sustainable Business Value*	Provides ESG insights and considerations.	2010	www.unepfi.org
The United Nations Principles for Responsible Investment (UNPRI)	*Principles for Responsible Investment*	Establishes principles, focused on the provision and use of ESG information.	2005	www.unpri.org/principles
International Corporate Governance Network (ICGN)	*ICGN Statement and Guidance on Non-Financial Business Reporting*	Provides disclosure criteria to assist companies in meeting investor expectations.	2008	www.icgn.org
Carbon Disclosure Project (CDP)	Global climate change reporting system	Harmonizes climate-change data from organizations and develops international carbon reporting standards.	2003	www.cdproject.net
Investor Network on Climate Risk (INCR)	*Investors Analyze Climate Risk and Opportunities: A Survey of Asset Managers' Practices*	Provides overview of investment practices, highlighting best practices and drivers for change.	2010	www.ceres.org/incr/
Ceres	*The 21st Century Corporation: The Ceres Roadmap for Sustainability*	Provides a comprehensive platform for sustainable business strategy.	2010	www.ceres.org

(continued)

EXHIBIT 1.1 *(Continued)*

Organization	Publications/Activities	Description	Year	Web Address
Extractive Industries Transparency Initiative (EITI)	*The EITI Principles and Criteria*	Establishes global standard for transparency in oil, gas, and mining.	2003	eiti.org
Harvard Law School – Pensions and Capital Stewardship Project	*Quantifying Labor and Human Rights Portfolio Risk*	Explores how investors can obtain data on the long-term sustainability risks posed by labor and human rights activities of global corporations.	2009	www.law. harvard.edu/ programs/lwp
National Roundtable on the Environment and Economy (NRTEE)	*Capital Markets and Sustainability: Investing in a Sustainable Future*	Encourages the integration of ESG factors into capital allocation decisions.	2007	nrtee-trnee.ca
International Federation of Accountants (IFAC)	*Sustainability Framework 2.0*	Supports integration of sustainability in relation to business strategy, operations, and reporting.	2011	http://www .ifac.org/ publications-resources/ifac-sustainability-framework-20
The European Federation of Financial Analysts Societies (EFFAS) and Society of Investment Professionals in Germany (DVFA)	*KPIs for ESG: A Guideline for the Integration of ESG into Financial Analysis and Corporate Valuation*	Develops standard reporting framework for ecological, social, and corporate governance aspects built on requirements of investment professionals.	2010	www.effas-esg .com
CFA Institute Centre for Financial Market Integrity	*Environmental, Social and Governance Factors at Listed Companies*	Provides a manual to help investment professionals identify and evaluate risks and opportunities that ESG issues present for investors.	2008	www.cfapubs. org/toc/ccb /2008/2008/2

EXHIBIT 1.2 A Sampling of Global Companies Disclosing Their Sustainability Initiatives

Name	Description	Website
BHP Billion	Discloses sustainability issues of health, safety, the environment, and the community as to how management addresses them.	www.bhpbilliton.com/bb/ sustainabledevelopment.jsp
Veolia Environment	Discloses both financial and nonfinancial sustainability information.	www.sustainable-development .veolia.com
Vancouver City Saving (Vancity)	Received the first Ceres-ACCA North America sustainability award for incorporating the triple-bottom-line strategy into its financial institution reports.	www.vancity.com/AboutUs/ OurBusiness/Ourreports
Telefonica S.A.	Received a Corporate Register reporting award for obtaining a third-party assurance on sustainability.	http://www.telefonica.com/en/ home/jsp/home.jsp
Gap, Inc.	Dedicates a section on its website to social responsibility. The company focuses its social responsibility in four key areas: supply chain, employees, environment, and community investment.	http://www.gapinc.com/ GapIncSubSites/csr/ EmbracingOurResponsibility/ ER_Our_Focus.shtml
Chili's	The popular casual dining restaurant is becoming well known for its partnership with St. Jude Children's Research Hospital.	http://www.brinker.com/ company/givingback.asp
The Hershey Corporation	Discloses corporate strategic initiatives suggested by CSR/ sustainability leadership team and four issue-specific subgroups charged with responsibility for climate change tracking and GHG emissions reduction.	http://www.marketwatch.com/ story/hershey-issues-first-corporate-social-responsibility-report-2010-09-13? reflink=MW_news_stmp http://www.thehersheycompany .com/social-responsibility.aspx
Starbucks	Environmental Stewardship. 2009 and 2011 Shareholders Annual Meeting on sustainability initiatives to create value for all stakeholders including shareholders, customers, and communities by promoting social responsibility, ethical sourcing goals, and environmental stewardship.	http://www.starbucks.com/ responsibility

list of global companies that have made progress in their sustainability initiatives in recent years.

PRINCIPLES OF BUSINESS SUSTAINABILITY

The three overriding principles of business sustainability are: value creation, performance enhancement, and accountability assurance. The value creation principle suggests corporations should create the maximum number of products and services with the least utilization of scarce resources, while maintaining the highest quality and efficiency to yield the utmost customer satisfaction. The primary goal of any organization should be creation of value for all stakeholders including investors, employees, customers, and society. An accountability assurance principle means conducting business in an ethical and socially responsible manner. A proper assurance process requires timely and deliberate planning, bold actions, effective implementation, enforceable accountability, continuous monitoring, and an independent third-party assurance on sustainability reports. The performance enhancement principle indicates achievement of sustainable EGSEE performance by enhancing corporations' positive impacts and minimizing negative effects on society and environment.

BUSINESS SUSTAINABILITY AND CORPORATE ACCOUNTABILITY FRAMEWORK

The business sustainability and accountability framework for an organization consists of performance in five overriding dimensions: economic, governance, social, ethical, and environmental (EGSEE), as depicted in Exhibit 1.3. Exhibit 1.4 introduces the sustainability framework consisting of sustainability performance goals, reporting, and assurance that will be discussed in detail in Chapter 2. The most important dimension is economic viability, the cornerstone of business sustainability. Organizations can survive and produce sustainable performance only when they continue to be profitable, creating shareholder value. Although the primary goal of many business entities will continue to be improving economic performance by enhancing shareholder value, they must also effectively deal with ethical, social, and environmental issues to ensure adding value for their shareholders and other stakeholders. Business sustainability not only ensures long-term profitability and a competitive advantage, but also helps in maintaining the well-being of society as a whole.

EXHIBIT 1.3 Five EGSEE Dimensions of Sustainability Performance

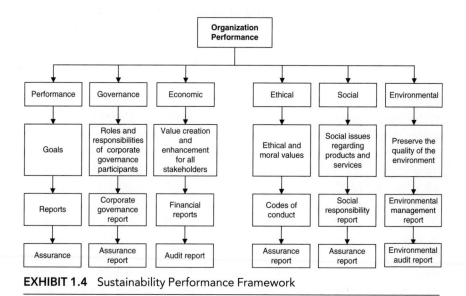

EXHIBIT 1.4 Sustainability Performance Framework

The sustainability framework presented in Exhibits 1.3 and 1.4 is consistent with "Sustainability Framework" of the International Federation of Accountants (IFAC), which addresses four perspectives:

1. The business strategy perspective by focusing on the achievement of long-term strategic decisions, objectives, goals, and performance;
2. The internal management perspective of directing and integrating management activities to ensure sustainability performance;
3. The investors' perspective of effective communications with shareholders regarding sustainability performance; and
4. The stakeholders' perspective of presenting both financial and nonfinancial sustainability KPIs as well as providing assurance on disclosed information.[20]

KEY PERFORMANCE INDICATORS

The primary goal of an organization is to operate effectively and efficiently in generating sustainable performance. Key performance indicators are measures that are critical to the success of the organization and assessment of its performance. Applying KPIs to sustainability initiatives is a way to monitor and track them. KPIs can be very useful as a means of assessing an organization's current position and deciding on new strategies to achieve future objectives, goals, and targets. Proper use of KPIs enables an organization to define its goals and establish metrics to measure its performance in achieving them sustainably. KPIs are developed to reflect the critical success factors and are normally classified into financial and nonfinancial KPIs. Financial KPIs deal with information that can be measured in monetary values and reflect key financial positions and results of operations. Examples of financial KPIs are movements in stock prices, sales growth, earnings, return on equity, earnings per share, dividends, and return on assets. Nonfinancial KPIs are relevant to information that cannot be measured in monetary values. Examples of nonfinancial KPIs include information on environmental and social matters, customer satisfaction activities, employee training and turnover, supplier satisfaction, and ethics compliance.

The key to creating usable nonfinancial KPIs is to offer stakeholders sufficient measures to assess sustainable performance. For example, an organization that desires to present a KPI for the generation of wastewater from a manufacturing process can use the volume of wastewater generated each year along with an estimate of the total treatment costs of annual wastewater. In an attempt to assist organizations in developing effective and adequate nonfinancial KPIs, the Prince of Wales's Accounting for Sustainability Project (A4S) has worked with over 150 organizations to develop best practices to embed sustainability into an organization's structure.[21] A4S is collaborating with the IFAC in promoting sustainable organizations by embedding sustainability into strategy, governance, performance management, and reporting processes. One of the organizations that the project worked with was Carillion PLC, a construction and facilities maintenance firm. Carillion PLC was an equity partner that was created to build a new hospital. The company was tasked with providing design, construction, maintenance, and ongoing facilities management services. From the beginning of the project, Carillion PLC worked with the end users of the facility to understand their strategic objectives and then designed a Sustainable Action Plan that was monitored by nonfinancial KPI's for various sustainability objectives.

In measuring a company's success, it is important to link its stated goals to implemented strategies, reported KPIs, and compensation policy. For example the 2010 PwC report "Insight or Fatigue?" revealed that about 88 percent of ETSE 350 companies identified their KPIs; of these, only 25 percent clearly align KPIs to their strategic priorities and an even smaller percentage (14 percent) disclose the link between KPIs and the metrics that determine executive compensation, operations, and nonfinancial KPIs which often reflect strategic decisions made by management.[22]

KPIs should be used in conjunction with related contexts of narrative information. KPIs should meet the following six criteria:

1. Be prepared for each component of sustainability performance.
2. Consist of both financial and nonfinancial performance metrics.
3. Be prepared based on best practices shared by many stakeholders and procedures.
4. Be conceptualized and supported by narrative description.
5. Measurable in terms of volume and monetary value.
6. Implemented consistently and effectively beyond a check-the-box mentality.

EMERGING ISSUES IN SUSTAINABILITY REPORTING

Reporting business sustainability has gained significant attention and acceptance throughout the world in recent years due to support and promotion from the Global Reporting Initiative (GRI), the Prince of Wales's Accounting for Sustainability Project, the International Integrated Reporting Committee, and the IFAC, among other organizations. The emerging issues in sustainability reporting, according to GRI, are the three I's: integration, implementation, and integrity.[23]

Implementation

Sustainability laws, rules, regulations, and best practices are evolving and their effective implementation plays an important role in the future of reporting. Proper implementation of applicable laws, regulations, standards, and best

KEY**GUIDANCE**

Integration

Integration means the adoption of a single set of globally accepted sustainability reports presenting all dimensions of sustainability performance. Integration consists of the three following parts:

1. **Integrated reporting and XBRL *(Extensible Business Reporting Language).*** The future of sustainability reporting will be an integrated report on all dimensions of EGSEE performance in compliance with the International Financial Reporting Standards (IFRS) prepared on the XBRL platform. This integrated sustainability reporting requires the adoption of the IFRS and the establishment of XBRL taxonomies for all dimensions of EGSEE.

2. **Global standards with teeth.** The establishment of globally accepted and enforced sustainability standards is needed to successfully implement all dimensions of sustainability EGSEE performance. The future of sustainability reporting depends on the recognition, implementation, and enforcement of a set of globally accepted sustainability reporting standards.

3. **Better integration of digital technology and social media** for reporting and engagement purposes. The entire corporate reporting world is rapidly moving toward digital applications with the use of XBRL platforms and sustainability reporting is no exception. The future success of sustainability reporting depends on whether online reporting is used.

practices requires organizations to align their external sustainability reporting practices with internal daily operational culture and behavior. Organization gatekeepers including the board of directors, legal counsel, and internal and external auditors play an important role in ensuring proper implementation and alignment of actual performance with expected performance in compliance with related rules, regulations, and standards.

Integrity

The future success of sustainability reporting is determined by the integrity of the process of preparing transparent and reliable reports. The integrity of the reporting process and the transparency of the reports themselves can significantly influence stakeholder confidence and public trust in EGSEE sustainability performance reports. Integrity of sustainability reporting can be strengthened by:

- Broadening the scope of sustainability reporting to include the stakeholder perspective.
- Disclosing sustainable performance in all dimensions of EGSEE to enable stakeholders to assess the overall performance.
- Expanding management's discussion and analysis on all dimensions of sustainability performance (EGSEE) by putting the numbers into a sustainable context.
- Developing an integrated sustainability and accountability reporting system to reflect comprehensive performance.
- Disclosure of more continuous and electronic business reporting.
- Providing assurance on all dimensions of sustainable performance.
- Expanding the audit to all dimensions of business sustainability beyond the financial statements.

Emerging trends in business sustainability include: (1) supply-chain business sustainability; (2) board strategic initiatives in business sustainability and accountability; (3) employee involvement; (4) technological development; (5) regulations; and (6) investors' demands for sustainability information.

1. Supply chain sustainability management.

High-profile companies such as IBM, Wal-Mart, and P&G, among others, are now more engaged in all areas of EGSEE. Supplier carbon management programs are one way these corporations are managing sustainable supply chains, while demanding that their trading partners follow suit.

2. Sustainability board strategies.

Boards of directors are now considering sustainability as an integral component of board strategies. A study conducted by the Conference Board shows that during the 2011 proxy season, the number of shareholder proposals on social and environmental policy issues has increased from 28.1 percent in 2007 to 29.1 percent in 2010.[24] Sustainability is a strategic plan that demands attention and commitment from the board of directors, who need to include it in the organization's vision for future viability.

3. Employee involvement.

Organization employees, from the senior executives to entry-level staff, are now more conscientious about business sustainability.

4. Technological development.

Tech companies and software developers are now investing more in sustainability initiatives, so it can be expected that new technologies will be utilized in this area.

5. Sustainability regulations and standards.

Regulations on climate change (e.g., SEC rules, ISO 14000), guiding standards on corporate social responsibility (ISO 2600), and regulatory reforms on corporate governance (SOX, 2002; Dodd-Frank Act, 2010) are shaping business sustainability and sustainability reporting. However, the main force behind sustainability initiatives as of now is market-driven. Many businesses have implemented sustainability best practices voluntarily to satisfy their stakeholders' demands for sustainability development. Effective, efficient, and scalable sustainability regulations are expected to bring more uniform, standardized, and globally accepted practices of business sustainability and sustainability reporting and assurance.

6. Investor interest in and demand for sustainability information.

Global investors show more interest in and demand for sustainability information regarding environmental, social governance, and ethics performance. The 2011 survey by Institutional Shareholder Services (ISS) indicates that a high majority of both surveyed global investors (81 percent) and issuers (76 percent) believe that disclosure of their companies' environmental, social, and governance information has significant impacts on their long-term investment decisions and shareholder value.[25]

PROMOTION OF SUSTAINABILITY DEVELOPMENT, PERFORMANCE, AND DISCLOSURES

There is a growing call from corporate stakeholders (including investors) for integrated sustainability performance information in corporate reporting models. Meaningful and sound sustainability development and reporting require organizations to:

- Establish an appropriate tone at the top to ensure commitment and vigilant oversight of the sustainability program and performance by the board of directors and executives.
- Integrate sustainability initiatives and activities into the organization's strategic decision by employing best practices of sustainability policies, programs, and activities.
- Define clearly the organization's mission, goals, policies, and programs relevant to EGSEE sustainability performance.
- Establish financial and nonfinancial KPIs relevant to sustainability performance and design proper metrics to measure sustainability KPIs.
- Develop and maintain sound sustainability reports and obtain independent sustainability assurance on sustainability reports.
- Communicate sustainability initiatives, practices, and performance to all relevant stakeholders and consider shareholder proposal on sustainability-related performance.
- Work with credit rating agencies (e.g., Moody's, S&P, and Fitch) to ensure important sustainability initiatives and programs are considered in their ratings.
- Be proactive rather than reactive regarding emerging regulatory reforms and standards pertaining to sustainability.
- Coordinate sustainability programs and activities with finance and accounting functions to ensure proper financing, measurement, recognition, and reporting.

Following are some suggestions for promoting business sustainability and accountability reporting:

- Investigate input and insight from institutional investors and financial analysts on all aspects of sustainability performance and how it is integrated into their investment decisions.

- Integrate all dimensions of sustainability initiative into corporate reporting.
- Encourage research in business sustainability and corporate reporting.
- Evaluate the link between all dimensions of sustainability performance.
- Integrate business sustainability and accountability reporting into the business curriculum.

CONCLUSION

Business sustainability has emerged as a central, multifaceted theme of the 21st century. Organizations of all types and sizes are focusing on business sustainability as a means of creating enduring value for shareholders and managing the interests of other stakeholders, including creditors, employers, suppliers, governments, and societies at large. Business sustainability and corporate accountability as presented in this chapter set a framework for organizations to achieve their goals of adding value in all areas of economic, governance, social, ethical, and environmental matters and events. Business sustainability is a process of enabling organizations to design and implement strategies that contribute to enduring performance in all areas. Business sustainability not only ensures long-term profitability and competitive advantage but also helps in maintaining the well-being of the society, the planet, and its inhabitants. This chapter presented a framework for business sustainability and corporate accountability reporting, as well as assurance and risk management in the five key areas of strategy, operations, compliance, reputation, and financial management.

ACTION**ITEMS**

1. Establish appropriate tone at the top, promoting business sustainability as creating value for shareholders while protecting the interests of other stakeholders, including creditors, suppliers, customers, employees, government, the environment, and society.
2. Make sure business strategies focus on the achievement of all dimensions of sustainability performance.
3. Identify key drivers of your business sustainability initiatives.

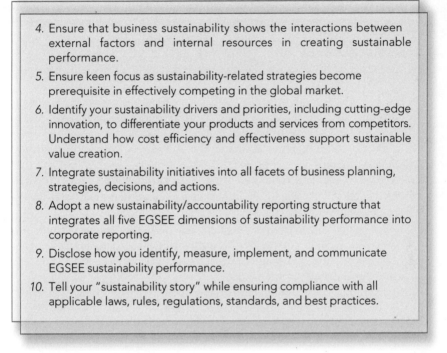

4. Ensure that business sustainability shows the interactions between external factors and internal resources in creating sustainable performance.

5. Ensure keen focus as sustainability-related strategies become prerequisite in effectively competing in the global market.

6. Identify your sustainability drivers and priorities, including cutting-edge innovation, to differentiate your products and services from competitors. Understand how cost efficiency and effectiveness support sustainable value creation.

7. Integrate sustainability initiatives into all facets of business planning, strategies, decisions, and actions.

8. Adopt a new sustainability/accountability reporting structure that integrates all five EGSEE dimensions of sustainability performance into corporate reporting.

9. Disclose how you identify, measure, implement, and communicate EGSEE sustainability performance.

10. Tell your "sustainability story" while ensuring compliance with all applicable laws, rules, regulations, standards, and best practices.

NOTES

1. United Nations. 2010 United Nations Conference on Trade and Development, "Corporate Governance in the Wake of the Financial Crisis," viii. Available at http://www.unctad-docs.org/files/CG-in-Wake-of-Fin-Crisis-Full-Report.pdf.
2. Ibid.
3. International Federation of Accountants (IFAC). 2009. "Sustainability Framework." Available at http://www.ifac.org/publications-resources/ifac-sustainability-framework-20.
4. Ibid.
5. World Commission on Environment and Development (WCED). 1987. *Our Common Future* (New York: Oxford University Press), Chapter 2.
6. As discussed in: Canadian Institute of Chartered Accountants (CICA). 2004. "Financial Reporting Disclosures about Social, Environmental and Ethical (SEE) Issues: Background Paper for the Capital Markets and Sustainability Program of the National Round Table on the Environment and the Economy"

(Toronto: CICA) and UNEP FI. 2009. "AMWG Fiduciary Responsibility Legal and Practical Aspects of Integrating Environmental, Social and Governance Issues into Institutional Investment" (Geneva: UNEP FI).

7. Southwest Airlines. 2011. "Southwest Airlines One Report 2010," 115. Available at http://www.southwestonereport.com/_pdfs/SouthwestOneReport2011.pdf.

8. Ernst & Young and GreenBiz. 2012. "Six Growing Trends in Corporate Sustainability." Available at http://www.ey.com/Publication/vwLUAssets/Six_growing/$FILE/SixTrends.pdf.

9. KPMG. 2010. "Corporate Sustainability: A Progress Report." Available at www.kpmg.com.

10. Ernst & Young and GreenBiz. 2012. "Six Growing Trends in Corporate Sustainability." Available at http://www.ey.com/Publication/vwLUAssets/Six_growing/$FILE/SixTrends.pdf.

11. United Nations Environment Programme. 2012. Brazil, Denmark, France and South Africa Join in a Committee to Sustainability Reporting. (June 20, 2012). Available at http://www.unepfi.org/fileadmin/events/2012/Rio20/Press_release_Rio_outcome_document.pdf.

12. United Nations. 1992. "Framework Convention on Climate Change," Article 2.

13. United Nation Global Compact and Accenture. 2010. "A New Era of Sustainability." Available at http://www.unglobalcompact.org/docs/news_events/8.1/UNGC_Accenture_CEO_Study_2010.pdf.

14. Clark, W.H., and L. Vranka. 2011. The Need and Rationale for Benefit Corporation: Why it Is the Legal Form. Benefit corporation white paper. Available at www.benefitcorp.org.

15. PricewaterhouseCoopers (PwC). 2010. "Insight or Fatigue?: FESE 350 Reporting." Available at http://www.pwc.com/gx/en/corporate-reporting/integrated-reporting/publications/reporting-survey-2010.jhtml.

16. Chartered Institute of Management Accountants (CIMA), American Institute of Certified Public Accountants (AICPA), and Canadian Institute of Chartered Accountants (CICA). 2010. "Global Survey Findings on Accounting for Sustainability Practices," press release, December 16, 2010. Available at http://www.aicpa.org/Press/PressReleases/2010/Pages/GlobalSUrveyFindingsOnAcctforsustainability.aspx.

17. Canadian Institute of Chartered Accountants. 2010. "Environmental, Social and Governance (ESG) Issues in Institutional Investor Decision Making." Available at www.cica.ca.

18. de Morsella, Tracey. 2011. "CEOs See Sustainability as Engine for Growth but Industry Sectors Split on Priorities." *Fast Company*, May 25, 2011.

19. Ibid.

20. International Federation of Accountants (IFAC). 2009. "Sustainability Framework." Available at http://www.ifac.org/publications-resources/ifac-sustainability-framework-20.

21. The International Federation of Accountants (IFAC). 2011. "Sustainability Framework 2.0." Available at http://web.dev.ifac.org/sustainability-framework/imp-sustainability-performance.
22. PricewaterhouseCoopers (PwC). 2010. "Insight or Fatigue?: FESE 350 Reporting." Available at www.corporatereporting.com.
23. Murninghan, Marcy. 2010. "The Three 'I's of Sustainability Reporting's Future" Global Reporting Initiative website, November 3, 2010. Available at https://www.globalreporting.org/information/news-and-press-center/Pages/The-Three-Is-of-Sustainability-Reporting%E2%80%99s-Future.aspx.
24. Tonello, M., and M. Augilar. 2012. "Shareholder Proposals: Trends from Recent Proxy Seasons (2007–2011)" (The Conference Board: February 2012). Available at http://ssrn.com/abstract=1998378.
25. Institutional Shareholder Services, Inc. (ISS) 2011. "2011-2012 Policy Survey Summary of Results." Available at www.issgovernance.com.

CHAPTER TWO

Brief History of Sustainability Reporting

EXECUTIVE**SUMMARY**

The history of sustainability reporting and assurance is presented in this chapter. The conventional corporate reporting model reflects only financial information with regards to the bottom line. Sustainability reporting model provides financial and nonfinancial information on key performance indicators pertaining to economic, governance, social, ethical, and environmental (EGSEE) performance. Sustainability reporting is evolving from its initial focus primarily on environmental issues to corporate social activities and now disclosing information on all multiple bottom line EGSEE dimensions of sustainability performance. Sustainability reporting reflects performance not only in long-term profitability, but also discloses information on the well-being of the society, the planet, and people.

HISTORICAL PERSPECTIVES

The history of sustainability reporting can be traced back to as early as the 1960s and 1970s in Europe and slightly later in the United States when organization started to recognize their role in the society above and beyond profit maximization. The sustainability movement and reporting in the United States dates back to the first Earth Day held on April 22, 1970.[1] After that, the movement gained momentum with a 1987 United Nations report, *Our Common Future*, better known as the Brundtland Report.[2] This report promoted sustainability as a means of balancing economic and environmental issues and considering the tradeoff between short-term economic benefits and long-term impacts on future generations. The acceptance of corporate social responsibilities in France and the Netherlands encouraged the introduction of environmental reports in countries such as Austria, Germany, and Switzerland during the 1970s.[3]

The creation of the U.S. Environmental Protection Agency (EPA) and the passage of the Clean Air, Clean Water, and Endangered Species Acts in the United States in the early 1980s were big steps in the development of the environmental aspect of sustainability reporting.

The first country that adopted a mandatory sustainability reporting law was Finland, which did so in 1997.[4] Other countries adopting similar laws are Australia, Austria, Canada, China, Denmark, France, Germany, Greece, Indonesia, Italy, Malaysia, Netherlands, Norway, Portugal, Sweden, and the United Kingdom.[5]

Ethical investment funds in the United States and the United Kingdom during the 1980s promoted ethical and social performance by excluding firms that operated in the tobacco or alcohol industries. Due to the 1989 Exxon Valdez disaster, the U.S.-based Coalition for Environmentally Responsible Economies (Ceres), a Boston-based nonprofit organization, established the "Ceres/Valdez Principles." These principles defined a set of environmental reporting guidelines on behalf of the Social Investment Forum (SIF).

During the 1990s, reporting on both financial and nonfinancial key performance indicators gained some acceptance through the introduction of values reporting, with a primary focus on social, environmental, and animal protection issues.[6] In 1997, Ceres started a Global Reporting Initiative (GRI) aimed at developing a sustainability information disclosure framework. In 1999, the United Nations Environment Programme (UNEP) joined with Ceres as a partner in the GRI project. In 2000, the first GRI Sustainability Reporting Guidelines were issued and almost 50 companies issued sustainability reports using these guidelines. A year later, the GRI became an independent organization and subsequently relocated in the Netherlands. GRI was launched to establish reporting guidelines for the *triple bottom line*: economic, social, and environmental performance. During this period, voluntary corporate social responsibility reports gained momentum due to demands by socially responsible investors as well as managerial initiatives on brand reputation building and encouragements from policymakers, regulators, and standard-setters.

RECENT DEVELOPMENTS AND INITIATIVES

In the first decade of the 21st century, much progress has been made in sustainability reporting, including the introduction of the sustainable stock exchanges initiative by the United Nations Principles for Responsible Investment (UNPRI). The UNPRI initiative facilitates dialogue between exchanges and investors, companies, and regulators to improve corporate transparency on sustainability performance by encouraging responsible long-term and sustainable approaches to investment. This type of interaction can support sustainability initiatives. For example, in January 2011 a group of investors representing $1.6 trillion in assets under management sent a letter to the top 30 global stock exchanges requesting them to demand better internal corporate governance by their listed companies. The investors asked for disclosure of how the boards address sustainability issues and also for exchanges to consult with listed companies on how sustainability and integrated reporting can be infused into long-term strategic decision making and corporate reporting.[7]

The Global Reporting Initiative (GRI) was launched in 1997 to bring consistency and global standardization to sustainability reporting. GRI initially focused on incorporating environmental performance into corporate reporting and with its "Sustainability Reporting Guidelines," which were published in 2000, 2002, 2006, and 2011. GRI is now considered the sole global standard-setter in sustainability reporting. The current version, the "G3.1 Guidelines," was issued in 2006 and the next generation, the G4 Guidelines, are scheduled to be released in 2013. The proposed fourth generation (G4) of GRI's guidelines will cover economic, governance, social, and environmental performance.[8]

In February 2010, the Securities and Exchange Commission (SEC) issued the report "Commission Guidance Regarding Disclosure Related to Climate Change," which requires public companies to disclose material financial and reputational risks associated with global climate change.[9] This rule along with the BP Gulf of Mexico oil spill in April 2010, encourages regulators to establish rules requiring more disclosure on sustainability performance.

The International Integrated Reporting Committee (IIRC) was formed in August 2010 with the primary goal of establishing a globally accepted integrated reporting framework to standardize reporting on sustainability performance information. The IIRC promotes integrated reporting, which is intended to make the link between sustainability and economic value by focusing on the interrelationships between all aspects of business

KEY**GUIDANCE**

A survey conducted by Ernst & Young indicates the following global themes regarding climate change:

- Executive leadership and effective governance are critical to fully understand and realize the full potential of the business response to climate change. More than 90 percent of executives surveyed indicate that climate change governance should be addressed at the board and top-management level.
- Business drivers are dominated by the top-line and bottom-line impacts of climate change initiatives, with keen focus on meeting changes in customer demand.
- Business executives are committed to addressing the ever-increasing challenges of climate change.
- Climate change investments have increased despite regulatory uncertainty.[10]

sustainability.[11] The International Organization for Standardization (ISO), in November 2010, developed "ISO 26000,"guidelines for social responsibility reporting. The guidelines focus primarily on relevance and the value of public reporting on social responsibility performance to both internal and external users.[12]

ISO 26000 is a globally accepted guidance document for social responsibility relevant to all types and sizes of entities, from governmental to nongovernmental organizations and private businesses to public companies, small to large. ISO 26000 also covers a broad range of activities, including economic, social, governance, ethical, and environmental issues. ISO 26000 goes beyond profit maximization and social performance to cover all EGSEE dimensions of sustainability. Social responsibility performance, as promoted in ISO 26000, correlates to sustainability performance because each requires the other.

In July 2011, the Singapore Exchange (SGX) introduced a "Sustainability Reporting Guidance" framework, requiring its listed companies to disclose accountability for their operations and conduct business in a sustainable manner. This framework provides the policy statement that sets out principles, questions, and answers to assist listed companies in expanding their conventional financial reports to emerging EGSEE sustainability reports.[13]

Adoption of sustainability reporting has made significant progress during the past decade. In 2000 about 44 organizations followed the GRI guidelines to report a range of sustainability information, whereas in 2010, the number of organizations disclosing sustainability reports grew to 1,973. As of September 2011, more than 3,000 global companies disclose sustainability information.[14] The terms "sustainability reporting," "integrated reporting," "environmental, social, and governance (ESG) reporting," "corporate social responsibility (CSR) reporting," and "risk compliance and governance (RCG)" have been used interchangeably in the business literature to describe reports with a wide range of coverage and different degrees of focus on risk, environmental, social, or governance issues. In this book, we will take a holistic and integrated approach to sustainability reporting by discussing all five dimensions of sustainability performance of economic, governance, social, ethical, and environmental (EGSEE) issues.

STATUS OF BUSINESS SUSTAINABILITY AND SUSTAINABILITY REPORTING AND ASSURANCE

Reporting of sustainability performance has been for most part voluntary, as more than 3,000 business organizations worldwide are now issuing stand-alone sustainability reports. This trend is expected to continue as investors demand more sustainability information.

An overall and comprehensive sustainability performance report can be achieved when organizations focus on satisfying the needs of all stakeholders, including employees, clients, the environment, and society, as well as investors. Businesses should balance the priorities of all stakeholders and protect their interests. According to economic theory, the primary goal of businesses is to maximize profit to ensure value creation for shareholders. As such, any other activities that deviate from this goal (e.g., social, environmental) can damage investment value unless they contribute to the promotion of the business. In some instances, corporations engage in social and environmental activities in an anticipation of preventing government interferences with their business through more regulation.

Sustainability reporting enables companies to disclose their strategies, commitments, and performance in all EGSEE areas, therefore ensuring the achievement of long-term financial targets while also mitigating negative social and environmental impacts. The idea is that a company must extend its focus beyond making profits by considering the impact of its operation on the community, society, and the environment.

The 2011 annual sustainability global executive survey conducted by the *MIT Sloan Management Review* and the Boston Consulting Group reports the following four trends:

1. Sustainability is gaining in importance. Over 75 percent of more than 4,700 executives said sustainability-related strategies are necessary to be competitive.
2. More than 68 percent of respondents stated that their commitment to sustainability has increased to 59 percent in 2010 (from 25 percent in 2009).
3. About 74 percent believe that their sustainability commitments will increase in the future.
4. Nearly 50 percent said that their sustainability commitments could influence their employment choices.[15]

The widening focus on sustainable performance and long-term, value-adding strategies has driven a need for new reporting and accountability structures, which extend beyond financial statements into nonfinancial key performance indicators based on environmental impact and social responsibility.

The GRI reporting process enables organizations to disclose sustainability information based on one of three application levels (i.e., A, B, or C) depending on the extent of information provided. GRI also recommends that external experts provide assurance, which can be designated with a + added to the application level declared. Alternatively, GRI can examine the declared content of sustainability reports and express an opinion on the extent of compliance with GRI guidelines, but not comment on the quality or reliability of the disclosed sustainability information.

GOING FORWARD

The concept of business sustainability has become an overriding factor in successful strategic planning for many organizations worldwide. The idea is that an organization must extend its focus beyond making profits by considering the impact of its operation on the community, society, and the environment. This concept of the *triple bottom line* is often used to assess an organization's success from three perspectives—profit, people, and the planet.

This book provides an introduction on the importance, relevance, and benefits of business sustainability and accountability reporting in all areas of economic, governance, social, ethical, and environmental performance (EGSEE). We will identify financial and nonfinancial key performance indicators (KPIs) for each of the five areas of EGSEE and their integration into the organization's strategic mission, goals, operations, and culture. Traditionally, business enterprises have focused on earnings as the only bottom line and the major KPI for measuring sustainable performance. As businesses have evolved, their role in society as good citizens has developed and their impact and possible external costs have become more noticeable. In light of this, refocusing on multiple bottom lines has become inevitable. The multifaceted bottom line does not replace the conventional one but supplements it by measuring performance in all areas of EGSEE.

CONCLUSION

In summary, under the conventional model, businesses have reported information to their shareholders concerning only the financial bottom line. The sustainability and accountability reporting method covers a broad range of corporate stakeholders and reflects a broader bottom line, incorporating complete EGSEE performance. Business sustainability is a process of enabling organizations to design and implement strategies that contribute to enduring performance in all EGSEE areas. Business sustainability not only ensures long-term profitability and competition advantage but also helps in maintaining the well-being of the society, the planet, and its people.

ACTION**ITEMS**

1. Develop a corporate reporting model that is comprehensive and integrated enough to reflect past, present, and expected future sustainable performance.
2. Consider the impact of emerging regulatory reforms (e.g., Sarbanes-Oxley Act of 2002, Dodd-Frank Act of 2010), as well as emerging developments and initiatives in sustainability reporting and your business strategies.
3. Comply with GRI reporting framework guidelines in preparing your sustainability reports.

4. Accept that the sustainability reporting and assurance process is an evolving corporate practice with significant potential and challenges.

5. Follow global professional organizations, including the Global Reporting Initiative (GRI) and the International Integrated Reporting Committee (IIRC), that are working to develop a set of globally accepted, uniform, and standardized sustainability reporting guidelines.

6. Adopt the 2011 GRI guidelines that focus on the triple bottom line of economic, social, and environmental performance ("Sustainability Reporting Guidelines, Version 3.1). Look ahead to the fourth generation (G4) of GRI's guidelines, which cover economic, governance, social, and environmental performance.

7. Consider the IIRC's integrated reporting strategy, which is aimed at making the link between sustainability and economic value by focusing on interrelationships between all economic, social, environmental, and governance dimensions of sustainability performance.

■ NOTES

1. Brownlee, E. R. 2011. "Corporate Sustainability Reporting: Becoming Mainstream." *Ernst & Young Faculty Connection* 33. Available at http://www.ey.com/US/en/Careers/EY-Faculty-Connection-Issue-33---Corporate-Sustainability-Reporting-Becoming-Mainstream.

2. Ibid.

3. Ioannou, Ioannis, and George Serafeim. 2010. "The Consequences of Mandatory Corporate Sustainability Reporting." Harvard Business School working paper. Available at: http://www.hbs.edu/research/pdf/11-100.pdf.

4. Sustainable Development Commission. 2011. "Looking Back, Looking Forward: Sustainability and UK Food Policy 2000–2011." Available at http://www.sd-commission.org.uk/publications.php?id=1187.

5. Ioannou, Ioannis, and George Serafeim. 2012. "The Consequences of Mandatory Corporate Sustainability Reporting." Harvard Business School working paper. Available at: http://www.hbs.edu/research/pdf/11-100.pdf.

6. For one example see: David Nicholson-Lord. 1996. "Stake-out at the Body Shop." *The Independent*, January 21, 1996. Available at http://www.independent.co.uk/news/business/stakeout-at-the-body-shop-1324992.html.

7. See the letter at: http://www.unpri.org/files/SSE%20Letters%20to%20exchanges%20-%20public%20version.pdf.

8. Global Reporting Initiative (GRI). 2010. "Sustainability Reporting Guidelines, RG, Version 3.1."Available at https://www.globalreporting.org/reporting/latest-guidelines/g3-1-guidelines/Pages/default.aspx.

9. Securities and Exchange Commission (SEC). 2010. "Commission Guidance Regarding Disclosure Related to Climate Change; Final Rule," 17 CFR Parts 211, 231, and 241, *Federal Register* 75(25). Available at http://www.sec.gov/rules/interp/2010/33-9106.pdf.

10. Ernst & Young. 2010. "Action Amid Uncertainty: The Business Response to Climate Change." Available at http://www.ey.com/GL/en/Services/Specialty-Services/Climate-Change-and-Sustainability-Services/Action-amid-uncertainty--the-business-response-to-climate-change.

11. International Integrated Reporting Committee (IIRC). 2010. "Integrated Reporting Academic Network Response to IR Discussion Paper December 2011. Available at www.theiirc.org/wp-content/uploads/2012/02/Global-Integrated-Reporting-Academic-Network-United-Kingdom.pdf.

12. International Organization for Standardization (ISO). (2010). "ISO 2600: 2010 – Guidance on social responsibility." Available at http://www.iso.org/iso/catalogue_detail?csnumber=42546.

13. See "Guide to Sustainability Reporting for Listed Companies." Available at http://rulebook.sgx.com/en/display/display_viewall.html?rbid=3271&element_id=5863

14. Global Reporting Initiative (GRI). For a complete listing of organizations currently providing sustainability reports. Available at http://database.global reporting.org.

15. Kruschwitz, N., and K. Haanaes. 2011. "First Look: Highlights from the Third Annual Sustainability Global Executive Survey." *MIT Sloan Management Review* 53(1).

CHAPTER THREE

Business Sustainability and Accountability Initiatives, Reporting, and Assurance

EXECUTIVE**SUMMARY**

B usiness sustainability addresses five dimensions of corporate performance reporting, as discussed in the previous chapters. These dimensions are economic, governance, social, ethical, and environmental (EGSEE). Conventional financial statements provide historical information on economic performance, reflecting an entity's financial condition and results of operations in assessing future business performance. Nonetheless, investors and other corporate stakeholders demand forward-looking financial and nonfinancial information on key performance indicators (KPIs) concerning the entity's governance, economic, ethical, social, and environmental activities. This chapter presents emerging initiatives and best practices of sustainability reporting in all five EGSEE sustainability performance categories and also offers suggestions relevant to providing assurance reports on all five EGSEE dimensions of sustainability performance.

MULTIPLE BOTTOM-LINE DIMENSIONS OF BUSINESS SUSTAINABILITY

Chapter 1 introduced a framework for business sustainability performance and accountability and a reporting model with a multiple bottom-line (MBL) focus. Although the primary focus of corporate reporting continues to be financial, the inclusion of social, ethical, and environmental performance is gaining momentum. In fact, there is a growing understanding that sustainable efforts positively impact the bottom line. For example, by promoting environmentally friendly practices today, the organization can avoid the unnecessary future costs of remediating environmental damage. Likewise, by investing in the community, the organization develops goodwill in its customers, driving market share.

Business sustainability is driven by increasing consumer demand for sustainable products, improved efficient practices, emerging social responsibilities, ever-increasing scarcity of resources, and ever-growing environmental concerns. The recent global economic downturn, along with increasing pressures from the public and regulators, is also driving companies to seek sustainable strategies. Sustainability efforts at an organization may put various stakeholders at odds with one another. A shareholder, for example, may believe that the purpose of the company is to create value in order to generate a desired return on investment. Customers, on the other hand, may expect that the company not only provides the product or service advertised but also gives back to society in a meaningful way. Customer satisfaction, business reputation, brand value, environmental initiatives, and social responsibility are often considered intangible business assets that cannot be adequately described in purely economic terms. As such, these assets and their value should be linked to related economic value over the long term.[1] Shareholders are better off in the long term to recognize the various financial benefits derived from the intangible business assets generated through sustainability efforts and development.

There are three significant ways that firms can create value through sustainability development and efforts. First, by adopting sustainable practices, an organization can be prepared for the inevitable policy and taxation initiatives enacted by governments. For example, the climate change conversation garners increased attention, legislation will certainly be enacted to penalize those organizations that do not have sustainable business practices. Those firms that are ahead of the curve will already have practices in place and will be ready to meet the requirements of stricter legislation, earning them an advantage over lagging competitors. Second, sustainability practices are generally viewed as positives by current and prospective stakeholders, providing an edge over competitors. When two firms produce essentially the same product, customers would generally prefer to do business with the firm that appears to be more socially responsible and environmentally conscientious. Finally, one of the most important parts of an organization, its employees, are inspired by socially responsible initiatives and that can lead to longer and more engaged staff tenure. Stockholders would do well to recognize that sustainability practices must be incorporated into the purpose of the firm and that while they may not provide an immediate payback, they do in fact raise the value of the firm over time. Corporate reporting can be used to illustrate the environmental impact of their products and the processes undertaken to become more sustainable. The concept of a connected reporting framework (CRF) provides direction for reporting strategically important financial and nonfinancial sustainability KPIs.[2] The framework is intended to provide a mechanism by which EGSEE sustainability performance can be communicated to all stakeholders. The CRF also recommends a three-phase decision-making model of assessing the potential impacts of the organization's products and services, the life cycle of each product and service, and ways that sustainability performance can be improved.

USEFULNESS OF SUSTAINABILITY INFORMATION

Investors, particularly institutional investors who typically have a long-term investment horizon, are demanding corporate disclosures beyond conventional financial information, including more sustainability information.[3] Traditionally, socially responsible investors have focused on sustainability information, whereas such interest is gaining global attention as more investors consider the planet, its people, and profits. For example, Colin Monks, Head of European Equity Research of HSBC, stated in 2005 that, "it is becoming increasingly clear that sustainable development will be one of the major drivers of industrial change over the next 50 years."[4]

An interview of 17 institutional investors and financial service providers conducted in 2009 gathered sustainability information including where sustainability information can be found, how the information is used, and the degree of satisfaction with the information disclosed.[5] Interviewees reported that while there is a wide range of available sustainability information, the most common and standardized is regarding the governance dimension of business sustainability. There is currently more demand and regulatory requirements for disclosing standardized environmental information, whereas social responsibility information is less standardized and regulated.

Sustainability information can normally be found in the following sources:[6]

1. **Companies:** Organizations typically provide sustainability information either on their websites and/or in the management discussion and analysis (MD&A) section of their annual reports. The 2012 survey conducted by the *MIT Sloan Management Review* and The Boston Consulting Group indicates that 31 percent of surveyed companies report that sustainability is contributing to their profits, whereas 70 percent have considered sustainability permanently on their management agenda.[7] These results suggest that business sustainability is gaining momentum in 2012 and onwards and will continue to be the main theme of corporate boardrooms.

2. **Data providers:** A growing number of data providers including financial data stalwarts Thomson Reuters and Bloomberg offer sustainability information that are being used by buy and sell side analysts as a factor in their recommendations for the holding or selling of equities. Between Reuters and Bloomberg they provide information to over 800,000 financial terminals.[8,9]

3. **Sustainability research firms:** A growing number of research firms provide sustainability performance information. Among them are MSCI (which in 2010 purchased RiskMetrics, which had purchased the pioneering Innovest), Jantzi Sustainalytics, Governance Metrics International, EIRIS, ECPI, FTSE-4Good, and Sustainable Asset Management (SAM). Some of these research firms have developed sustainability indices.

4. **Pension consultants:** For example, Mercer (financial advisory firm business of March and McLennen) has developed a pool of sustainability ratings regarding environmental, social, and governance spanning all asset classes.

5. **Investment firms with sustainability products:** Sell-side or broker research firms such as Goldman Sachs, Société Générale, Deutsche Bank, and Citi among numerous others provide sustainability research reports that are available to the market.

6. **Non-governmental organizations (NGOs):** Many NGOs, such as CERES, the World Resources Institute, and the the Pembina Institute, Heidelberg Institute, Pacific Institute, and the World Wildlife Fund regularly research and present sustainability-related information.

7. **Academic institutions such as Harvard Business School, ERB School of Michigan, MIT, Cambridge, etc.**

Reported sustainability information can be used for a variety of purposes including:

1. Providing risk and return potential.
2. Evaluating management quality.
3. Engaging with companies and inform proxy voting.
4. Developing customized investment products or portfolios.
5. Assessing asset managers.[10]

THE SUSTAINABILITY REPORTING PROCESS

Businesses are searching to find an effective, efficient, and feasible way to improve the quality of their financial reporting while ensuring compliance with all applicable rules, laws, regulations, and standards. Sustainability reporting can offer solutions to emerging and widening corporate reporting challenges facing businesses. The sustainability reporting process is very similar to the conventional reporting process consisting of three elements of inputs, process, and outputs as depicted in Exhibit 3.1.

Inputs to sustainability reporting are source documents, events, and transactions pertaining to performance. The processing element classifies measures, recognizes, and reports activities in accordance with sustainability reporting guidance. Outputs are sustainability reports on performance that disclose both financial and non-financial KPIs.

The Global Reporting Initiative (GRI) defines the purposes of sustainability reports as follow:

1. Benchmarking and assessing sustainability in compliance with applicable laws, rules, regulations codes, standards, norms, and guidance and best practices of sustainability initiatives.

EXHIBIT 3.1 Sustainability Reporting Process

2. Demonstrating how the organization affects and is affected by emerging sustainability developments and initiatives.
3. Comparing sustainability performance within an organization and across different organizations over time.
4. Indicator Protocols defining key performance indicators of performance to ensure consistency of sustainability reports.
5. Sector Supplements of complementing the Sustainability Reporting Guidelines and the applications of Guidelines to specific sectors including key performance indicators of the sectors.
6. Technical Protocols in providing technical details and guidance on issues (reporting boundary) pertaining the application and implementation of the Sustainability Reporting Guidelines.[11]

Sustainability reporting should reflect both positive and negative aspects of performance by disclosing:

1. Key successes and shortcomings
2. Overriding organizational risks and opportunities
3. Significant changes in the reporting period to better reflect EGSEE performance
4. Major policies, strategies, and procedures to achieve sustainability goals
5. Key obstacles and ways to mitigate their effects

Sustainability reporting reflects the commitment of organizations and their directors and officers to measure, recognize, and report on all dimensions of performance. In reporting business sustainability, management should decide on the content, scope, and format of the report and aim to address the issues of who will use the report and for what purposes. The business sustainability report should be useful, relevant, reliable, and transparent. The usefulness and relevancy of the report are determined by the accuracy of the content and its standardized format.

In 2011 GRI issued "Sustainability Reporting Guidelines, Version 3" (also known as G3), which provide reporting principles for non-financial sustainability performance.[12] These reporting principles are: materiality, stakeholder inclusiveness, context, completeness and accuracy, measurability and verifiability, and transparency. These principles are applicable to both financial and non-financial dimensions of sustainability and are described in the following paragraphs.

Materiality

Sustainability reports should reflect all relevant performance information that could influence stakeholders' decision-making process when determining sustainable and enduring performance in all EGSEE dimensions. This materiality concept is relatively well defined in financial reporting but has yet to be defined for non-financial dimensions of sustainability performance.

Materiality is determined by professional judgment and its qualitative and quantitative measures for all EGSEE performance dimensions require the proper use of professional judgment. The materiality concept applies to sustainability and accountability reporting covering a wide range of economic, governance, social, ethical, and environmental performance measures recently being reported by corporations. These multiple bottom-line (MBL) measures should enable stakeholders to make appropriate and informed decisions relevant to their interests. When reporting on their MBL sustainability performance, companies should focus on issues that are important and material to their stakeholders. Unlike financial reports, which are primarily prepared in detail for the purpose and benefit of shareholders, sustainability reports are intended to provide relevant and material MBL information on KPIs to a wide range of stakeholders, including shareholders, bondholders, employees, creditors, customers, suppliers, government, and society. Thus, sustainability reports should be concise and relevant, with a focus on only material issues that reflect the company's EGSEE performance and assist its stakeholders in understanding and assessing such performance. The Committee on Capital Markets Regulation urges the SEC to establish rules and interpretations to raise the threshold of materiality required to determine if a misstatement meets a level that is subject to litigation.[13] A reasonable materiality standard should be established for all EGSEE dimensions of business sustainability.

In 1999 the SEC issued Staff Accounting Bulletin (SAB) No 99, which requires independent auditors to consider both qualitative factors (e.g., nature of items, trend in earnings, circumstances) and quantitative factors (e.g., absolute size, relative size, cumulative effects) in assessing materiality. The SEC issued its SAB No. 108, in September 2006, in addressing: (1) diversity in practice in quantifying materiality concerning misstatements on financial reports; and (2) the potential under such practice for proper financial statements.[14] SAB No. 108 provides interpretive guidance on how public companies should quantify the materiality of misstatements on financial reports. SAB No. 108 addresses only financial reporting materiality, but it can also be used for other dimensions of sustainability reporting. It identifies two prevailing methods commonly used in practice to accumulate and quantify misstatements, namely rollover and iron curtain approaches.[15] Under the rollover approach, a misstatement is quantified based on the amount of the error occurring in the current year's income statement regardless of the carryover effects of prior-year misstatements. The rollover approach focuses primarily on the effects on income and thus can result in the accumulation of material misstatements on the balance sheet that are considered immaterial primarily because the amount that originates in each year is quantitatively small.

The iron curtain approach focuses primarily on the balance sheet effect of misstatements and thus quantifies a misstatement based on the effects of correcting the error as of the current-year balance sheet date regardless of the year(s) in which the misstatement originated. The primary shortcoming of the iron curtain approach is its failure to consider the correction of prior-year misstatements in the current year as errors. Therefore, neither the rollover approach nor the iron curtain approach properly quantifies all misstatements that could be material to users of financial statements and particularly stakeholders of sustainability reporting.

SAB No. 108 suggests the use of a combination of both the rollover and iron curtain approaches to provide a more appropriate quantification of materiality assessment for the discovery of misstatements including both the carryover and reversing effects of the prior- and current-year misstatements. SAB No. 108 also provides transition accounting and disclosure guidance, where the application of the dual approach (rollover and iron curtain) may result in a material misstatement in the prior-period financial statements. Under SAB 108 companies are allowed to restate prior-period financial statements or recognize the cumulative impact of its initial application through an adjustment to beginning retained earnings in the year of adoption.

Materiality guidelines and thresholds are fairly developed for financial reporting; however, their applications in sustainability reporting are not well established. Comprehensive and globally accepted materiality guidelines for all EGSEE dimensions need to be developed. The International Standard for Assurance Engagements (ISAE) 3000[16] and AccountAbility's Guidance AA1000 Assurance Standard[17] provide some guidance as to the extent and type of sustainability disclosures and the assessment and attestation of such disclosures. The Global Reporting Initiative (GRI) in its G3 Sustainability Reporting Guidelines asserts the following in relation to materiality: "The information in a report should cover topics and Indicators that reflect the organization's significant economic, environmental, and social impacts or that would substantively influence the assessments and decisions of stakeholders."[18]

Stakeholder Inconclusiveness

Sustainability reports should reflect all dimensions of EGSEE and address the interests of all stakeholders that affect or are affected by sustainability performance, including shareholders, creditors, customers, suppliers, competitors, government, environment, society, and the global community.

Sustainability Context

Sustainability reports should be all-inclusive in reflecting all five EGSEE dimensions of sustainability performance. These dimensions are not mutually independent and exclusive. For example achieving employee and customer satisfaction will also have positive effects on growth and financial performance. Compliance with environmental laws is not only the right thing to do, but it also reduces the likelihood of financial penalties resulting from noncompliance risk or remediation efforts. By being perceived as good citizens through philanthropy, business organizations can earn better reputations that make them more sustainable and profitable.

Completeness and Accuracy

Sustainability reports should be complete and accurate in presenting all dimensions of sustainability performance.

Measurable and Verifiable

Sustainability reports should reflect only measurable and verifiable sustainability performance. Sustainability activities that are not measurable and verifiable are neither auditable nor comparable and thus do not provide relevant and objective information to stakeholders.

Transparency

Sustainability reports should provide transparent information about all EGSEE dimensions of performance.

Standardization

Currently sustainability reports are typically voluntary, prepared, and often audited based on the company's preferences, needs, and specifications, with no compliance to a set of globally accepted standards. These reports vary in terms of structure, content, format, accuracy, and assurance level.

A survey of corporate secretaries of 54 companies in 16 industries conducted in 2010 by Conference Board suggests six areas of sustainability reporting can be easily standardized. These areas and their impotence in terms of percentage of total respondents are:

1. Evaluating sustainability activities (76.5 percent).
2. Procedures for integrating the sustainability initiatives and programs into the organization's vision, strategies, and policies (70.6 percent).
3. Defining the scope of the sustainability activity (58.8 percent).
4. Communication with stakeholders regarding their sustainability interests and concerns (52.9 percent).
5. Disclosing sustainability initiatives and programs (47.1 percent).
6. Overseeing the implementation of the sustainability integration procedures (41.2 percent).[19]

Standardization can provide a wide range of benefits including:

- Creating uniformity for both internal and external sustainability information.
- Improving comparability of sustainability information.
- Establishing consistency in proving assurance on sustainability reports.
- Promoting transparency, reuse, and analysis of sustainability information.
- Creating an opportunity for a broader use of sustainability information.
- Enabling the use of structured and standardized electronic reporting formats, such as extensible business reporting language (XBRL).

One area this is expected to further standardization is the assurance of sustainability reporting as well as to the entities undertaking the assurance.

SUSTAINABILITY REPORTING IN ACTION

Recently, the Big Four accounting firms have promoted variations of sustainability reporting. In 2010 PricewaterhouseCoopers (PwC) launched a comprehensive integrating reporting (CIR), which discloses both financial and nonfinancial KPIs. CIR focuses on capturing and disclosing relevant information on strategic corporate objectives and performance in assessing opportunities and risk, ensuring sustainable performance, maintaining a good reputation, and being a good citizen. An Ernst & Young study reveals that more than two-thirds of the Fortune Global 500 companies publish some form of sustainability report as defined in this book. It is expected that a growing number of entities including business corporations, not-for-profit organizations, and even private companies will provide some sort of sustainability and accountability reports above and beyond conventional financial reports. More than 3,000 companies worldwide currently prepare and disclose sustainability reports, according to the E&Y study, including U.S. companies Microsoft, Cisco, Ford, Johnson & Johnson, Procter & Gamble, Best Buy, Chevron, ConocoPhillips, Xerox, HP, and Disney. Internationally, Shell, BASF, ArcelorMittal, Novartis, Carrefour, Nokia, Siemens, HSBC, and Novo Nordisk prepare sustainability reports.[20]

Sustainability reporting with a focus on environmental issues originated in mining, utilities, and energy industries and is now widely used in all sectors, including financial services, telecommunications, health care, logistics, construction, and even not-for-profit entities. The Ernst & Young study also suggests that equity analysts increasingly consider sustainability practices such as climate change and CSR strategies when valuing and rating public companies.

As sustainability reporting gains widespread acceptance and is used by many high-profile companies in almost all industrial sectors, the reliability, relevance, and comparability of sustainability reports become crucial. As rating agencies and financial analysts in particular utilize sustainability information, reasonable assurance plays an important role in the accuracy of their ratings and valuations, which eventually affect the company's cost of capital and stock value. Thus, the third-party audit and assurance reports on sustainability disclosures can be beneficial to all stakeholders, including companies, investors, creditors, suppliers, customers, government, and society. Public accounting firms have traditionally provided audit reports on mandated financial statements and they are well qualified and prepared to provide assurance reports on all EGSEE dimensions of sustainability and accountability performance.

PROMOTION OF SUSTAINABILITY REPORTING

Several organizations have provided guidelines for sustainability reporting including the GRI's Integrated Reporting Framework and Accountability for

Sustainability's Connected Reporting Framework. Sustainability reporting can be promoted in several ways. The most effective and natural way to promote sustainability reporting is through market forces; investors and other stakeholders will drive demand. Another way would be for policy-makers and regulators to mandate a range of measures to promote compulsory sustainability reporting. This could be achieved through four different methods:

1. Regulatory measures and reforms intended for corporations to comply with.
2. Regulatory endorsement and strong encouragement of the adoption of GRI sustainability guidelines by organizations, and particularly by business corporations worldwide.
3. A process of complying with a set of mandatory sustainability reporting measures or explaining why not.
4. Requiring stock exchanges to establish sustainability reporting listing standards (e.g., the Singapore Exchange).

While voluntary disclosure of sustainability performance information may have firm-specific effects, mandatory sustainability reporting can generate positive systemic effects, such as an ability to compare and contrast entities at the industry, market, country, and global levels.[21]

FUTURE OF SUSTAINABILITY REPORTING

Best practices in sustainability reporting and assurance are evolving. Currently there is no globally accepted set of reporting and assurance guidance regarding the content and format of the reports. Relevant questions to be addressed are:

1. What dimensions of sustainability performance should be reported on?
2. What framework should be used?
3. How prescriptive should sustainability standards be (e.g., principles-based versus rules-based)?
4. What sustainability reporting system should be used (e.g., voluntary versus mandatory)?
5. What level and type of sustainability assurance should be required?
6. Who should provide sustainability assurance (e.g., internal versus external providers)?[22]

Sustainability reports are expected to be value-relevant to both external and internal users. Investors and other stakeholders, including suppliers, customers, government, and society, can have more transparent information about performance, which enables them to make more informed decisions. Sustainability reporting can also improve internal management practices by enabling companies to establish better relationships with investors, customers, suppliers, employees, regulators, and society. Sustainability reporting can also create more incentives for management to refocus its goals, strategic decisions, and actions from a short-term and long-term prospective.

Sustainability reporting can be used as a tool for more effective risk management of identifying both opportunities and risks associated with operations. Thus, more transparent sustainability disclosures on performance create opportunities to identify and correct operational inefficiencies, as well as reputational and financial risks that would improve economic performance. Best practices of sustainability suggest that companies that ignore their social, governance, ethical, and environmental dimensions often suffer in a number of ways:

- Not be sustainable in the long term
- Be subject to higher risk of regulatory actions
- Lose their license to operate
- Lose customer confidence in their products and services and suffer from a damaged reputation
- Not be able to attract the most qualified and talented human capital and workforce
- Incur a higher cost of capital, both debt and equity
- Experience decreased analyst interest, which may affect their market valuation
- Not attract investors with long-term horizons
- Encourage managerial practices of not being sensitive or accountable for EGSEE performance
- Not set an appropriate tone at the top, with directors, officers, and corporate leaders failing to promote behavior that is ethical, accountable, and socially and environmentally responsible, impacting practices throughout the organization.

The format and content of existing sustainability reports are not standardized and range in quality and reliability. There are six major improvements needed in sustainability disclosures:[23]

1. **Format Standardization:** Standardizing all aspects of sustainability performance where there is no set of globally accepted guidelines is a challenging task. Currently companies provide ad hoc reports on dimensions of sustainability performance (excluding economic performance) including ratios, graphs, and charts without sufficient numerical values and narrative description. The value relevance of sustainability reports would significantly improve if the reports were more standardized and prepared based on globally accepted guidelines (e.g., GRI).

2. **Comparability:** Sustainability reports would be useful and relevant to stakeholders when they reflect uniform and comparable performance metrics. Performance metrics should be exactly identified, correctly measured, consistently measured, and comparably reported.

3. **Availability and Transparency:** Currently only a small portion of public companies provide any sustainability disclosures pertaining to their performance. In many cases sustainability disclosures are not consistent, comparable, and transparent. Lack of availability and transparency of sustainability information place many global companies in competitive disadvantage as more market participants are evaluating companies based on overall integrated performance and not just economic performance.

4. **Timeliness:** Sustainability performance reports should be integrated and timely so they are useful for decision making by stakeholders. Currently, except for mandatory reporting requirements for economic performance in a standardized set of audited financial statements, other dimensions of sustainability performance are normally voluntarily and inconsistently reported. Some companies only report on their environmental and social responsibility every two years. Sustainability reports should be comprehensive, prepared and integrated in one report, and disclosed regularly and continuously on a timely basis.

5. **Reliability:** Completeness, accuracy, and timeliness of sustainability reports strengthen the reliability of such reports. The reliability of sustainability reports plays an important role in determining stakeholders' trust and confidence in them. While management is primarily responsible for the reliability of sustainability reports any external and independent assurance should improve the reliability of such reports.

6. **Analysis:** An integrated and holistic sustainability report should analyze the link between all dimensions of sustainability performance. For example, well-governed and ethical companies should also achieve more sustainable economic and financial performance.

The International Integrated Reporting Committee (IIRC) has developed its integrated reporting as a framework for sustainability reporting that intends to meet the following five criteria:

1. Satisfy the information needs of long-term investors by presenting sustainability information that affects long-term decision-making.
2. Make the link between sustainability and economic value by focusing on interrelationships between all aspects of business performance including social, financial, and environmental.
3. Present the framework for social and environmental factors to be considered in reporting and decision making.
4. Refocus performance metrics from short term to long term and broader sustainability.
5. Bring corporate reporting closer to information needs of management in managing the business.[24]

Sustainability reporting is now gaining acceptance and emerging as the best way to communicate EGSEE performance information to interested users. As previously mentioned, more than 3,000 companies worldwide now issue sustainability reports, including two-thirds of the Fortune Global 500 companies.[25] One way to communicate sustainability information is to integrate it with financial reporting and issue a comprehensive corporate report on all five dimensions of sustainability performance.

MANDATORY VERSUS VOLUNTARY SUSTAINABILITY REPORTS

There is no mandatory guidance at this time for sustainability reporting. However, there are several voluntary guidelines for sustainability reporting, including the reporting frameworks released by GRI, the Connected Reporting Framework, and the reporting publications of AccountAbility, as discussed in previous sections.

C-level management of public companies has stepped up its efforts in achieving sustainable shareholder value creation and enhancement, improving the reliability of financial reports in the post-Sarbanes-Oxley (post-SOX) era. Moreover, countries worldwide have either revised or established business sustainability and corporate accountability best practices or codes. For example, global companies, in compliance with ISOs 9000, 14000, 26000, and

31000, are paying more attention to improving the quality of their products, addressing their environmental issues, fulfilling their social responsibilities, and managing their risks, respectively. The moves toward integrated sustainability reports, independent directors serving on corporate boards, increased disclosure of executive compensation, and rotation of audit partners are other examples of progress. There is a global trend toward sustainability performance improvement.

Mandatory sustainability reporting can be evaluated in two opposing ways. It can be viewed as over-burdensome legislation that will impose unneeded and costly obligations on public companies for providing sustainability performance disclosures. Or it can be argued that mandatory sustainability reporting can improve the quality, reliability, consistency, timeliness, transparency, and usefulness of sustainability performance information. It would also encourage the use of sustainability information by all stakeholders including regulators, institutional investors, companies, and other financial market participants. The benefits of disclosing sustainability information, which are often hard to quantify, should exceed preparation costs, which are easy to measure.

Regulators worldwide have taken initiatives to make at least some elements of sustainability reporting mandatory for public companies. Examples are the guidelines for external reporting by state-owned companies in Sweden and the Danish Financial Statements Act in Denmark. Other countries also have mandatory integrated reporting (e.g., the King Code III in South Africa and the Grenelle II Act in France). The Singapore Exchange in July 2011 released its "Sustainability Reporting Guide" for its listed companies, which requires disclosure of accountability for conducting business in a sustainable manner. In the United States, the Securities and Exchange Commission (SEC) in February 2010 released an interpretive guide regarding climate change disclosures in management's discussion and analysis (MD&As). In 2009, regulators in Canada required corporate disclosures for both quantitative and qualitative environmental, social, and governance information. The International Accounting Standards Board (IASB) has released guidance on management commentary that recommends sustainability disclosures in some dimensions of sustainability performance.[26]

Several laws and regulations in the United States mandate sustainability disclosure compliance. The most established regulations pertain to financials including: the Securities Act of 1933, the Securities and Exchange Act of 1934, the Sarbanes-Oxley Act of 2002 (SOX), and the Dodd-Frank Act of 2010 and related SEC rules. Taken together, these regulations require that listed public companies measure their economic performance and prepare a set of financial statements (see Chapters 4 and 5). The corporate governance dimension of EGSEE is governed by SOX, the Dodd-Frank Act, and SEC-related regulations and best practices. The ethical sustainability performance dimension is required under SEC rules. Environmental rules, regulations, standards, and best practices will be presented in Chapter 9.

Companies typically report on a variety of dispersed financial and non-financial sustainability KPIs and use a wide range of formats, structures, and metrics for disclosing them across different time horizons. Currently, disclosed sustainability reports are not adequate and effective in providing systematic, uniform, and comparable sustainability information. An alternative mandatory sustainability report should be considered to accomplish the following:

- Standardize dispersed sustainability reports that are currently issued.
- Establish a globally accepted reporting framework for sustainability information.
- Create uniformity in objectively reporting all five dimensions of EGSEE performance.
- Ensure that a wide range of users, including investors, have access to uniform and comparable sustainability reports.
- Facilitate uniform sustainability assurance.

It is documented that existing regulations governing sustainability reporting are neither adequate nor effective in promoting and enforcing mandatory sustainability disclosures.[27] The effectiveness, reliability, relevance, and uniformity of sustainability reports are greatly influenced by the level of disclosure (voluntary versus mandatory), the extent of enforcement (inadequate versus adequate), and the extent of uniformity (less uniform versus more uniform) as depicted in Exhibit 3.2

SUSTAINABILITY ASSURANCE

As more organizations produce sustainability reports to meet the needs of a variety of stakeholders, while complying with regulatory measures, the assurance on these reports becomes more credible. Corporate stakeholders may demand assurance on sustainability reports even if it is not legally

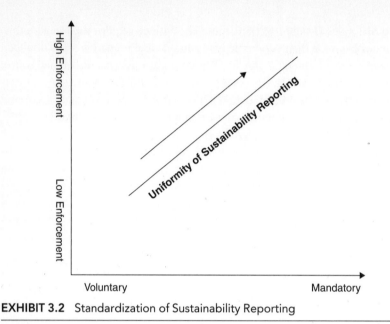

EXHIBIT 3.2   Standardization of Sustainability Reporting

required by a regulator or standard setter. Assurance services can play a vital role in helping stakeholders obtain performance information that is as reliable, accurate, and timely as they desire.

The objectivity, reliability, transparency, credibility, and usefulness of sustainability reports are important to both internal and external users of reports. Sustainability assurance can be provided internally by the internal audit function of the organization or by external assurance providers. Internal auditors are well qualified to assist management in the preparation of sustainability reports and provide assurance on the integrity and credibility of the reports. Nonetheless, external users of sustainability reports may demand more independent and objective assurance. This type of assurance must be provided by certified public accountants (CPAs), professional assurance providers, or equivalent accredited individuals, groups, or bodies.

GRI advocates the use of external assurance for sustainability reports.[28] It also recommends the following key qualities of external assurance on sustainability reports:[29]

- Sustainability assurance is provided to the organization by competent, external professional groups or individuals.

- Assurance providers have conducted their work in systematic, documented, and evidence-based procedures.
- Assurance providers assess whether the sustainability report discloses a reasonable and balanced presentation of EGSEE performance.
- Assurance providers can render independent and impartial opinions on sustainability reports.
- Assurance providers assess the extent to which the sustainability report is prepared in compliance the GRI reporting framework.
- Assurance providers submit a written report expressing their opinion on the sustainability report and their relationship to the report preparer.

Financial statements have traditionally been accompanied by an audit report from a third-party independent auditor who provides an opinion on the fair presentation of financial statements in compliance with accounting standards. In the post-SOX era (after 2004) large companies in the United States also include an audit report on internal control over financial reporting, which lends more credibility to published audited financial statements. As third-party assurance has been an integral component of corporate reporting, it makes sense to require the same level of third-party assurance on all performance dimensions of sustainability. Consequently, more credible sustainability information improves the level of trust and confidence that stakeholders have in a company's disclosure.

Factors that may influence the company's decision to obtain third-party assurance include the type of assurance—in terms of either a review of sustainability data (negative assurance) or audit of sustainability data (positive assurance)—as well as the cost of assurance and the ability and availability of accounting and consulting firms to audit or review all dimensions of sustainability performance. The type of third-party sustainability assurance (audit or review) is determined by mandatory or voluntary sustainability reporting guidelines and related costs. Typically, audits of sustainability data are more rigorous and costly, and thus more appropriate for providing positive assurance on mandatory sustainability reports. The review of sustainability data is less rigorous and costly, and thus more appropriate for voluntary reporting on sustainability performance.

AA1000's 2008 Assurance Standard (AS) was established by the not-for-profit professional institute AccountAbility (AA), which provides assurance-related services to its members.[30] The International Standard on Assurance Engagements (ISAE 3000) is intended to offer a basic framework for audits associated with financial and nonfinancial data.[31] These types of audits can be conducted on dimensions of sustainability performance data including financial and economic data and environmental, social, and governance reports. ISAE 3000 was developed to further address governance and ethical requirements, quality control, engagement acceptance, planning, expert materials, evidence-gathering processes, documentation, and preparing assurance reports. The American Institute of CPAs's (AICPA's) AT101[32] and the Canadian Institute of Chartered Accountants's *Handbook* Section 5025[33] have also been used in providing assurance on nonfinancial information disclosed by organizations.

Assurance standards on the nonfinancial dimensions of sustainability including EGSEE standards are yet to be fully developed and globally accepted. Nonetheless, there are currently two global standards providing assurance guidance for business sustainability. The International Standard on Assurance Engagements (ISAE) 3000, issued by the IAAS Board in 2004, provides guidance for assurance on nonfinancial dimensions of sustainability. Also, global sustainability assurance standard AA1000AS, issued in 2008 by AA, a global nonprofit organization, provides reporting and assurance guidance for nonfinancial dimensions of sustainability performance. In addition to these globally related sustainability assurance standards, there are national sustainability standards, including the American Certified Public Accountants (AICPA) AT 101 and the Canadian Institute of Charted Accountants (CICA) *Handbook* Section 5025.

Types of Assurance Opinions

There are three types of assurance opinions on sustainability information. The first type is referred to as *negative assurance*, where the accountants opine that they are not aware of any modifications that need to be made to sustainability performance disclosures to ensure compliance with a set of globally accepted sustainability standards (e.g., ISO 26000). In the second type, known as *positive assurance*, accountants opine whether or not sustainability performance disclosures are fairly presented in conformity with a set of globally accepted sustainability standards.

The third type is the *integrated* and/or *universal audit* approval, in which accountants provide limited assurance as to compliance with all applicable sustainability standards based on agreed-upon procedures. This type is filed with an international public registry.

CONTINUUM OF ASSURANCE ON SUSTAINABILITY INFORMATION

The concept of a continuum of assurance, where the level of assurance is determined by a set of integrated factors, was first introduced by the International Auditing Practices Committee (IAPC) in its exposure draft entitled "Reporting on the Credibility of Information" in 1997.[34] The level of assurance, from limited to high-level, is determined by the interrelationships among four variables of subject matter, reported criteria, auditing aspects (nature, timing, and extent of procedures), and quality and quantity of evidence available. This concept of continuum assurance is relevant and applicable to sustainability performance information as depicted in Exhibit 3.3.

Exhibit 3.3 shows that the level of assurance provided by accountants on sustainability performance is determined by the type of sustainability category.

The level of continuum assurance from low to high depends on the type of assurance from social to economic, as well as the extent and nature of evidence-gathering procedures. In general, obtaining assurance requires an objective examination of subject matters and gathering of sufficient and competent evidence to provide an impartial assurance on the subject matter. For example, audit of financial statements reflecting economic sustainability performance requires an integrated audit on both financial statements and

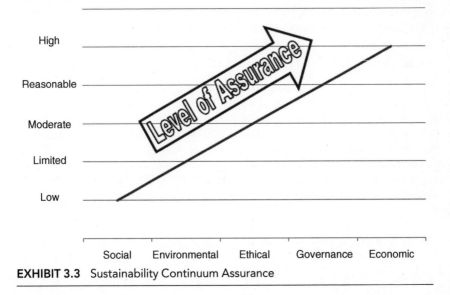

EXHIBIT 3.3 Sustainability Continuum Assurance

internal control over financial reporting as further discussed in Chapter 4. An integrated audit requires auditors to gather sufficient and competent evidence in order to provide reasonable assurance about the reliability of financial statements and the effectiveness of internal control over financial reporting. Examination of corporate social responsibility performance requires assurance providers to offer limited assurance indicating that the third-party provider is not aware of noncompliance with stated social criteria. Regardless of the level of assurance, at minimum the third-party assurance provider should gather adequate evidence to ascertain correspondence between the subject matter (EGSEE) performance and established criteria and communicate the appropriate level of assurance to the interested parties. In other words, audit of financial statements reflecting economic dimension of business sustainability has a high to reasonable level of assurance, whereas the review of social dimension of sustainability performance can offer only a low to limited level. Thus, economic performance audited by an independent auditor is more reliable than internally prepared reports on social and ethical performance.

INTERNAL CONTROLS RELEVANT TO SUSTAINABILITY PERFORMANCE

Internal controls relevant to sustainability performance can be classified as internal control over financial reporting (ICFR) and internal control over non-financial sustainability performance, such as governance, ethics, social, and environmental issues. ICFR standards are well established, globally accepted, and widely practiced. PCAOB Auditing Standard (AS) No.5 and its superseded AS No.2 provide guidance for auditors to opine on ICFR.

Internal controls over nonfinancial dimensions of sustainability performance and related reporting and auditing have yet to be established and globally practiced. Nonetheless, such internal controls need to be adequately designed and effectively implemented to ensure the credibility, integrity, transparency, and reliability of the process and content of sustainability reporting. Such controls are important in improving stakeholders' confidence.

SUSTAINABILITY RISK MANAGEMENT

Risk management is an overriding component of managerial functions affecting every transaction, economic event, and all dimensions of sustainability performance. Management's educated risk-taking and risk tolerances have a great impact on growth and stability of the organization. The Committee of Sponsoring Organizations of the Treadway Commission (COSO) issued its framework for enterprise risk management (ERM) in 2004 to assist organizations in managing their risk while achieving sustainable strategic objectives, creating shareholder value, and protecting stakeholder interests.[35] The International Organization for Standardization (ISO) released its ISO 31000 standards entitled "Risk Management – Principles and Guidelines" in 2009. ISO 31000 offers principles and guidelines on risk management in all areas of sustainability EGSEE performance.[36]

Investors and other stakeholders, including suppliers, customers, government, and society, can have more transparent information about economic, governance, social, ethical, and environmental performance, which enables them to make more informed decisions. Sustainability reporting can also improve internal management practices by enabling companies to establish better relationships with investors, customers, suppliers, employees, regulators, and society. Sustainability reporting can also create more incentives for management to refocus its goals, strategic decisions, and actions from a short-term to a long-term prospect.

Sustainability reporting can be used as a tool for more effective risk management by identifying both opportunities and risks associated with operations. Thus, more transparent sustainability disclosures on performance create opportunities to identify and correct operational inefficiencies and reputational and financial risks that would impact economic performance. Organizations should identify risks and opportunities relevant to all five dimensions of sustainability performance and use proper risk-management techniques to take advantage of opportunities. ERM and ISO 31000 frameworks enable organizations to accomplish the following:

- Assess risks.
- Monitor risk and develop policies and procedures to address risk.
- Communicate risk-assessment policies and procedures to managers throughout the organization.
- Encourage managers to manage their risks relevant to their business strategies, operations, customer satisfaction, reputation, and stakeholder trust.
- Take educated risk in minimizing business failures while achieving desired growth.

Brockett and Rezaee (2012) discuss the five risks (strategic, operations, compliance, finance, and reputation) relevant to sustainability, as depicted in Exhibit 3.4.[37]

1. Strategic risks associated with business sustainability are those risks pertaining to long-term objective-setting, marketing position, and changing consumer demand, strategic investments, investor relations, and stakeholder communications. The Ernst & Young 2010 survey indicates that executives believe a strong sustainability strategy aligned with their broader business strategy is a critical component of managing business, which is driven by changes in customer demand, operational costs, and revenue opportunities.[38]

2. Operations risks are those related to business operations that impact sustainability performance, including risks associated with IT, the supply chain, and production facilities.

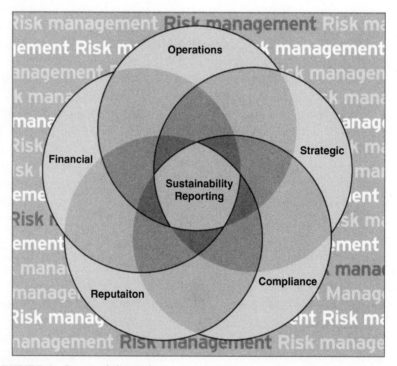

EXHIBIT 3.4 Sustainability Risks

Source: Adapted from Brockett and Rezaee, *Sustainability Reporting's Role in Managing Climate Change Risks and Opportunities.*

3. Compliance risks are those pertaining to failures to comply with local, national, and international laws, rules, regulations, and standards, dealing with issues ranging from climate change to social responsibility and financial activities. The 2010 Ernst & Young survey shows that 94 percent of respondents see national policies as "important" or "very important" in shaping their sustainability strategies and 81 percent recognize the importance of global or international policies in implementing sustainability strategies.[39]

4. Reputation risks are associated with an organization's reputation and brands, and its failure to meet the expectations of a range of stakeholders including investors, competitors, society, employees, customers, suppliers, local communities, and the media.

5. Financial risks are risks that adversely affect the organization's financial performance. This can be caused by a lack of commitment by the board and management in achieving sustainable performance. The 2010 Ernst & Young global survey of 300 executives at large companies showed that 43 percent believe that equity analysts consider factors related to climate change when valuing a company.[40]

Ioannou and Serafeim surveyed more than 4,100 publicly traded companies over a 16-year period and found that, since 1997, analysts have viewed corporate social responsibility (CSR) strategies as creating value and reducing uncertainty about future profitability and cash flow. They also found that analysts have issued more favorable ratings to companies that have sustainability strategies in place.[41]

CONCLUSION

An increasing number of organizations worldwide are issuing sustainability reports, which enable them to measure, recognize, and report on all five EGSEE dimensions of sustainability performance. Disclosure of sustainability performance can reduce the risk of noncompliance with applicable laws, rules, and regulations pertaining to financial, governance, ethical, social, and environmental issues. It can also enhance dialogue with all stakeholders on all aspects of sustainability performance and ensure that performance is incorporated into the company's overall ratings and valuation. Business sustainability and its reporting and assurance are evolving. As sustainability gains global acceptance, its measurement, recognition, reporting, and assurance will become more unified and standardized.

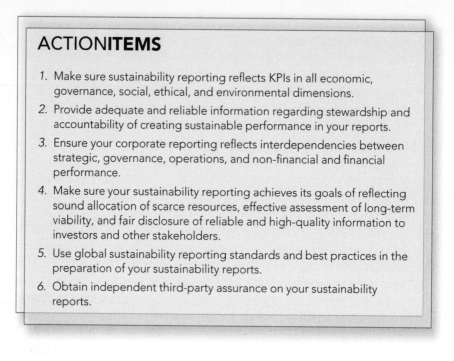

ACTION**ITEMS**

1. Make sure sustainability reporting reflects KPIs in all economic, governance, social, ethical, and environmental dimensions.

2. Provide adequate and reliable information regarding stewardship and accountability of creating sustainable performance in your reports.

3. Ensure your corporate reporting reflects interdependencies between strategic, governance, operations, and non-financial and financial performance.

4. Make sure your sustainability reporting achieves its goals of reflecting sound allocation of scarce resources, effective assessment of long-term viability, and fair disclosure of reliable and high-quality information to investors and other stakeholders.

5. Use global sustainability reporting standards and best practices in the preparation of your sustainability reports.

6. Obtain independent third-party assurance on your sustainability reports.

NOTES

1. Wheeler, D., B. Colbert, and E. Freeman. 2003. "Focusing on Value: Reconciling Corporate Social Responsibility, Sustainability and a Stakeholder Approach in a Network World." *Journal of General Management* 28(3).

2. The Prince's Charities. 2010. *Accounting for Sustainability: Practical Insights.* Available at: http://www.accountingforsustainability.org/embedding-sustainability/accounting-for-sustainability-practical-insights-book.

3. The International Corporate Governance Network (ICGN). 2008. "Statement and Guidance on Non-financial Business Reporting." Available at: http://www.icgn.org/files/icgn_main/pdfs/best_practice/buss_reporting/icgn_statement_&_guidance_on_non-financial_business_reporting.pdf.

4. Quoted in Canadian Institute of Chartered Accountants. 2010. "Environmental, Social and Governance (ESG) Issues in Institutional Investor Decision, Making." Available at: www.aicpa.org/InterestAreas/BusinessIndustryAndGovernment/Resources/Sustainability/DownloadableDocuments/CICA_ESG_Issues_in_Decision_Making.pdf.

5. Ibid.

6. Ibid.

7. The Boston Consulting Group (BCG). 2012. "Nearly a third of companies say sustainability is contributing to their profits, says *MIT Sloan Management Review*–Boston Consulting Group report," press release, January 24, 2012. Available at: http://www.bcg.com/media/PressReleaseDetails.aspx?id=tcm: 12-96246.

8. Bloomberg. 2012. "At a Glance," Bloomberg Press Room website. Available at: http://www.bloomberg.com/pressroom/facts/index.html.

9. Shayon, Sheila. 2010. "Thomson Reuters vs. Bloomberg: A Terminal Fascination." *BrandChannel*, May 11, 2010. Available at: http://www.brand channel.com/home/post/2010/05/11/Thomson-Reuters-Insider.aspx.

10. Ibid.

11. Global Reporting Initiative (GRI). 2011. "G3 Sustainability Reporting Guidelines." Available at https://www.globalreporting.org/reporting/latest-guidelines/g3-guidelines/Pages/default.aspx.

12. Ibid.

13. The Committee on Capital Markets Regulation. 2006. "Interim report of the Committee on Capital Market Regulation," November 30, 2006. Available at: www.capmktsreg.org/research.html.

14. U.S. Securities and Exchange Commission (SEC). 2006. Staff Accounting Bulletin (SAB) No. 108. Available at: www.sec.gov/interps/account/sab108.pdf.

15. Ibid.

16. The International Standard on Assurance Engagements 3000 (ISAE 3000, Revised). 2011. *Assurance Engagements Other Than Audits or Reviews of Historical Financial Information*, April 2011: Available at http://www.ifac .org/sites/default/files/publications/exposure-drafts/IAASB_ISAE_3000_ ED.pdf.

17. Global Reporting Initiative (GRI). 2011. "G3 Sustainability Reporting Guidelines." Available at: https://www.globalreporting.org/reporting/latest-guidelines/g3-guidelines/Pages/default.aspx.

18. Global Reporting Initiative (GRI). 2011. "G3 Sustainability Reporting Guidelines." Available at: https://www.globalreporting.org/reporting/latest-guidelines/g3-guidelines/Pages/default.aspx.

19. Tonello, Matteo. 2010. *Sustainability in the Boardroom*. Available at: http:// www.conference-board.org/retrievefile.cfm?filename=DN-008-10. pdf&type=subsite.

20. Ernst &Young. 2011. "TBL Technology considers sustainability reporting," Ernst & Young What Do you Think? Series, June 2011. Available at www.ey .com/Publication/vwLUAssets/CCaSS_case_study_first_time_sustainability_ reporting/$FILE/CCaSS_case_study_first_time_sustainability_reporting.pdf.

21. AccountAbility. 2011. The Future of Sustainability Assurance. ACCA Research Report No.86. Available at: www.accountability.org/images/content/1/2/ 121/FOSA%20-%20Full%20Report.pdf.

22. Ernst & Young. 2010. "Seven questions that CEOs and board should ask about 'triple bottom line' reporting," press release, October 28, 2010. Available at: http://www.ey.com/US/en/Newsroom/News-releases/Seven-questions-CEOs-and-boards-should-ask.

23. Ibid.

24. International Integrated Reporting Committee (IIRC). 2011. "Integrated Reporting." Available at: http://www.theiirc.org/.

25. Ernst &Young. 2011. "How Sustainability Has Expanded the CFO's Role: Climate Change and Sustainability." Available at: http://www.ey.com/US/en/Services/Specialty-Services/Climate-Change-and-Sustainability-Services/How-sustainability-has-expanded-the-CFOs-role.

26. International Accounting Standards Board (IASB) and the International Financial Reporting Standards (IFRS) Foundation. 2012. "Management Commentary." Available at: http://www.ifrs.org/Current | Projects/IASB+Projects/Management+Commentary/Management+Commentary.htm.

27. Ibid.

28. Global Reporting Initiative (GRI). 2011. "G3 Sustainability Reporting Guidelines." Available at: https://www.globalreporting.org/reporting/latest-guidelines/g3-guidelines/Pages/default.aspx.

29. Ibid.

30. AccountAbility. 2008. "AA1000 Assurance Standard 2008," 1–26. Available at: www.accountability.org/standards/aa1000as/index.html.

31. ISAE. 2005. "Assurance Engagements Other than Audits or Reviews of Historical Financial Information," 1–57. Available at: www.ifac.org/sites/default/files/publications/exposure-drafts/IAASB_ISAE_3000_ED.pdf.

32. American Certified Public Accountants (AICPA). 2001. "Attest Engagements AT 101," 1085–1115. Available at: www.aicpa.org/Research/Standards/AuditAttest/DownloadableDocuments/AT-00101.pdf.

33. Canadian Institute of Chartered Accountants. 2011. "Assurance," *CICA Handbook*. Toronto: Canadian Institute of Chartered Accountants.

34. The Institute of Chartered Accountants in England and Wales (ICAEW). 2011. "Alternatives to Audit: Audit and Assurance Faculty." Available at: www.icaew.com/~/media/Files/Technical/Audit-and-assurance/assurance/sustainability-assurance-your-choice.ashx.

35. Committee of Sponsoring Organizations of the Treadway Commission (COSO). 2004. "Enterprise Risk Management – Integrated Framework. Available at: www.coso.org.

36. International Organization for Standardization (ISO). 2009. "ISO 31000: Risk Management Principles and Guidelines." Available at: www.iso.org/iso/catalogue_detail.htm?csnumber=43170.

37. Brockett, A., and Z. Rezaee. 2011. "Sustainability Reporting's Role in Managing Climate Change Risks and Opportunities," *Managing Climate Change,*

Business Risk and Consequences: Leadership for Global Sustainability, edited by J.A Stoner and C. Wankel (Hampshire, England: Palgrave Macmillan): Chapter 7.

38. Ernst & Young. 2010. "Action Amid Uncertainty: The Business Response to Climate Change." Available at: http://www.ey.com/GL/en/Services/Specialty-Services/Climate-Change-and-Sustainability-Services/Action-amid-uncertainty--the-business-response-to-climate-change.

39. Ibid.

40. Ibid.

41. Ioannou, Ioannis, and George Serafeim. 2012. "The Consequences of Mandatory Corporate Sustainability Reporting." Harvard Business School working paper. Available at: http://www.hbs.edu/research/pdf/11-100.pdf.

PART TWO

Dimensions of Sustainability Performance

4

Sustainability, Corporations, Capital Markets, and the Global Economy

EXECUTIVE**SUMMARY**

In this chapter, we further investigate the concept of the multiple bottom lines (MBL) of economic, governance, social, ethical, and environmental (EGSEE) sustainability performance and their measurement, reporting, and assurance. A sustainable business is one that takes a long-term view, considering the impact of its operations and long-term strategy on the environment, community, society, and economy. The single objective of improving the organization's profit has been replaced with the concept of improving the widely known triple bottom line of measuring sustainable performance in terms of making profit while considering the impact on the planet and its inhabitants, thus in turn making the organization more economically sustainable for the long run.

GLOBAL ECONOMY AND FINANCIAL CRISIS

Recent financial crises and resulting global economic meltdowns were caused by a variety of factors, including lack of adequate focus on transparent long-term sustainable performance, ineffective corporate governance, and troubled financial institutions. The responding government bailouts in the United States, the United Kingdom, and other countries have cost trillions of taxpayer dollars without effectively energizing and stimulating capital markets or the economy, or promoting sustainable business performance.

In the context of this book and our topic, two general approaches are suggested to address the global financial crises and resulting economic meltdown. The first is to establish more effective and globally enforceable regulations to monitor activities and performance of corporations and thus better protect investors. The second is for the global market to empower shareholders to change a company's legal jurisdiction, which will enable shareholders to choose countries that better protect investor interests with a more robust corporate governance system.

The existence and persistence of the global financial crisis requires bold responses by policymakers, regulators, central banks, and the business community worldwide. More efforts must focus on the achievement of all five dimensions of EGSEE sustainability performance. In the aftermath of the global financial crisis and new regulatory reforms (e.g., Dodd-Frank Act of 2010), corporations are searching to find an effective and efficient way to improve long-term performance, minimize systemic risk, and strengthen the quality of their financial reporting while ensuring compliance with all applicable rules, laws, regulations, and standards. Sustainability reporting can offer solutions to emerging and widening corporate reporting challenges and risks facing business firms. Sustainability has become a business imperative and is demanded by investors, consumers, regulators, and the business community. Many factors have caused more interest in business sustainability, including pressure on effective use of natural and scarce raw materials; corporate reputation; and consumer awareness of corporate social responsibility, energy prices, and regulatory reforms. Business sustainability not only ensures long-term profitability and competition advantage but also helps in maintaining the well being of society, the planet, and people.

Business sustainability should focus on all five types of risks discussed in Chapter 2 (strategic, operational, compliance, financial, and reputation). Furthermore, risks related to globalization—including risks pertaining to political instability, intellectual property infringement, bribery and corruption, disaster recovery, the timing of product development, and the availability of scarce resources—should be properly assessed and considered in sustainability development. Other globalization factors, including population growth, political movement, regional differences in aging, and global warming, should also be addressed in the development of sustainability strategies.

CAPITAL MARKETS

Confidence in the sustainability and financial health of public companies is essential in keeping investor confidence high and requires public trust in the reliability of financial reports. This section discusses the importance of the capital markets to global economic prosperity, the promotion of the free enterprise system, the vital role of financial information as the lifeblood of the capital markets, and the relevance and importance of sustainability information to facilitate an efficient capital market.

The U.S. capital markets have traditionally been regarded as the deepest, safest, and most liquid in the world, and for many decades have required stringent regulatory measures for protecting investors, which has also raised the profile and status of its listed companies. However, recent competition from capital markets abroad has provided global companies with a variety of choices regarding where to list. This allows them to opt for places where they may be less subject to vigorous regulatory measures. As these markets abroad become better regulated, more liquid, and deeper, they provide companies worldwide with a preference to raise their capital needs under a different jurisdiction.

The global competitiveness of U.S. capital markets depends, to a significant extent, on the reliability of information—including financial and nonfinancial disclosures—in assisting investors to make sound decisions. Cost-effective regulation to protect investors and efficiency in attracting global investors and companies also support the United States' competitive position. Transparent and high-quality information demonstrating the sustainability of a company are the lifeblood of the capital markets. The efficiency of the markets depends on the reliability of that information, which enables the markets to act as signaling mechanisms for proper capital allocation and the potential (perhaps not yet fully realized) fulfillment of social responsibilities and achievement of governance, ethical, and environmental performance. Investor confidence in the level playing field of all market participants has encouraged investors to own stock and, as such, billions of shares trade hands every day in providing capital to businesses.

The IBM Institute for Business Value conducted a survey of more than 2,700 financial services industry participants to address the important issues of transparency and sustainability in that sector. Results of the survey indicate that the financial markets industry has profited by capitalizing on "pockets of opacity" through buying and selling complex products during the past two decades. These business strategies have generated very high returns but also resulted in extreme risk-taking and did not produce sustainable value.[1]

Adopting a framework that balances stability with innovation would be a great step for the financial services industry. Investor confidence in sustainability information will drive willingness to invest, and America's and, ultimately, the world's economic future is tied to how successfully companies respond to this call for greater transparency and reliability in sustainability information. Financial markets should continue promoting and enforcing sustainability performance along with demanding accountability reporting to ensure transparent flows of reliable, accurate KPI information to the markets. This requires policymakers, standard setters, regulators, investors, businesses, and educators to collaborate in promoting sustainability performance and accountability reporting. It would be a strong step toward rebuilding public trust and investor confidence in corporate America.

ROLE OF CORPORATIONS IN SOCIETY

The role of corporations has evolved over time from profit maximization in the 1960s and 1970s to enhancement of shareholder wealth during the 1980s and 1990s. Integrating and recognizing shareholder value includes protecting interests of all stakeholders including creditors, suppliers, customers, governments, and society at large and now adding value to all stakeholders. There used to be a saying: "What was good for General Motors (GM) was good for America." Pubic companies are expected to add value to our society and capital markets through their interactions with all stakeholders as depicted in Exhibit 4.1. The effective interactions with all stakeholders demand measurement, recognition, and disclosure of sustainability performance.

Public companies are viewed as creators of value for all stakeholders and as the major engine of economic growth and prosperity. This important role of corporations underscores the importance of business sustainability in all dimensions of performance. As separate legal entities, corporations obtain their financial capital from their investors and creditors. They get their human capital from their employees, and other resources from stakeholders including suppliers, government, and society. All stakeholders contribute to sustainable performance and the successful operation of corporations in creating value. For example, equity and debt holders provide financial capital; management provides managerial skills; the boards of directors oversee corporate affairs; employees offer labor capital; suppliers provide operational resources; and the government sets rules to protect stakeholders. In return, corporations grant desired return on investment to shareholders; compensation to directors,

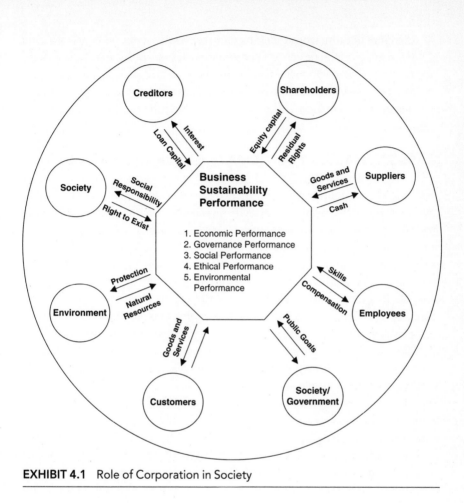

EXHIBIT 4.1 Role of Corporation in Society

officers, and employees; and fulfill their obligations to customers, suppliers, government, environment, and society. Recent corporate governance reforms, including the Sarbanes-Oxley Act of 2002 (SOX), Dodd-Frank Act of 2010, Securities and Exchange Commission (SEC) rules, listing standards, and global best practices, have shifted the power balance between the company's shareholders, directors, management, employees, and other stakeholders, whereby:

■ Shareholders have been more proactive in monitoring and scrutinizing their corporation's sustainable performance and thus heightened their expectations for directors' performance on their behalf.

- Directors have improved their commitment and accountability in fulfilling their fiduciary duties to all corporate stakeholders by overseeing management's strategic plans and decisions.
- Management has stepped up its efforts in achieving sustainable shareholder value creation and protecting the interests of other stakeholders.

SUSTAINABILITY INFORMATION NEEDS OF INVESTORS

Traditionally, sustainability performance has been of significant interest to investors who prefer to invest in socially responsible companies. Recently many institutional investors, fund managers, and investment organizations have shown interest in sustainability information beyond the conventional financial information disseminated to the capital markets. A large number of institutional investors and portfolio managers are now using sustainability information in their investment decisions. Sustainability issues can affect the company's performance and investment portfolios and be considered in assessing operating and investment decisions. To address this important global issue, in 2005, the United Nations Secretary-General invited a group of representatives from 20 investment organizations in 12 countries to establish the Principles for Responsible Investment (PRI), a set of global best practices.[2] The PRI are voluntary and inspirational rather than prescriptive, providing a framework for incorporating sustainability information into investment decision-making and ownership practices. Compliance with the PRI is expected to lead not only to more sustainable financial returns but also to a close alignment of the interests of investors with those of global society at large. The PRI provide a common framework for the integration of sustainability information into portfolio analysis and it consists of:

- Integration of sustainability information into investment analysis and the decision-making process.
- Incorporation of sustainability information into investment ownership policies and practices.
- Promotion of appropriate disclosure on sustainability information by the entities in which institutional investors invest.
- Promotion of acceptance and implementation of the principles within the investment industry.
- Collaboration among institutional investors to enhance the effectiveness of implementing the principles.

▪ Reporting on initiatives, activities, and progress toward implementing these principles.

As of 2009, there were 650 signatories to the UN PRI, representing over $18 trillion in assets compared to 20 signatories with assets of $2 trillion in 2006.[3]

In 2009, the CICA conducted interviewers of 15 financial analysts, 15 institutional investors, and two service providers and found that, generally, investors use sustainability information in their investment decisions, including those dealing with public equities, corporate debt, and private equities. In particular, investors use sustainability information in the following five investment-related areas:

1. **Identification and assessment of risk and return potentials:** Evaluating carbon price risk, identifying new investment themes (alternative energy), assessing risks related to different geographical or political issues, identifying promising new technologies and identifying and assessing red flags or relevant to investment strategies and decisions.
2. **Evaluation of management quality:** Investors often consider sustainability information as a proxy for management effectiveness. For example, governance sustainability dimensions provide information on board oversight function of managerial activities and leadership effectiveness. Risk management offers information about environmental issues and reputation.
3. **Shareholder communication, proposals, and proxy voting:** Sustainability information can be helpful in communicating related performance to shareholders in proposals, such as asking shareholders to vote on important environmental issues (e.g., climate change) or corporate governance initiatives (e.g., executive compensation).
4. **Development of customized investment products or portfolios:** Customized and targeted products can be created based on reported sustainability information pertaining to related performance data.
5. **Evaluation of asset managers:** Establishing sustainability performance benchmarks and assessing asset manager activities in relation to these targets can reveal the success of a manager's investment portfolios.[4]

The sustainability information needs of investors in making investment decisions are in all dimensions of sustainability performance. The economic performance dimension of business sustainability in terms of reported earnings and cash flows has traditionally been used by investors when assessing future cash flows and return on investment. The financial performance dimension of business sustainability will be discussed in detail in Chapters 4 and 5.

Corporate governance has received significant attention in recent years and investors have paid more attention to the responsibilities of all participants in the corporate governance process who share collective responsibility for producing reliable, transparent, and high-quality financial information. The participants in the corporate governance process are the board of directors, the audit committee, executives, internal auditors, external auditors, financial analysts, legal counsel, regulators, investing bankers, and other stakeholders. Corporate governance has transformed from a compliance process to a strategic business imperative and an integral component of investment decision-making process. The passage of the Sarbanes-Oxley and Dodd-Frank Acts and related regulations are aimed at improving the governance dimension of business sustainability. Such regulations can make that governance more useful and relevant to investors and capital markets. The governance dimension of business sustainability will be further discussed in Chapter 6.

Other dimensions of business sustainability performance—including the socially responsible, environmental, and ethical dimensions—are less standardized, and as such they have not adequately been used in investment decision-making. Regulators' recent focus on climate change initiatives is expected to promote the use of the environmental dimension of sustainability performance by investors and capital markets. The ethical dimension of sustainability performance is expected to receive more attention from investors in fostering the corporate culture integrity and competency. In their study, Ioannou and Serafeim (2011), using sustainability data from 58 countries, find that sustainability development and reporting are associated with enhanced social responsibility, improved sustainable performance, more effective employee training and corporate governance, enhanced managerial credibility, more ethical practices, and reduced bribery and corruption.[5] Capital markets and market participants are now using sustainability information in many ways, including the following:

- Assessing risks and opportunities associated with sustainability issues pertaining to all five dimensions of EGSEE.
- Integrating sustainability performance into investment decision making.
- Enhancing dialogue with management and directors on all aspects of sustainability performance.

- Determining to what extent financial institutions are using sustainability information in general and how each component of EGSEE performance impacts their investment decision making.
- Ensuring the tone of the board of directors' top commitments meets investors' preferred sustainability performance.
- Promoting executive commitment to shareholders' proposals on preferred sustainability performance.
- Electing directors with keen focus and qualifications on various aspects of sustainability performance.
- Ensuring management consideration of shareholder proposals on preferred sustainability performance.
- Encouraging integration of sustainability performance dimensions into the ratings of agencies such as DJSI and CRD Global Sustainability Index.
- Ensuring financial analysts are using sustainability performance in the company's valuation process.
- Encouraging investment research service providers to gather and analyze sustainability performance data.
- Promoting the integration of sustainable performance initiatives, programs, policies, procedures, and reporting into all corporate strategies and corporate disclosures.

CORPORATE REPORTING

Effective and transparent corporate reporting is the lifeblood of capital markets. Reliable and useful information on corporate performance is vital to maintain sustainable and healthy capital markets. Corporate reporting should be value-relevant to all stakeholders and help them achieve their goals. The conventional corporate reporting model reflects historical financial performance. This rules-based approach is complicated, not concise, and cannot support global comparisons. It also fails to present relevant nonfinancial KPIs on many critical aspects of business and is not effectively overseen by regulatory authorities. Traditionally, corporate reporting has been directed toward protecting the interests of one important group of stakeholders: the shareholders. Consequently, shareholders have shown more interest in financial reports. In recent years, other stakeholders have also shown interests in corporate reporting and the traditional model may not be adequate to respond to needs of the diverse stakeholders of the 21st century.

The 2007 PwC survey reveals that investors would like generally accepted accounting principles (GAAP) to remain as the primary guidance for financial reporting and analysis. They would also like to see improvements in revenue recognition and become more engaged in the standard-setting process.[6] More specifically, investors expect to see some improvements in different sections of financial reports. Five suggested improvements in the income statement are:

1. Better assessment of whether an increase in revenues or earnings is sustainable.
2. More breakdowns of costs to better reflect the operational leverage of the business.
3. Separate revaluations of assets and liabilities to avoid obscuring underlying operating performance.
4. More detailed information on net income and other summary earnings numbers including earnings before interests, taxes, depreciation, and amortization (EBITDA).
5. Less management discretion in the determination of the company's performance.

Investors rely on the balance sheet to provide relevant information as an input into a cash-flow model, calculating return on invested capital and assessing debt levels and working capital. There are two primary preferred balance sheet improvements. First, providing current values for liquid financial assets and investments while retaining historical costs for certain assets used in ongoing operations can be useful to investors. Second, presenting key assumptions enables comparison across companies and assessment of the reasonableness of fair values.

Suggested improvements for the statement of cash flow are supported by two simple changes: (1) preparing the statement of cash flow base on the income statement model; and (2) and providing more detailed cash flow information and related notes.

There are four suggested improvements in voluntary disclosures involving management discussion and analysis (MD&A):

1. Adding management's strategic and nonfinancial information, which is value-relevant to investors.
2. Enhancing the contextual understanding of the company's nonfinancial KPIs, including information about competitors, market research, and face-to-face management briefings.

3. Fostering investor interest in social and environmental issues.
4. Improving the value-relevance of management reports on governance by reflecting management behavior in practice.

The conventional financial reporting model has been criticized for presenting historical data rather than disclosing market performance. This provides only a portion of relevant financial information. The current reporting process relies on a predominately historical cost-based framework, which was established many years ago when business transactions were not complicated, corporations operated nationally, assets were mostly tangible in nature, and a manual accounting system was the norm. Many things have changed since then; businesses are becoming extremely complicated and operating globally and electronically. This new business model requires a new financial reporting process capable of capturing complicated global transactions online and based on their fair value and in accordance with a set of globally accepted accounting standards.

In recent years, corporate reporting has been broadened beyond financial reporting to address a wide range of stakeholders with a variety of dimensions relevant to EGSEE issues. Many global businesses are now recognizing that reporting their financial performance through the use of the conventional single bottom line is no longer adequate. Concerns over a range of scandals and erosion of public trust have encouraged businesses to focus on achieving bottom-line sustainability performance in all EGSEE dimensions. A few examples include business-related financial fraud, human rights abuses, and environmental degradation, which have shaken investor confidence and public trust.

RECENT INITIATIVES IN CORPORATE REPORTING

The International Federation of Accountants (IFAC) commissioned a project on the financial reporting supply chain to address people and processes associated with the preparation, oversight, approval, audit, analysis, and use of financial reports. All supply-chain links, from preparation to the final use, should function effectively and collectively to produce high-quality financial reports.

According to a 2010 PwC report about 35 percent of reviewed FTSE 350 Index companies did not disclose their business models in the 2010 reporting period.[7] There is no uniform standard on how companies should disclose their goals (e.g., creating shareholder value) and strategies for implementation. The PwC 2010 report indicated that about 29 percent of FTSE 350 companies clearly disclose the key resources and relationships they need to effectively implement their business strategies. Investors need to have data on operational as well as financial KPIs to be able to understand and assess their companies' sustainability performance in creating value. The business model may describe a company's life cycle, its strengths and resources, its value chain, how it generates profits, how it implements strategies, how it manages value-adding activities and outcomes, and how it generates performance in all sustainability dimensions.

The International Federation of Accountants (IFAC), during the past several years, has taken several initiatives in improving the quality of financial reports, auditing, and governance for global companies in the post-financial-crisis era. In 2008, the IFAC published its report "Financial Reporting Supply Chain: Current Perspectives and Directions" and subsequently established a Business Reporting Project Group to study global progress in the areas of governance, financial reporting, and auditing. The IFAC's 2008 global research study indicates that while there have been some improvements, the following challenges remain:[8]

Corporate governance: Inadequate focus on risk and control systems; ineffective integration of governance measures into the business model; insufficient safe-harbor protection for those charged with governance; and inadequate link between remuneration for directors, executives, and corporate sustainable performance.

Financial reporting: Inadequate move toward the adoption of a set of globally accepted accounting standards; slow move toward the use of principles-based reporting standards; and persistent challenges of fair value accounting.

Financial auditing: Persistent challenges for small and medium accounting practices to comply with ever-increasing international standards on auditing (ISAs) and other national auditing standards; inconsistent implications and enforcements of various sets of auditing standards for multinational clients; inadequate understanding and appreciation of benefits of audits by the financial reporting stakeholders; widening auditor litigation risks in today's turbulent environment; and audit challenges of fair-value accounting estimates.

The usefulness of financial reports: Inadequate reporting on nonfinancial KPIs, risks, and sustainability performance; lack of a robust link between reporting and an organization's objectives, strategies, and actions; and ineffective use of fair-value measurements in current market situations.

Improvements needed in financial reporting are:

- More relevant and understandable financial reports for various users.
- The use of a direct method in the preparation of the cash-flow statement.
- More support for retail investors.
- Simplification of financial reporting standards by standard-setters.
- Limited financial reporting burden on smaller and nonlisted entities.
- Support for the use of fair value in financial reporting.
- Support for the use of principles-based financial reporting standards.
- Convergence to one set of globally accepted, principles-based, high-quality financial reporting standards.
- Preparers of financial statements maintain professional behavior and qualification.[9]

The global business community and accounting profession demands more comprehensive and integrated sustainability and accountability reporting. This emerging corporate reporting consists of regulatory reporting requirements and voluntary disclosures for public companies, including:

- SEC mandatory filing
- SEC interpretive guidance on climate change disclosure
- The Ontario Securities Commission Corporate Sustainability Reporting Initiative
- The Climate Registry and Carbon Disclosure Project voluntary reporting
- Climate Disclosure Standards Board (CDSB) Climate Change Reporting Framework
- GRI framework
- The Prince of Wales' Accounting for Sustainability Project (A4S) and International Integrated Reporting Committee
- ISO 9000, 14000, and 26000 reporting requirements

A new corporate sustainability model should be developed to meet the following 10 objectives:

1. Serve and satisfy the needs of all stakeholders including shareholders, suppliers, customers, governments, the environment, and society.

2. Present both financial and nonfinancial KPIs in all EGSEE dimensions.
3. Be guided by principles-based standards of accounting that are flexible enough to adequately and effectively reflect performance in EGSEE dimensions.
4. Provide transparent and easily understandable financial and non-financial KPIs.
5. Present comprehensive and integrated information on financial statements and internal controls.
6. Be cost-efficient, effective, and scalable while providing useful, relevant, and reliable information.
7. Be prepared on a set of high-quality and globally accepted financial and nonfinancial standards.
8. Improve risk management.
9. Enhance operational efficiency.
10. Improve investor confidence and stakeholder trust.

The following five improvements were made to increase the usefulness of financial reports:[10]

1. More useful and relevant financial information due to improved standards, regulation, and oversight.
2. More disclosure and better comparability in financial reports.
3. Enhanced reliability of financial reports.
4. Increased emphasis on narrative reporting.
5. Easier access to financial information.

Seven challenges in the usefulness and understandability of financial reports are:

1. Reduced usefulness and readability of financial reports due to complexity.
2. Excessive use of fair value in financial reporting.
3. Companies' focus on compliance with applicable laws, rules, regulations, and standards rather than a focus on the essence of the business and sustainability.
4. Regulatory disclosure overload.
5. Difficult and often-changing financial reporting standards.
6. Lack of forward-looking information.
7. Focus on measuring short-term performance instead of sustainable performance.

Five needed improvements are:

1. Improving communication among all participants in the financial reporting supply chain.
2. Including more business-driven information in financial reports.
3. Better alignment of internal and external reports.
4. More readily and easily accessible electronic data (e.g., XBRL).
5. Focus on short-form reporting and the material issues.

WEB-BASED CORPORATE REPORTING

Use of the Internet in corporate reporting has progressed during the past decade. Many multinational corporations have established websites for financial reporting.[11] Unlike conventional printed annual reports, web-based corporate reports offer opportunities to communicate relevant financial and nonfinancial information and allow a wealth of up-to-date, unofficial, critical, and alternative channels of accounting information to compete with the official channels. The Internet may also serve as an important tool to facilitate a better functioning of financial markets by enhancing companies' ability to disseminate relevant and useful information to investors, which reduces agency risk that results from information asymmetries. In addition to reducing information asymmetry to the capital market, sufficient information is also essential for shareholders to monitor the behavior of management. The use of web technologies in disseminating the financial reports makes the presentation of financial reporting through the Internet similar to paper-based reporting except for its much greater speed of distribution. The widespread use of the Internet in corporate reporting encouraged the SEC to release its guidance on the use of company websites in 2008.

Connected Reporting

Connected reporting is a new concept introduced by the Prince of Wales's Accounting for Sustainability[12] to provide an alternative way to focus on the needs of long-term investors and management. Connected reporting is aimed at aligning interests of management with those of long-term investors by identifying and assessing the link between the organization's strategic objectives, performance, governance, reward, and risks and opportunities.

Connected reporting links the organizational strategies to the company's financial (economic) and nonfinancial (environmental and social) performance. Connected reporting is intended to address business sustainability by evaluating the impacts of environmental and social activities on the organization's strategic objectives, determining how these objectives and related actions contribute to a more sustainable economy and society. Connected reporting objective is to connect the broken link between strategic directions, financial performance, and the achievement of social and environmental goals. Connected reporting provides the link between important sustainability issues, the organization's strategic objectives, the measurement of sustainability performance in terms of KPIs, and continuous improvement to achieve sustainability targets.

PREDICTIVE BUSINESS ANALYTICS

The International Federation of Accountants (IFAC) in May 2011 released its[13] International Good Practice Guidance (IGPG) in an attempt to apply predictive business analytics (PBA) to assessment of relevant business data and drivers that can influence financial results and operational performance. The PBA focuses on the achievement of high-quality performance in four core performance areas:

1. **Economic.** Economic performance focuses on creating value for all key stakeholders (shareholders, customers, creditors, government, environment, and employees) by optimizing revenues on all significant economic events.
2. **Strategic.** Strategic performance relates to making strategic decisions based on future changes, industry practices, opportunities, business models, customer markets, regulatory reforms, and external developments.
3. **Operational.** The operational performance can be tracked by properly managing and measuring operational activities and achieving the proper balance of operational efficiency and effectiveness.
4. **Organizational and reputational.** The organizational and reputational performance promotes a culture of honesty, fairness, integrity, and competency to enhance the company's public image and reputation as well as to fulfill social responsibilities and environmental obligations.

NARRATIVE REPORTING

The 2011 PwC study "A Snapshot of FTSE 350 Reporting" reveals that the vast majority of surveyed companies (FTSE 350) provide the key bases of narrative reporting with less depth and understanding of major drivers of sustainable performance (e.g., strategic decisions; the link between KPIs and remuneration). The study concludes that an opportunity exists for improvement in the integrated reporting model in all areas of external drivers: strategy, risks, KPIs, and sustainability.[14] The study suggests that corporate reporting should reflect strategy and objectives; external drivers—including economics, governance, society, the environment, sources, and relationships—KPIs, and sustainability performance.

PwC conducted a review of both FTSE 250 and FTSE 100 companies' narrative reporting in their annual reports for periods ending between April 1, 2009, and March 31, 2010. The PwC review focuses on nine areas of reporting: (1) external drivers for business sustainability performance and reporting; (2) corporate reporting strategy; (3) risk management; (4) delivering strategy; (5) measures of success; (6) performance fundamentals; (7) sustainability; (8) segment reporting; and (9) remuneration reporting.[15]

PwC suggests narrative reporting as an important element of corporate communication with stakeholders. The review of FTSE 350 indicates that there is a need for a reporting model that provides all relevant information to market participants by focusing on business sustainability development and strategic information. Narrative reporting can provide a competitive mechanism for reporting relevant information during the post-crisis era, which has caused economic and business uncertainties. The PwC report finds some improvements in the post-crisis. For example, 74 percent of companies present some forward-looking information on market trends in 2010 compared to 49 percent the year before; over 90 percent report information relevant to their strategic priorities.[16]

Reporting corporate strategy or strategic priorities is gaining momentum in corporate reporting. PwC's 2010 review shows that 88 percent of FTSE 350 companies disclosed their overall goal or objective (e.g., creating shareholder value) in 2010. This is also important in explaining corporate strategic priorities. In 2010, about 40 percent of the reviewed FTSE 350 companies reported their strategic priorities (e.g., customer satisfaction, R&D investments).[17] Explanation of the business model should be an integral part of disclosing corporate strategies.

The UK corporate governance code requires companies to include in their annual report an explanation of the business model defined as "the basis on which the company generates or preserves value over the longer term and the strategy for delivering the objectives of the company."[18] Disclosing the business model should be included in all corporate governance reporting.

GOVERNANCE, RISK MANAGEMENT, AND COMPLIANCE (GRC) REPORTING

KPMG, in cooperation with Economist Intelligence Unit (2011), has opined that the future of corporate reporting is the convergence of governance, risk management, and compliance (GRC), and discusses the drivers, perceived benefits, potential costs, and possible obstacles of related reporting. To assess the feasibility of GRC reporting, KPMG and the Economist Intelligence Unit conducted a global survey of 542 executives in different industries in 2009.[19]

The GRC reporting addressed the ever-increasing business complexity, regulatory reforms, and seemingly excessive executive risk-taking. The GRC is all about continuous improvement of sustainable performance through effective governance, risk assessment, and compliance. The survey reveals that:

- About 64 percent of executives believe that GRC is driven by widening business complexity, the need to reduce risk exposure, and mission to improve performance.
- More than 11 percent reported full convergence of GRC throughout their organization.
- About 50 percent estimate the cost of full convergence of GRC to be around 5 percent of their annual revenue, with a majority (77 percent) expecting GRC costs to increase in the next two years.
- The perceived benefits of GRC convergence is not fully realized by respondents as only about one-third considered GRC expenditure as an investment rather than an expense.
- Resistance to change rather than technology is viewed by a high percentage of respondents (44 percent) as the major obstacle to successful GRC convergence. This was followed by the complexity of the convergence process (39 percent) and the lack of available experts (36 percent).[20]

SUSTAINABILITY REPORTING

Corporate and financial reporting since the financial crisis is subject to the close scrutiny of policy makers, regulators, and users of the reports. Investors demand more accurate, reliable, and relevant financial and nonfinancial information on KPIs such as corporate governance, risk assessment, business models that create sustainable performance, and issues of strategic and significant importance to all stakeholders. Investor confidence and public trust in corporate reporting determine the perceived reliability and usefulness of corporate reports.

Many professional organizations, regulators, and standard-setters worldwide have suggested ways to improve quality, reliability, comprehensiveness, transparency, and usefulness of corporate reporting, as discussed in the previous sections. Globalization and economic, social, and technological developments in the 21st century demand a new type of corporate accountability reporting, revealing KPIs through both financial and nonfinancial information. An effective sustainability performance and accountability reporting model that reflects the EGSEE aspects of business while addressing the interests of all stakeholders is the bedrock of the capital market. Significant opportunities exist for businesses to improve the value-relevance of their corporate reporting to better meet the needs of global investors and enhance investors' understanding of their MBL sustainable performance.

There are three important ways that sustainability development and reporting can affect long-term economic performance and thus shareholder value. First, by adopting sustainable practices, management can be prepared for inevitable regulations. For example, in 2010, the SEC issued guidance reiterating the need and importance for companies to disclose their material risk associated with climate change.[21] As the climate change rules are implemented, regulators penalize those firms that do not have sustainable business practices.

Second, sustainability initiatives and practices are generally viewed positively by investors and other stakeholders as the evidence of management commitment to long-term sustainable economic performance, social responsibility, and customer satisfaction create an edge over competitors. When two companies report the same earnings, socially responsible investors typically invest in the company that appears to be more environmentally conscientious and socially responsible.

Finally, customers, employees, suppliers, and other stakeholders are generally inspired by environmentally friendly, ethically driven, and socially responsible companies. Shareholders realize that management focus on EGSEE performance is incorporated into earnings management activities that will likely generate short-term gains and also deliver sustainable value over time.

Regulations and best practices pertaining to business sustainability vary significantly worldwide, but one global trend is emerging: investors' desire for more transparent and reliable sustainability information. Organizations of all types and sizes are working with their sustainability teams to develop and communicate their sustainability policies and practices to all stakeholders. Sustainability reports can provide investors and the capital markets with relevant information regarding performance. Sustainability reports provide persuasive information to investors and stakeholders in order for them to make sound investment decisions. The most persuasive information is reliable, useful, transparent, timely, and relevant to all five dimensions of performance.

CONCLUSIONS

Since the turn of the century, corporate reporting has been broadened beyond mere financial reporting. It now addresses a wide range of stakeholders and a variety of dimensions of sustainability performance relevant to economic, governance, social, ethical and environmental (EGSEE) issues. Many global businesses now recognize that reporting their financial performance through the use of the conventional financial bottom line is no longer adequate.

ACTIONITEMS

1. Make sure your sustainability report focuses on long-term strategic goals, addresses all stakeholders, and discusses sustainable value creation.

2. Work toward inclusion strategies to protect the interests of all stakeholders.

3. Establish, promote, and implement an MBL strategy of achieving performance in all EGSEE sustainability dimensions.

4. Focus on disclosing both financial and nonfinancial KPIs.

5. Good performance on sustainability ensures good business overall.

6. Use sustainability reporting as a vehicle to tell your stories about commitments to social responsibilities, environmental initiatives, customer trust, and employee satisfaction.

7. Revisit your corporate mission to reconcile divergent views of the purposes of your corporation, including creating shareholder value and protecting interests of other stakeholders (e.g., employees, customers, suppliers, the environment, and society).

NOTES

1. Duncan, Suzanne L., Daniel W. Latimore, and Shanker Ramamurthy. 2009. "Toward Transparency and Sustainability." Somers, NY: IBM Global Business Services. Available at: www.ibm.com/smarterplanet/global/files/ie__en_ie__banking__gbe03214-usen_financialorder.pdf.

2. United Nations Environment Programme Finance Initiative (UNEP FI) and the UN Global Compact. 2006. "Principles for Responsible Investment." Available at: www.unglobalcompact.org/principles.

3. The Canadian Institute of Chartered Accountants (CICA). 2010. "Environmental, Social and Governance Issues in Institutional Investor Decision Making." July 2010. Available at: http://www.cica.ca/publications/list-of-publications/manual/item41881.pdf.

4. Ibid.

5. Ioannou, Ioannis, and George Serafeim. 2010. "The Consequences of Mandatory Corporate Sustainability Reporting." Harvard Business School working paper. Available at: http://www.hbs.edu/research/pdf/11-100.pdf.

6. PricewaterhouseCoopers (PwC). 2007. "Corporate reporting: Is it what investment professionals expect?" Available at: http://www.pwc.com/gx/en/ifrs-reporting/publications/corporate-reporting-pwc-survey.jhtml.

7. PricewaterhouseCoopers (PwC). 2010. "Insight or Fatigue?: FTSE 350 Reporting." Available at: http://www.pwc.com/gx/en/corporate-reporting/integrated-reporting/publications/reporting-survey-2010.jhtml.

8. The International Federation of Accountants (IFAC). 2009. "Developments in the Financial Reporting Supply Chain – Results from a Global Study among IFAC Member Bodies." Available at http://www.ifac.org/publications-resources/developments-financial-reporting-supply-chain-results-global-study-among-ifac.

9. International Federation of Accountants (IFAC). 2011. "Integrating the Business Reporting Supply Chain." Available at: http://www.ifac.org/publications-resources/integrating-business-reporting-supply-chain-summary-key-recommendations.

10. Ibid.

11. Ettredge, M., V.J. Richardson, and S. Scholz. 2001. "The presentation of financial information at corporate web sites," *International Journal of Accounting Information Systems* 2: 149–68.

12. The Prince of Wales's Accounting for Sustainability (A4S). 2011. "Connected reporting: A practical guide with worked examples." Available at: http://www.accountingforsustainability.org/wp-content/uploads/2011/10/Connected-Reporting.pdf

13. The International Federation of Accountants (IFAC). 2011. "International Good Practice Guidance (IGPG): Predictive Business Analytics: Improving

Business Performance with Forward-Looking Measures." Available at: www
.ifac.org/sites/default/files/publications/files/20111114-PAIB-IGPG-Predictive
%2520Business%2520Analytics%2520-%2520FINAL.pdf.

14. PricewaterhouseCoopers(PWC). 2010. "A Snapshot of FTSE 350 Reporting."
    Available at: http%3a//pwc.blogs.com/files/a-snapshot-of-ftse-350-reporting
    .pdf.

15. PricewaterhouseCoopers (PwC). 2010. "Insight or Fatigue?: FTSE 350
    Reporting." Available at: http://www.pwc.com/gx/en/corporate-reporting/in-
    tegrated-reporting/publications/reporting-survey-2010.jhtml.

16. Ibid.

17. Ibid.

18. Financial Reporting Council (FRC). 2010. "The UK Corporate Governance
    Code," p. 21. Available at: http://www.frc.org.uk/documents/pagemanager/
    Corporate_Governance/UK%20Corp%20Gov%20Code%20June%202010.pdf.

19. KPMG and The Economist Intelligence Unit. 2011. "The convergence challenge:
    Global survey into the integration of governance, risk and compliance."
    Available at: http%3a//www.kpmg.com/Global/en/IssuesAndInsights/Articles
    Publications/Documents/The-convergence-challenge.pdf.

20. Ibid.

21. Securities and Exchange Commission (SEC). 2010. "17 CFR Parts 211, 231
    and 241: Commission Guidance Regarding Disclosure Related to Climate
    Change." *Federal Register* 75(25). Available at: http%3a//www.sec.gov/
    rules/interp/2010/33-9106.pdf.

CHAPTER FIVE

Economic Vitality as a Component of Sustainability

EXECUTIVE**SUMMARY**

T he primary function of business entities is to create shareholder value through continuous sustainable economic performance. This chapter discusses the importance of economic performance, its key performance indicators (KPIs), measurement, recognition, and reporting in the form of financial statements. We will also examine the roles of assurance in the framework of audit reports on financial statements and internal control over financial reporting (ICFR). The reliability of financial statements, the effectiveness of ICFR, and the efficacy of audits are vital if public companies are to attract investors and build confidence in the capital markets. This applies to both financial statements and ICFR that are under integrated financial and internal control reporting (IFICR). This chapter also discusses the role of gatekeepers (e.g., board of directors, management, internal and external auditors) in preparing reliable, relevant, useful, and timely IFICR.

INTRODUCTION

Investor confidence in capital markets is the key driver of economic growth, prosperity, and financial stability. This confidence is earned over time and "the ability of the U.S capital markets to attract capital over time depends on investors having confidence in the integrity and transparency of the markets."[1] The global competitiveness of U.S. capital markets depends significantly on the reliability of information on KPIs, which assist investors in making sound decisions. Financial markets should continue promoting and enforcing sustainability performance while also demanding accountability reporting to ensure transparent flows of reliable, accurate, and relevant financial and nonfinancial KPI information to the markets.

ECONOMIC KPIs

Proper measurement of the sustainability process and its integration into corporate reporting can be achieved by focusing on KPIs. Traditional financial KPIs are probably not sufficient to monitor sustainability development and efforts. Organizations must look at their specific circumstances and needs in order to decide about the relevant KPIs. The key to creating usable financial KPIs is to offer stakeholders sufficient measures to assess sustainable performance. For example, an organization that desires to track the generation of carbon dioxide (CO_2) in metric tons from a smoke stack compares the estimated costs to offset the pollution with those to reduce it through equipment upgrades. These numbers can be benchmarked against the market cost of CO_2 emissions allowances. Important economic KPIs consist of conventional financial information and nonfinancial information presented in the financial statements and management discussion and analysis (MD&A), as summarized in Exhibit 5.1.

PUBLIC TRUST AND INVESTOR CONFIDENCE IN FINANCIAL INFORMATION

The reliability of financial reports and the quality of audit reports are essential to maintaining investor confidence and promoting efficient capital markets. As stated by three former Securities and Exchange Commission (SEC) chief accountants, "In our capital markets, a single catastrophic reporting failure is a disaster in which losses to investors and the public can be, and often are, overwhelming, wiping out decades of hard work, planning, and saving."[2] Financial scandals of the late 1990s and early 2000s and the 2007–2009 financial crisis raised serious concerns and questions about where the boards of directors, audit committees, and auditors were and why didn't they prevent or detect these serious problems. The ever-increasing demand for high-quality

EXHIBIT 5.1 Examples of Economic/Financial KPIs

Economic KPIs on Financial Statement	Economic KPIs on MD&A
1. Economic value generated.	1. The current and potential impacts of emerging environmental initiatives and reforms on financial, operational, and capital expenditures.
2. Revenues earned.	
3. Resources consumed.	
4. Costs recognized.	
5. Resources obtained (assets).	
6. Capital raised.	2. The median compensation for top executives and their relation to the median for average employees.
7. Liabilities assumed.	
8. Expenses incurred.	
9. Earnings retained.	3. Information on capital and human resources including the number of employees and their average compensation.
10. Earnings distributed.	
11. Compensations paid.	
12. Financial risk assessed.	
13. Donations given.	4. Information on social, governance, ethical, and environmental policies, programs, and operations.
14. Market share secured.	
15. Taxes paid.	
16. Financial assistance received.	5. Risk factors and their assessment and management as related to environmental, health, political, and regulatory initiatives and reforms.
17. Research and development (R&D) invested.	
18. New products discovered.	
19. Market information, such as market growth, market share, and regulatory environment.	
	6. The optional impacts of global economic and financial market conditions on the current year's and foreseeable future years' operations and performance.
20. Corporate governance information, such as the board of directors' composition, structure, and committees.	
21. Strategic information, such as goals and objectives.	7. Description of any current penalties and sanctions imposed and pending litigations.
22. Information about management, such as the track record, compensation plans, and incentive plans.	8. Description of corporate governance policies and practices.
23. Value-creating information, such as customers, employees, suppliers, innovative brands, and supply chain.	9. Description of the established and implemented business code of conduct.
24. Corporate responsibility information, such as environmental, ethical, and social information.	10. Description of compliance with regulatory requirements.
25. Forecasts, projections, and other technical and quantitative market information.	11. Market information, such as market growth, market share, and regulatory environment.
26. Financial statements (balance sheet, income statement, statement of cash flow, owners' equity).	

(continued)

EXHIBIT 5.1 *(Continued)*

Economic KPIs on Financial Statement	Economic KPIs on MD&A
27. Note disclosures.	12. Corporate governance information, such as board of directors' composition, structure, and committees.
28. Accounting policies.	
29. Segment information.	
30. Changes in business structure (e.g., business combination, discontinued operation).	13. Strategic information, such as goals and objectives.
31. Material and unusual items.	
32. Post-balance-sheet events.	14. Information about management, such as track record, compensation plans, and incentive plans.
33. Executive compensation.	
34. Stockbased compensation.	
35. Dividend policy.	15. Value-creating information regarding customers, employees, suppliers, innovative brands, and supply chain.
36. Budget and performance evaluation.	
37. Earnings releases.	
38. Non-GAAP financial measures.	
39. Operational information.	16. Corporate responsibility information regarding environmental, ethical, and social information.
40. Quantitative analysis.	
41. Forward-looking data.	
42. Market information.	17. Forecasts, projections, and other technical and quantitative market information.
43. Stock prices.	
44. Risk management.	
45. Codes of conduct and ethics.	

financial information makes the role of individuals involved in the corporate financial reporting supply chain (including the board of directors, the audit committee, management, and auditors) a value-added function under intense scrutiny.

Public trust and investor confidence in public financial information is a complex issue that "cannot be legislated . . . the investment community is requiring individual companies, one by one, to earn back market trust."[3]

In the United States, several initiatives have been taken to address the use of aggressive accounting practices by public companies and to restore public trust in corporate America and its financial reports. Recent corporate governance reforms, including the Sarbanes-Oxley Act of 2002 (SOX), Dodd-Frank Act of 2010, Securities and Exchange Commission (SEC) rules, listing standards, and best practices worldwide, have shifted the power balance between a company's shareholders, directors, and management.

In addition, shareholders have been more proactive in monitoring and scrutinizing their corporations and thus heightened their expectations for directors' performance on their behalf. Directors have strengthened their commitment and accountability in fulfilling their fiduciary duties by overseeing management's strategic plans, decisions, and performance and spending more time on their duties, particularly in overseeing the financial reporting process.

Management also has stepped up its efforts in achieving sustainable shareholder value creation and enhancement, and improving the reliability of financial reports through executive certification of internal controls and financial statements. Executive certifications, vigilant oversight of the audit committee, and improved audit quality together have significantly enhanced the quality of public financial information and investor confidence in the capital markets.

Early evidence indicates that the effects of SOX legislation are positive and should remain positive over the long term for the U.S. economy.[4] Some provisions of SOX that were not previously practiced by public companies and are intended to benefit all companies include:

- Creating the Public Company Accounting Oversight Board (PCAOB) to oversee the audit of public companies and to improve the ineffective self-regulatory environment of the auditing profession.
- Improving corporate governance through more independent and vigilant boards of directors and responsible executives.
- Enhancing the quality, reliability, transparency, and timeliness of financial disclosures through executive certifications of both financial statements and internal controls.
- Prohibiting nine types of nonaudit services considered to adversely affect auditor independence and objectivity.
- Regulating the conduct of auditors, legal counsel, analysts, and their potential conflicts of interest.
- Increasing civil and criminal penalties for violations of security laws.

Six provisions of SOX address the quality, reliability, transparency, and timeliness of public companies' financial reports:

1. The board of directors should adopt a more active role in the oversight of financial reports.
2. The audit committee is responsible for overseeing financial reports and related audits.

3. Management (CEO, CFO) must certify the completeness and accuracy of financial reports in conformity with generally accepted accounting principles (GAAP).
4. Pro forma financial information must be presented in a manner that is not misleading and that is reconciled with GAAP items.
5. All material correcting adjustments identified by the independent auditor must be discussed with the audit committee and reflected in any reports that contain financial statements.
6. Management must assess the effectiveness of internal controls, audit of ICFR, communication of significant deficiencies to the audit committee, and public disclosure of material weaknesses in ICFR.

The potential effects of SOX, therefore, range from sweeping measures that will eventually reform corporate governance and the financial reporting of public companies to patchworks, codifications, and further studies of the existing governance and financial disclosures regulations and requirements.

Promoting Transparency in Financial Reporting

Investors normally want transparency in financial and nonfinancial reports regardless of their attitude towards risk (e.g., risk-averse, risk-tolerant, or risk-embracing). A 2005 Ernst & Young survey of 137 investors indicates that they prioritize transparency in their investment decisions as follows, in order of importance:

1. Transparency of company
2. Long-term track record
3. Business model
4. Characteristics of markets
5. Overall management approach
6. Track record of executive directors
7. Company's exposure to risk
8. Customer base (e.g., repeat business)
9. Company's approach to risk management
10. Directors' stake
11. Quality of nonexecutive directors[5]

Overall, investors wish to make informed analysis and educated decisions on risk/reward aspects of their investment targets.

Lack of transparency and complexity in financial reporting encouraged the U.S. Congress to pass the Promoting Transparency in Financial Reporting Act February 28, 2007.[6] Congress found that:

- Transparent financial reporting is vital to the continued growth and strength of the capital markets and investor confidence.
- The increasing detail and volume of accounting, auditing, and reporting guidance (standards) pose a major challenge.
- The complexity of accounting and auditing standards has been a major contributing factor in the increasing costs and effort involved in financial reporting.

This Act requires annual oral testimony before the Financial Services Committee, composed of the chairpersons of the SEC, PCAOB, and FASB, relevant to their efforts to promote transparency in financial reporting beginning in 2007 and for five years thereafter.

Global Financial Reporting Language

Financial reporting has traditionally been governed by national accounting standards. In recent years, there has been a move toward accepting the International Financial Reporting Standards (IFRS) as globally accepted accounting standards. As of 2011, more than 97 countries require IFRS compliance by all or some domestic companies and 25 countries permit IFRS compliance for financial reporting.

Recent initiatives by the SEC in considering eliminating reconciliation for foreign companies and the possibility that even U.S. companies could be allowed to choose to report under international financial reporting standards (IFRS) are positive steps toward convergence of IFRS and U.S. GAAP and also pave the way for the development of one global financial reporting language. We should expect significant changes in financial reporting as both the FASB and IASB move toward convergence in their standards, and as the SEC promotes the idea of giving U.S. companies the choice between U.S. GAAP and IFRS compliance in their filings.

Forward-Looking Financial Reports

Investors demand forward-looking financial and nonfinancial information on KPIs concerning an entity's economic, governance, social, ethical, and environmental (EGSEE) activities. Standard setters worldwide are considering overhauling financial reporting and restructuring financial statements by focusing on KPIs and providing information concerning how businesses are actually run.[7] Regarding improving financial disclosures, SEC Chairman Christopher Cox states that we should "go out of our way to listen to retail customers [corporate governance participants] and ask them what they think. What do they find useful in current disclosure? What do they find useless? What would they like to see that they don't presently have?"[8] These questions are an important starting point to improve the quality of financial reports.

The U.K. Companies Act 2006 significantly expands corporate responsibility reporting to include both financial and other KPIs concerning information about the company's policies pertaining to environmental matters, employee activities, and social and community issues.[9]

Investors demand forward-looking financial and nonfinancial information and companies have strived to provide it. PricewaterhouseCoopers (PwC) has recently published a practical guide based on best practices for providing a view of the future that investors need.[10] PwC's guide is based on following the seven pillars of effective communication between public companies and their stakeholders:

1. Resources available to the company and how they are managed.
2. Key risks and uncertainties that may affect the company's sustainable performance.
3. Significant relationships with principal stakeholders that are likely to affect the company's sustainable performance.
4. Quantified data pertaining to trends and factors that are likely to influence the company's future prospects.
5. Any uncertainties underpinning forward-looking information on how the report reflects the company's long-term objectives and the strategies to achieve them.

Exhibit 5.2 looks at some of the challenges in financial reporting.

INTERNAL CONTROL REPORTING

Legislators, regulators, and the accounting profession have traditionally advocated the establishment and maintenance of internal control systems by public companies and reporting on internal control systems by managers and auditors. The passage of SOX and the Dodd-Frank Act of 2010 requires

EXHIBIT 5.2 Financial Reporting Challenges and Improvements

Improvement Needed	Improvement Made	Challenges
1. More relevant and understandable financial reports for the various users.	1. More useful and relevant financial information due to improved standards, regulation, and oversight.	1. Reduced usefulness and readability of financial reports due to complexity.
2. The use of a direct method in the preparation of the cash flow statement.		2. Excessive use of fair value in financial reporting.
3. More support for retail investors.	2. More disclosure and better comparability in financial reports.	3. Focus by companies on compliance with applicable laws, rules, regulations, and standards instead of emphasis on the business and focus on sustainability.
4. Simplification of financial reporting standards by standard setters.		
5. The financial reporting burden on smaller and nonlisted entities should be limited.	3. Enhanced reliability of financial reports.	
6. The use of fair value in financial reporting should be supported.	4. Increased emphasis on narrative reporting.	4. Regulatory disclosure overload.
7. The use of principles-based financial reporting standards.	5. Easier access to financial information.	5. Difficult and often changing financial reporting standards.
8. Convergence to one set of globally accepted, principles-based, high-quality financial reporting standards.		6. Lack of forward-looking information.
9. Preparers of financial statements should maintain professional behavior and qualification.		7. Focus on measuring short-term performance instead of sustainable performance.
10. Improving communication with all participants in the financial reporting supply chain.		8. Effective transition to International Financial Reporting Standards (IFRS).
11. Including more business-driven information in financial reports.		9. Complying/reconciling accounts to different financial reporting standards.
12. Better alignment of internal and external reports.		10. Complexity of financial reporting standards.
13. More readily and easily accessible electronic data; for example, XBRL.		
14. Less focus on short-form reporting on the material issues.		
15. Move toward convergence to a single set of global financial reporting standards.		

(continued)

EXHIBIT 5.2 *(Continued)*

Improvement Needed	Improvement Made	Challenges
16. Enhanced regulatory and oversight of the financial reporting process.		11. Liability restricting process.
17. Board of directors/management taking ownership of financial reporting.		12. Value-relevance of financial reports.
18. Enhanced internal control over financial reporting systems.		
19. Improved technology in the financial reporting process.		
20. Complete convergence to one set of globally accepted financial reporting standards.		
21. Simplified and clarified financial reporting standards through more principles and fewer rules.		
22. Continuous oversight of financial reports by boards of directors, with particular attention to the quality of financial reports.		
23. Enhanced additional education and training for preparers of financial reports.		
24. Continued support for online and electronic financial reports.		
25. More quantitative and qualitative information on the quality of financial reports.		
26. Clarification on what financial statements do and do not disclose.		
27. Information on significant risks and trends that have affected the financial statements and will continue to affect financial statements.		
28. Discussion of quality and quantity of earnings and cash flows.		

management to step up its efforts in achieving sustainable shareholder value creation and enhancement, improving the reliability of financial reports through executive certification of internal controls, and improving financial statements.

INTERNAL CONTROL REPORTING REQUIREMENTS

Internal control reporting became mandatory only recently with the passage of SOX, which, among other things, requires executive certification of internal control in the periodic reports (e.g., quarterly reports, 10-Qs, annual reports, and 10-Ks) filed with the SEC under Section 302. Section 404 of SOX is intended to improve the effectiveness of design and operation of ICFR and compliance is now required for large U.S. public companies (companies with equity market capitalization in excess of $75 million, known as accelerated filers) for fiscal years ending on or after November 15, 2004. Other public companies are required to comply with Section 404(a) for their fiscal years ending on or after November 15, 2008.

In the United Kingdom, the 1999 Turnbull Guidance on Internal Control ("the Guidance") is intended to: (1) promote sound business practice by requiring internal control be embedded in business processes to ensure the achievement of the company's objective; (2) remain relevant over time by responding to changes in business environment; and (3) provide flexibility so companies may tailor it to their particular circumstances.[11] The Guidance mandates the following 16 requirements:

1. Companies must use a risk-based approach in establishing and maintaining a sound system of internal control, and their directors must exercise judgment in reviewing the company's compliance with the code provisions pertaining to internal control and related reporting to its shareholders.
2. The company's system of internal control must play a key role in the management of risks that are significant to the achievement of business objectives and contribute to safeguarding the company's assets and shareholders' investment.
3. The company's internal control must facilitate the efficiency and effectiveness of its operations, ensure the reliability of financial reporting (both internal and external), and assist with compliance with applicable laws and regulations.

4. Internal control must include, manage, and control risks; retain proper accounting records; safeguard assets; and prevent and detect fraud.

5. The company's board of directors must be responsible for its system of internal control by establishing adequate and effective internal control policies in achieving its goals and in managing risks.

6. The board's deliberations on the assessment of an effective internal control must include the nature and extent of the risks facing the company, the extent and categories of acceptable risks, the likelihood of risks to occur, the company's ability to reduce the incidence and impact of the materialized risks, and the costs of operating particular controls relative to the benefits in managing the related risk.

7. The company's management must be responsible for implementing its board policies and risk control. Management should design, operate, and monitor a suitable system of internal control based on board policies and identified risks.

8. All employees must have some responsibility for the effective design and operation of internal controls as part of their accountability for achieving the company's objectives.

9. An internal control system must consist of policies, processes, tasks, behaviors, and other aspects of a company designed to facilitate effective and efficient operation, ensure the quality of internal and external reporting, and assist compliance with applicable laws, regulations, and internal policies.

10. A company's internal controls must reflect its control environment including organizational structure, control activities, information, and communications processes.

11. The company must recognize that adequate and effective internal control reduces but cannot eliminate the possibility of poor judgment, human error, circumvention of the control process, management override of internal controls, and the occurrence of unforeseeable circumstances.

12. The company must accept that a sound system of internal control provides only reasonable assurance that a company will achieve its operating, financial reporting, and compliance objectives.

13. The board of directors must be primarily responsible for reviewing the effectiveness of the company's internal control system, and management must be accountable to the board for monitoring the system. The board is also responsible for disclosing proper information about internal control in the annual report and accounts.

14. Management must report to the board its assessment of significant risks and the effectiveness of the internal control system in managing those risks.

15. The company's board must conduct an annual assessment of the effectiveness of the internal control system and make public statements on its assessment.

16. The company's board must determine the cause and effect of weaknesses in internal control and reassess the effectiveness of internal control processes designed, operated, and monitored by management.[12]

Benefits of Mandatory Internal Control Reporting

Capital markets view mandatory internal control reporting by both management and auditors as a signal that the company is in control of managing its risk and achieving its business objectives. Academic research demonstrates that capital market participants view mandatory internal control reporting as a positive sign and that investors are willing to pay a premium for it, penalizing those companies that cannot comply with their mandatory internal control reporting.[13] A 2007 survey by Ernst & Young reveals that investments in internal controls are profitable:

- 89 percent of respondents reported improvement in their business processes and underlying control structures.
- 86 percent achieved a better understanding of major risk areas.
- More than 50 percent believed it had a positive impact on investor confidence.[14]

About 75 percent were planning additional investments to improve their internal controls over the next two years, particularly in key business/operational risk areas, IT, and entity-level controls (e.g., control environment). They are also planning better alignment of internal controls to company strategy and key risks.[15]

Effective internal control can be achieved when a company is operating efficiently, its financial reports are reliable, its business risk is managed properly, and its compliance with applicable laws and regulations is documented. The achievement of effective internal controls is the key to business success, long-term survival, and sustainable performance. Thus, better internal controls should secure better business and should not be viewed as a burden on management's time or budget, but rather as an investment to exceed business objectives and obtain a competitive advantage.

Internal Control over Business and Operations (ICBO)

Internal control over business and operations has not received the attention it should, as evidenced in the 2007 Ernst & Young survey, where the majority of respondents did not believe that their internal controls were effective in activities that are strategic in nature and fundamental to business success.[16] This suggests that there is a need for further investment. More specifically, the highest percentages of respondents cited the following nine areas as being effective:

1. Sales and marketing (66 percent)
2. Supply chain (61 percent)
3. Pricing and contract management (60 percent)
4. Acquisition diligence and processes (59 percent)
5. IT implementations and upgrades (49 percent)
6. Business continuity planning (46 percent)
7. Real estate and construction projects (45 percent)
8. Post-acquisition integration (42 percent)
9. Expanding into new international markets (41 percent)[17]

These results suggest that companies have not adequately invested in ICBO, as the majority of respondents (over 50 percent) said that their ICBO is not effective in areas of IT, real estate, post-acquisition and international markets.

Investment in Internal Control

It is expected that investment in internal control will continue to increase as the majority of respondents (over 75 percent) reported that they planned to make large investments in internal control in the near future. Survey respondents focus their investments on the following six areas of internal controls:

1. Strengthening controls over key business operational risks (51 percent)
2. Improving information technology controls (49 percent)
3. Achieving a better alignment of their internal controls to the company strategy and key risk areas (44 percent)
4. Strengthening company-level controls pertaining to oversight activities by the board of directors and managerial function by management in setting appropriate tone at the top (42 percent)

5. Improving assessment and testing programs (34 percent)
6. Enhancing controls over financial reporting (33 percent)[18]

These results suggest that companies place more investment focus on internal controls relevant to business strategies and risk assessment and less on traditional core financial reporting controls or compliance with applicable laws, rules, and regulations. The survey participants reported the top nine benefits of their current internal control investments:

1. Enhancement of processes and the underlying control structure (89 percent)
2. Better understanding of major risk areas (86 percent)
3. Better compliance with regulators (80 percent)
4. Improvement in the reliability of financial reporting (75 percent)
5. Improvement in the execution of change initiatives (54 percent)
6. More effective use of IT investments (52 percent)
7. Improvement in execution and integration of acquisitions (50 percent)
8. A positive impact on investor confidence (50 percent)
9. Improvement in execution of capital programs (43 percent)[19]

INTEGRATED FINANCIAL AND INTERNAL CONTROL REPORTING

Integrated financial and internal control reporting is financial information published in financial statements and reports about internal control over financial reporting. Reporting of financial statements and internal controls is vital as it assists shareholders in making appropriate investment and voting decisions, enables them to exercise their ownership rights on an informed basis, and protects them from receiving misleading financial information. Since 2004, the majority of public companies known as accelerated filers (those with $75 million or more in market capitalization) have been required to publish management and auditor reports on their internal controls. These two disclosure requirements are intended to facilitate companies to attract investors, strengthen their competitive edge, and maintain confidence in capital markets.

Regulations vary significantly throughout the world, but there is one emerging global trend: investors demand more transparent and reliable financial reports. Executives of global companies are being held more accountable for the effectiveness of internal controls and the integrity of financial statements through regulations such as SOX (e.g., executive certifications) and the European Union's Company Law Directives. Directors, particularly audit committees, are being held more responsible for overseeing their companies' internal controls, financial reporting, risk management, and audit activities. Global investors are provided with integrated financial and internal control reports from management and independent auditors. These integrated reports should be useful to investors and are vital in preventing and detecting financial misstatements, including fraud.

Integrated financial reporting and internal controls includes: (1) management report and certification of financial statements; (2) management report and certification of ICFR; (3) the independent auditor's opinion on fair and true presentation of financial statements; (4) independent auditor opinion on the effectiveness of ICFR; and (5) the audit committee's review of audited financial statements and both management and auditor reports on internal controls. The effectiveness depends on a vigilant oversight function by the board of directors, particularly the audit committee, and a responsible and accountable managerial function by senior executives, a credible external audit function by the independent auditor, and an objective internal audit function by internal auditors as depicted in Exhibit 5.3.

To facilitate the move toward cost-effective integration, the SEC and the PCAOB have taken several initiatives. The SEC issued interpretive guidance for management's assessment of the effectiveness of internal controls over financial reporting. On June 27, 2007, the SEC issued interpretive guidance (IG) and rule amendments to assist public companies' compliance with Section 404.[20] The IG provides guidance for management on how to conduct an assessment of the effectiveness of ICFR. The IG suggests management use a top-down, risk-based approach in evaluating ICFR and in satisfying the annual evaluation requirement in Exchange Act Rules 13a-15(c) and 15d-15(c). The PCAOB issued its Auditing Standard (AS) No. 5 in 2007, titled "An Audit of Internal Control over Financial Reporting that is Integrated with an Audit of Financial Statements" for audits of internal controls.[21] AS No. 5 is intended to improve the audit by: (1) focusing the audit on the matters most important to internal control; (2) eliminating unnecessary audit procedures; (3) simplifying the auditor requirements; and (4) scaling the integrated audit for smaller companies.

These initiatives were intended to make Section 404 of SOX on internal control compliance more cost-effective, efficient, and scalable and design a framework for effective implementation. The effective implementation requires a well-balanced functioning of all participants in the financial reporting process. It is expected that both the SEC's interpretive guidance and the

EXHIBIT 5.3 Integrated Financial and Internal Control Reporting Process

Oversight Function	Managerial Function	External Audit Function	Internal Audit Function
1. Establishes clear roles and responsibilities of the board of directors, particularly the audit committee, for the integrated financial reporting process.	1. Performs quarterly review and assessment of financial statements and ICFR.	1. Ensures that the audit committee is in charge of hiring, compensating, and overseeing the work of the independent auditor as related to the integrated audit of financial statements and ICFR.	1. Assists the board of directors, particularly the audit committee, in effectively overseeing IFICR.
2. Ensures that the audit committee reviews financial statements with the independent auditor and recommends to the board of directors that financial statements be released.	2. Performs quarterly assessment of ICFR to ensure effective ICFR is maintained throughout the year.	2. Plans the audit to gather sufficient and competent evidence to form an opinion on the effectiveness of ICFR.	2. Assists management with certification of both financial statements and ICFR, and the preparation of financial statements and report on internal controls.
3. Ensures that the audit committee reviews ICFR with the independent auditor and recommends to the board of directors that the auditor report on ICFR be released.	3. Provides management assurance for Section 302 reporting.	3. Plans the audit to gather sufficient and competent evidence to form an opinion on fair presentation of financial statements in conformity with GAAP.	3. Cooperates with external auditor for audits of both financial statements and ICFR.
	4. Assesses ICFR in compliance with Section 404 of SOX and the SEC's new interpretative guidance.		
4. Ensures that the audit committee reviews management's report on ICFR with management and recommends to the board that the report be released.	5. Identifies significant control deficiencies and takes remediation action.	4. Prepares an audit report on management's remediation of previously identified material weaknesses in ICFR.	4. Prepares internal auditor report on the adequacy and effectiveness of the overall internal controls.
	6. Builds SOX compliance into the financial reporting process.		
5. Ensures that the audit committee reviews management certifications on financial statements and ICFR, particularly in quarterly assessments in compliance with Section 302.	7. Develops standardized documentation methods including narratives, control flowcharts, and control matrices, for both financial statements and ICFR.	5. Documents audit evidence relevant to the integrated audit for at least seven years.	5. Assists management with enterprise risk management (ERM) assessment as pertains to internal controls.
	8. Works with the audit committee and the independent auditors to explore ways to improve the quality of financial statements and the effectiveness of ICFR.		

PCAOB's AS No. 5 will substantially improve IFICR by enabling management and auditors to fairly present their financial statements and to tailor their assessment of ICFR to the facts and circumstances of their company using a top-down, principles- and risk-based approach.

SEC interpretive guidance and AS No. 5 provide guidance for the effective implementation of Section 404 of SOX in the following six key areas:

1. Management must assess the effectiveness of the company's ICFR.
2. The independent auditor must opine only on the effectiveness of ICFR, not management's assessment.
3. The focus of the internal control audit should be on the matters that present the greatest risk that a company's internal controls will fail to detect, prevent, or correct material misstatements in financial statements by using a top-down, risk-based approach of focusing on company-level controls and its control environment.
4. Unnecessary audit procedures should be eliminated to achieve the intended benefits of the audit by using the experience gained in previous years' audits and from the work of others (e.g., internal auditors, management) and focusing on the assessment of the opinion on the effectiveness of internal controls rather than adequacy of management's process to reach its conclusion.
5. The integrated audit should be scaled to fit the size and complexity of the company, particularly making the auditing standards more scalable for smaller companies.
6. Auditing standards should be simplified by making them shorter, more transparent, and more clearly scalable to audits of companies of all sizes and levels of complexity.

The Dodd-Frank Wall Street Reform and Consumer Protection Act of 2010 (the Dodd-Frank Act),[22] Section 989G(b), directs the SEC to conduct a study to determine feasibility of complying with Section 404(b) of SOX (audit report on ICFR) for companies whose market capitalization is between $75 million and $250 million, while maintaining investor protections for such companies. The SEC released its study report in April 2011, suggesting that:

1. The existing investor protections for accelerated filers to comply with Section 404(b) of audit report on ICFR should be maintained for accelerated filers.

2. There is strong evidence that the auditor's role in ICFR improves the effectiveness of internal controls and thus the reliability of financial reporting, making it useful to investors.

3. There is no specific evidence that such potential savings associated with exemption of Section 404(b) would justify the loss of investor protections.

4. The available evidence does not suggest that granting an exemption to companies with between $75 million and $250 million in public float following an IPO would, by itself, encourage companies in the United States or abroad to list their IPOs in the United States.

5. The Dodd-Frank Act already exempted approximately 60 percent of reporting issuers with less than $75 million in market capitalization from Section 404(b), and the study does not recommend further extending this exemption.

6. The costs of Section 404(b) have declined since it was first implemented, particularly in response to the 2007 reforms of relaxing some of the unnecessary procedures of internal control reporting and auditing.

7. Investors generally view audit reports on ICFR as beneficial and value-relevant.

8. Efficiency and effectiveness of audit reporting on ICFR under Section 404 (b) of SOX should be improved.[23]

CONCLUSION

Integrated financial and internal control reporting covers both financial reporting and internal control reporting, which provides financial information disseminated to the capital markets by public companies. This part of the overall sustainability effort includes: (1) public trust and investor confidence in public financial information; (2) financial reporting; and (3) internal control reporting.

Corporate reporting can be used to illustrate the environmental impact of an organization's products and the processes undertaken to become more sustainable. Although the primary focus of corporate reporting will continue to be financial, the issues of social, ethical, governance, and environmental performance will gain momentum as we look ahead. The sustainability and financial health of public companies are essential to keeping investor confidence high.

ACTION**ITEMS**

1. Establish and implement a meaningful and sound sustainability accounting system to properly identify, classify, measure, recognize, and report relevant financial and nonfinancial sustainability performance indicators.

2. Convert your traditional financial reporting process to a more holistic sustainability- and accountability-driven reporting model.

3. Improve your sustainability reporting and assurance.

4. Ensure your sustainability-related strategies make you ready to compete in the global market now and in the future.

5. Change your reporting model to adopt emerging sustainability initiatives.

6. Ensure incorporation of sustainability development into your decision-making, planning, implementation, and evaluation processes.

7. Expand and redesign your corporate reporting to include sustainability and accountability with a keen focus on supporting the information needs of long-term investors.

8. Ensure that your audit strategies on ICFR are in compliance with both the SEC's Interpretive Guidance and PCAOB AS No. 5.

NOTES

1. Turner, L. E. 2006. "Stock Options Backdating," hearing held before the U.S. Senate Committee on Banking, Housing, and Urban Affairs. Available at: http://banking.senate.gov/public/index.cfm?FuseAction=Hearings.Hearing& Hearing_ID=a249d197-312a-46c2-8da3-3b504efeb589.

2. Turner, L. (2005). Costs and benefits of the Sarbanes-Oxley Act. Submitted by Glass, Lewis & Co., LLC, to the April 2005 SEC Roundtable. Available at: www .glasslewis.com.

3. Woodward, R., J. Dittmar, and C. Munoz. 2003. "The Currency of Good Governance," *Platts Energy Business and Technology* 5(4): 30.

4. Jain, P.K., & Rezaee, Z. 2006. "The Sarbanes-Oxley Act of 2002 and capital market behavior: Early evidence." *Contemporary Accounting Research* 23 (3), 629–54.

5. Ernst & Young. 2005. "Investors on Risk: The Need for Transparency." Risk Survey Series.

6. The Senate of the United States: Committee on Banking, Housing, and Urban Affairs. 2007. Promoting Transparency in Financial Reporting Act of 2007 (February 28). Available at: www.govtrack.us/congress/bill.xpd?bill=s110-834.

7. Reilly, D. 2007. "Profit as We Know It Could Be Lost with New Accounting Statements." *The Wall Street Journal* (May 12): A1. Available at: online.wsj .com/public/article/SB117893520139500814-m5r4gJLCTET50No6lq_tuIrv Fug_20070522.html?mod=blogs.

8. Solomon, D. 2005. "New SEC Chief Plans to Enforce Hedge-Fund Rule," *The Wall Street Journal* (September 19): A1. Available at: online.wsj.com/article/ SB112709476466344537.html.

9. Office of Public Sector Information. 2006. The U.K. Companies Act 2006. Available at: www.opsi.gov.uk/acts/acts2006/ukpga_20060046_en.pdf.

10. PricewaterhouseCoopers (PwC). 2006. "Guide to Forward-Looking Information: Don't Fear the Future – Communicating with Confidence." Available at: www.pwc.com/gx/en/corporate-reporting/assets/pdfs/uk-fl-info-guide.pdf.

11. Financial Reporting Council. 2003. UK Combined Code on Corporate Governance. Available at: www.frc.org.uk/documents/pagemanager/frc/combined-codefinal.pdf.

12. Ibid.

13. Rezaee, Z., R. Espahbodi, and P. Espahbodi. 2007. "Stock Price Reaction to Mandated Internal Control Reporting," working paper, the University of Memphis.

14. Ernst & Young. 2007. "From Compliance to Competitive Edge: New Thinking on Internal Control." Available at: www.eycom.ch/publications/items/ 2007_ics_brochure/2007_ey_ics_brochure.pdf.

15. Ibid.

16. Ibid.

17. Ibid.

18. Ibid.

19. Ibid.

20. Securities and Exchange Commission (SEC). 2007. Amendments to Rules Regarding Management's Report on Internal Control over Financial Reporting (June 20). Available at: www.sec.gov/rules/final/2007/33-8809 .pdf.

21. Public Company Accounting Oversight Board (PCAOB). 2007. Auditing Standard No. 5. *An Audit of Internal Control over Financial Reporting That is Integrated with an Audit of Financial Statements* (May 24). Available at: pcaobus .org/Rules/Rules_of_the_Board/Auditing_Standard_5.pdf.

22. 111th U.S. Congress. 2010. Dodd-Frank Wall Street Reform and Consumer Protection Act of 2010. Pub. L. No. 111-203 (Jul. 21, 2010). Available at: www.sec.gov/about/laws/wallstreetreform-cpa.pdf.

23. Securities and Exchange Commission (SEC). 2011. "Study and Recommendations on Section 404(b) of the Sarbanes-Oxley Act of 2002 for Issuers with Public Float between $75 and $250 Million." April 27, 2011. Available at: www.sec.gov/news/studies/2011/404bfloat-study.pdf.

CHAPTER SIX

The Corporate Governance Dimension of Sustainability

EXECUTIVE**SUMMARY**

In the aftermath of the 2007–2009 global financial crisis, countries worldwide have taken initiatives to improve their corporate governance by establishing more robust measures to strengthen their regulatory frameworks in order to promote economic stability, public trust, and investor confidence in their financial reporting. Examples of these corporate governance measures include the Dodd-Frank Act of 2010 and Basel III, which are intended to strengthen board oversight, positioning risk management as an important board responsibility. They also aim to link executive compensation schemes with sustainable long-term performance and encourage shareholders to take a more active role in corporate governance. These measures are designed to enable the convergence of a set of globally accepted corporate governance measures and the integration of business sustainability into corporate governance. These and other measures of corporate governance and their integration into the five EGSEE (economic, governance, social, ethical, and environmental) dimensions of sustainability performance will be presented in this chapter. This chapter also outlines professional accountability for all corporate governance participants including the board of directors, investors, management, internal auditors, external auditors, financial analysts, legal counsel, regulators, and standard-setters.[1] Furthermore, this chapter describes corporate governance key performance indicators (KPIs) and related reporting and assurance topics.

CORPORATE GOVERNANCE DEFINITION

Corporate governance is defined from a legal perspective as reforms and mechanisms that ensure compliance with all applicable laws, rules, regulations, and standards. In 2009, the Professional Accountants in Business (PAIB) and the Committee of the International Federation of Accountants (IFAC) approved the International Good Practice Guidance (IGPG) that adopted the following definition of corporate governance:

> the set of responsibilities and practices exercised by the board and executive management ('the governing body') with the goal of: (a) providing strategic direction, (b) ensuring that objectives are achieved, (c) ascertaining that risks are managed appropriately, and (d) verifying that the organization's resources are used responsibly.[2]

This definition of corporate governance covers both the conformance and performance aspects of governance:

- The *conformance* aspect of corporate governance reflects compliance with all applicable laws, rules, regulations, and standards, as well as accountability to all stakeholders.
- The *performance* aspect of corporate governance underscores the importance of policies and procedures in addressing opportunities and risks, best practices, resource utilization, strategy, value creation, and decision-making.

The IGPG definition of corporate governance is adopted in this chapter, which gives a broad definition describing the professional responsibilities and accountability of all "corporate gatekeepers." These corporate gatekeepers include the board of directors, management, legal counsel, internal auditors, external auditors, financial advisors, investment banks, credit agencies, regulators, policymakers, and standard-setters.

DRIVERS OF CORPORATE GOVERNANCE

The primary drivers and sources of standards for corporate governance in the United States are corporate law, securities law, listing standards, and best practices.[3]

- **State Corporate Laws:** In the United States, corporations are established and subject to the regulations under the state in which they were incorporated. State corporate law impacts corporate governance by defining authorities, fiduciary duties, and the responsibilities of shareholders, directors, and officers. This is accomplished by empowering shareholders to elect directors; inspect the company's ledgers, books, records, and financial reports; receive proxy materials; and approve major business transactions such as mergers and acquisitions.
- **The Federal Securities Laws:** Federal securities laws are intended to protect investors of public companies from receiving misleading information (e.g., financial statements). These laws improve investor confidence in the integrity and efficiency of the capital markets. Federal securities laws are primarily disclosure-based statutes that require public companies to file periodic reports with the Securities and Exchange Commission (SEC) and disclose certain information to shareholders so they can make educated investment and voting decisions. Congress responded to the wave of financial scandals during the late 1990s, and the early 2000s by passing the Sarbanes-Oxley Act of 2002 (SOX), which expanded the role of federal statutes in corporate governance by providing measures to improve corporate governance, financial reports, and audit activities. The global financial crisis of 2007–2009 prompted Congress to pass the Dodd-Frank Wall Street Reform and Consumer Protection Act of 2010[4] to minimize the probability of future financial crises and systemic distress. The Dodd-Frank Act empowers regulators to set higher capital requirements and establish new regulatory regimes and corporate governance measures for large financial services firms. These regulatory reforms and their impacts on corporate governance are discussed in the next section.
- **Listing Standards:** Listing standards adopted by national stock exchanges (NYSE, NASDAQ, and AMEX) are intended to establish standard corporate governance requirements for companies listed on the exchange. Listing standards often go beyond government reforms by addressing the uniform voting rights to majority voting practice, shareholder approvals of executive compensation, mandatory internal audit function, and risk assessment.
- **Global Exchanges:** Looking at exchanges globally, in November 2009, the United Nations (UN) invited the world's stock exchanges to open dialogue with investors, regulators, and companies to find creative ways for improving corporate environmental social and governance disclosure

and performance with the ultimate goal of encouraging responsible long-term approaches to investment. It was a call to recognize the momentum achieved by responsible investment as part of the solution to the global financial crisis. In 2010, Aviva Investors, with support from the UN-backed Principles for Responsible Investment (PRI), launched the Sustainable Stock Exchanges Initiative, which enlists the support of financial institutions that are PRI signatories to bring about change in global listing rules. All listing authorities and stock exchanges are encouraged to make it a listing requirement that companies should (1) consider how responsible and sustainable their business model is, and (2) put a forward-looking sustainability strategy to the vote at their AGM. At the same time, the PRI signatories are called upon to support the initiative by showing a commitment to trade on stock exchanges that maintain this listing provision. This last element is critical in making it clear to stock exchanges that there is a business case for them making changes. As a result, there is nascent movement by exchanges to require new listings to be more transparent in their governance of their sustainability footprint. The Johannesburg Stock Exchange and the Singapore Exchange (SGX) require their listed companies to report on sustainability considerations, and China's state-owned Assets Supervision and Administration Commission now expects the largest state-owned companies to report as well.

■ **Best Practices:** Corporate governance best practices are often developed and supported by professional organizations and investor interest groups. They are typically nonbinding guidelines intended to improve organizations' corporate governance practices above and beyond state and federal statutes and listing standards. Examples of some of these best practices include: shareholder approval of executive compensation ("say on pay"), a majority voting system, and separation of the roles of CEO and chairperson of the board of directors. These best practices intend to improve the effectiveness and objectivity of corporate governance.

GLOBAL CONVERGENCE IN CORPORATE GOVERNANCE

Globalization, technological advances, and the ever-growing regulatory reforms worldwide have promoted global convergence in corporate governance. The move toward convergence in corporate governance has become substantially more prevalent post-2007, since the global financial crisis. Recently, there have been influential attempts for improved corporate governance mechanisms worldwide. This prevalence, combined with globalization and increases in technology, has resulted in a trend towards a global corporate governance model. What has not been established, though, is whether or not global corporate governance convergence will actually occur any time in the near future. While there are numerous countries, organizations, and events that are working toward a consistent global governance model, there seems to be a greater number of forces (political and cultural differences) acting as a barrier at this point in time. As the world becomes a smaller place over the upcoming decades, this topic will need to be readdressed. Convergence may not only become a valid possibility; it may prove to be a global necessity.

Countries worldwide have their own corporate governance measures and best practices, which are typically reflective of their economic, political, cultural, and legal circumstances. The global regulatory responses to corporate scandals and financial crises demand convergence in corporate governance across borders. This convergence is particularly important in the areas of investor rights and protections, board independence and responsibilities, and uniform financial disclosures. While complete convergence in corporate governance reforms may not be possible, uniform global corporate governance measures and cross-border standards enforcements should be promoted to improve efficiency and liquidity in the global capital markets. An unaddressed issue is whether cross-border differences in corporate governance can be reconciled and whether full convergence in corporate governance is feasible.

A move toward convergence in corporate governance has been promoted since 1999 by the Organization for Economic Cooperation and Development (OECD). The OECD has established a set of corporate governance principles, which were later adopted by the International Corporate Governance Network (ICGN) designed to protect all global investors. The ICGN is a voluntary global membership organization of over 500 leaders in corporate governance including institutional investors who collectively represent funds under management of around $18 trillion and based in 50 countries.[5] The ICGN's mission is to strengthen and promote convergence in corporate governance standards worldwide.

SARBANES-OXLEY ACT OF 2002

Congress passed the Public Company Accounting Reform and Investor Protection Act of 2002, better known as the Sarbanes-Oxley Act (SOX), to rebuild investor confidence that had been eroded by a number of financial scandals. SOX is intended to restore trust in the financial reports of public companies and in the markets more generally.

SOX is viewed as a having three primary goals:

1. Minimizing conflicts of interest (e.g., independence of directors, formation of the audit committee, internal control reporting, the prohibition of non-audit services, regulation of the auditing profession, and rules for security analysts).
2. Establishing incentives for improving corporate governance and financial reporting (e.g., prohibiting loans to directors or executive officers; CEO/CFO certification of financial reports and internal controls; audit committees' responsibility for hiring, firing, compensating, and overseeing auditors; auditors' report to the audit committee).
3. Imposing penalties for violations of securities laws and fraud.

Sarbanes-Oxley provisions can be classified into corporate governance, financial reporting, auditing, and other provisions.

The corporate governance provisions of SOX are:

1. Enhanced audit committee responsibility for hiring, firing, compensating, and overseeing auditors and preapproval of non-audit services.
2. Disclosure, in periodic reports, as to whether the audit committee has at least one member who is a "financial expert" and if not, why.
3. CEO and CFO certification of the accuracy and completeness of quarterly and annual reports.
4. Management assessment and reporting of the effectiveness of disclosure controls and procedures.
5. Ban on personal loans by companies to their directors or executives, other than certain regular consumer loans.
6. Establishment of procedures by each audit committee for receiving, retaining, and handling complaints received by the company concerning accounting, internal controls, or auditing matters.
7. Review of quarterly and annual reports (forms 10-Q and 10-K) by officers.
8. Forfeiture of certain bonuses and profits by the CEO or CFO when the company restates its financial statements due to material noncompliance with reporting requirements.

9. Preventing and detecting improper influence on conduct of audits.
10. Remaining vigilant against insider trades during pension fund blackout periods.
11. Determining officers' and directors' penalties for violations of securities laws or corporate misconduct.

The Financial reporting provisions of SOX are:

1. Executive (CEO/CFO) certification of financial statements of public companies.
2. Executive certification of internal control over financial reporting.
3. Auditor's reports on both financial statements and internal control over financial reporting of large public companies.
4. Disclosures of off-balance-sheet arrangements.
5. Disclosures of contractual obligations.
6. Disclosures of reconciliation of non-GAAP financial measures pertaining to pro-forma financial information.
7. Disclosures of material correcting adjustments by auditors.
8. Disclosures of transactions involving management and principal stockholders.
9. Accelerated filing of changes in beneficial ownership by insiders.
10. Real-time disclosures of information concerning material changes in financial condition or operations (form 8-K disclosures).
11. Periodic review of published financial statements by the SEC, at least once every three years.
12. SEC-enhanced authority to determine what constitutes U.S. generally accepted accounting principles (GAAP).

Auditing provisions of SOX are:

1. Establishment and operation of the Public Company Accounting Oversight Board (PCAOB) to regulate the practices of professional auditors who work with public companies.
2. Registration with the PCAOB by public accounting firms that audit public companies in order to protect investors from receiving misleading reports and to strengthen the quality of audit of public companies.
3. Requirement that auditors be appointed, compensated, and overseen by the audit committee to ensure their independence and objectivity.

4. Many non-audit services are prohibited from being performed contemporaneously with an audit of financial statements to minimize the potential conflicts of interest between the auditors and public company clients.
5. Rotation of the lead (or coordinating) audit partner and the lead review partner every five years to preserve auditor independence and objectivity.
6. Auditors report to the audit committee regarding significant weaknesses in internal control over financial reporting and important accounting policies and practices.
7. Prohibition on hiring a C-level executive who was recently employed by auditor.
8. Auditor's report on the effectiveness of internal control over financial reporting.
9. Disclosure of fees paid to the auditor for all services (e.g., audit, taxes, consulting).
10. Requirements for preapproval of audit and permitted non-audit services by the audit committee.
11. Retention of audit work papers and documents for five years, with increased penalties for destruction of corporate audit records.

Other important provisions of SOX are:

1. Professional responsibilities for attorneys appearing and practicing before the SEC.
2. Disclosures of corporate code of ethics for executives and employees of public companies.
3. Collection and administration of funds for victim investors resulting from fraudulent financial statements.
4. Analyst conflicts of interest (e.g., Regulation Analyst Certification).
5. Establishment of internal policies and procedures that enable whistle-blowers to report violations of securities laws and to protect them from retaliation.
6. Handling of debts nondischargeable in bankruptcy.
7. SEC censure or bar of any person who is not qualified, lacks the requisite character or integrity, or with unethical conduct.
8. Lengthened statute of limitations for securities fraud.
9. Criminalization of corporate misconducts.
10. Criminal penalties for defrauding shareholders of public companies.

11. Increased criminal penalties under securities laws and mail and wire fraud.
12. Future studies on consolidation of public accounts by firm, audit firm rotation, accounting standards, credit rating agencies, and investment banks.

Corporations have benefited from the implementation of SOX through improved corporate governance, quality and transparency of financial reports, effectiveness of internal controls, and improved audit quality. More accurate and complete financial information allows investors to benefit from increased protection against misleading financial reports by being better able to assess the risk and return associated with their investment. The debate over the effectiveness and cost-efficiency of the implementation of provisions of SOX pertains to the increased compliance costs of SOX and the embedded benefits of compliance. If SOX has provided increased protection for investors and improved investor confidence through cost-effective compliance with its provisions, then we expect SOX to have positive effects on public financial reports, shareholder wealth, capital markets, and the nation's economic growth.

DODD-FRANK ACT

The 2007–2009 financial crisis spurred Congress into passing the Dodd-Frank Wall Street Reform and Consumer Protection Act in 2010. The legislation is over 2,300 pages and its provisions mainly pertain to financial services firms such as banks, hedge funds, credit rating agencies, and the derivatives market. The Dodd-Frank Act directs regulators to establish about 240 rules to implement its provisions and authorizes the establishment of an oversight council to monitor systemic risk of financial institutions and the creation of a consumer protection bureau within the Federal Reserve. It is intended to minimize the likelihood of future financial crises and systemic distress by empowering regulators to require more effective corporate governance and higher capital requirements for financial services firms. The Dodd-Frank Act also establishes new regulatory regimes for large firms and requires regulatory and market structures for derivatives, demanding systemic risk assessment and monitoring of financial markets.[6] The Dodd-Frank Act created the Financial Stability Oversight Council (FSOC), which identifies and monitors systemic risk in the financial sector.

The overarching goal is to make the financial markets safer, more stable, and more robust. In summary, the Dodd-Frank Act is expected to affect corporate governance measures and practices of public companies in many ways, including:

1. Strengthening the link between pay and performance with provisions empowering shareholders with a nonbinding vote on execution compensation (e.g., "say on pay," approval of golden parachutes). These are held every three years, at minimum, with the right to vote on the frequency of "say on pay" every one, two, or three years. In addition, institutional investment managers are required to disclose at least annually how they voted on the frequency of such votes.
2. Providing the rationale for choosing a combined or separate role of CEO and the chair of the board of directors (i.e., CEO duality).
3. Establishment of policies and practices on the hedging of company securities.
4. Disclosure of the internal executive compensation ratio (the ratio of the annual total compensation of the CEO and the median annual total compensation of all employees, excluding the CEO). All U.S. public companies are to incorporate so-called claw-back provisions into incentive compensation arrangements for executive officers. Public companies implement and report on their policies and practices for recouping payments to current and former executives in restatements of financial statements that have been caused by material noncompliance with standards.
5. Establishment and maintenance of more effective, rewarding, and protective whistleblowing policies and procedures.

More than a year after the passage of Dodd-Frank Act, only a small portion (about 12 percent) of its provisions has been implemented. A sluggish global economy, market volatility, and eroded public trust have contributed to the delay in implementation.

THE UNITED KINGDOM'S FINANCIAL REGULATORY FRAMEWORK

By comparison, the United Kingdom's government has taken initiatives to restructure its financial regulatory framework by replacing the Financial

Services Advisory (FSA) with two newly established bodies. The two regulatory bodies are the Prudential Regulation Authority (PRA) and the Financial Conduct Authority (FCA).[7] The PRA will be a subsidiary of the Bank of England (BoE), responsible for "micro-prudential," firm-specific regulation of regulatory capital and related oversight functions. The Financial Policy Committee (FPC) will be in charge of identifying, assessing, and monitoring financial services firms and taking proper action to minimize systemic risks at a macro level. The FCA will regulate financial services firms, performing many of the FSA's former functions. The primary objective of the FCA will be rebuilding confidence in the UK's financial system by securing an appropriate degree of protection for consumers, strengthening integrity, and enhancing efficiency and choice in the market.

LISTING STANDARDS RELATED TO CORPORATE GOVERNANCE

The New York Stock Exchange (NYSE) has conducted a comprehensive review of its adopted corporate governance principles since the 2007–2009 global financial crisis.[8]

CORPORATE GOVERNANCE IN THE POST-CRISIS ERA

Corporate governance has received significant attention since the financial crisis of 2007–2009 due to the perception that more effective governance measures could have mitigated some of the crisis's adverse effects. The Dodd-Frank Act of 2010 attempted to address corporate governance in the post-crisis era in many ways, as described in the previous sections.

The International Federation of Accountants (IFAC) has conducted several surveys and interviews in the pre- and post-crisis periods to determine the challenges related to corporate governance and to identify potential improvement opportunities. The IFAC has made the following recommendations for improvements in corporate governance in the post–financial-crisis era:

1. **Directors' primary duty is for performance not for conformance:** Although long-term survival of an organization is determined by improvements in performance and the effectiveness of conformance or

KEY**GUIDANCE**

NYSE's 10 corporate governance principles are:

Principle 1: The board's fundamental objective should be to create sustainable value and be responsible and accountable to shareholders for its performance in achieving this objective.

Principle 2: Management's primary responsibility is to create an environment where a culture of performance with integrity can flourish.

Principle 3: Shareholders have the right, responsibility, and long-term economic interest to exercise their voting rights to influence director behavior and corporate governance and to communicate their issues of concern.

Principle 4: Good corporate governance should be integrated with the company's business strategy and objectives.

Principle 5: Legislation and agency rulemaking are important to establish the basic tenets of corporate governance; market-based best practices of corporate governance should also be employed.

Principle 6: Corporate governance policies, practices, and performance should be effectively communicated to shareholders.

Principle 7: Listed companies should strike the right balance between the selection of independent and non-independent directors to take full advantage of expertise, diversity, and knowledge on the board.

Principle 8: Advisory should be held to appropriate standards of transparency and accountability.

Principle 9: The SEC should work with the NYSE and other exchanges to ensure an effective, efficient, useful, and transparent proxy voting process.

Principle 10: The SEC and/or the NYSE should periodically assess the impact of major corporate governance reforms on the achievement of sustainable performance.

Source: New York Stock Exchange (NYSE)/NYSE Euronext. 2010. "Report of the New York Stock Exchange Commission on Corporate Governance." Available at: http://www.nyse.com/about/listed/1265973393069.html.

compliance with all applicable laws, rules, regulations, and standards, performance creates sustainable stakeholder value. This necessitates that the board of directors find a balance between performance and conformance activities with a keen focus on creating and enhancing sustainable performance.

2. **Expand from a shareholder perspective to stakeholder perspective:** The primary goal of corporate governance is to protect interests of all stakeholders including shareholders, creditors, employees, customers, suppliers, governments, and society. Corporate governance measures should be in place to create and enhance stakeholder value.

3. **Achieve sustainable performance objectives in all areas of economic, social, and environmental activities:** Organizations should take into consideration the dimensions of sustainability performance of economic, governance, social, ethics, and environmental activities.

4. **Integrate governance and sustainability into the organization's strategy, operations, and disclosures:** Organizations should integrate sustainability and governance into their reporting process, producing a comprehensive report that reflects financial, social, and environmental performance.

5. **Create ethical and competent organization culture:** Organizations should establish codes of conduct to ensure a value-based culture. The established codes of conduct must be communicated throughout the organization to ensure compliance.

6. **Improve the organization's communications with all its stakeholders:** Organizations should expand their financial reporting and communication channels to include integrated and holistic reports on economic, governance, social, ethics, and environmental performance.[9]

Corporate governance participants and corporate gatekeepers have been criticized for the occurrence and persistence of the 2007–2009 global financial crises. Two overriding reasons for the persistence of the crises were ineffective risk management and inappropriate executive pay practices in the financial services industry. Several corporate governance reforms (e.g., the Dodd-Frank Act of 2010) in the post-crisis era have changed the relationship between shareholders and their boards in the United States by creating an appropriate "balance of authority" exercised by boards, management, and shareholders in corporate governance and decision-making processes. Traditionally, the shareholder model of corporate governance has suggested that decision oversight should be separated from decision management. This has been accomplished by holding the board of directors accountable for effective oversight of managerial decisions made when creating shareholder value. This model worked well when there was less widely dispersed stock ownership and investor value-creation was the only objective of corporations.

Today, directors are now accountable to a wide array of stakeholders, including shareholders, creditors, employees, customers, suppliers, governments, and communities where the corporation operates. Under this new view of corporate governance, directors are responsible to protect the interests of all stakeholders, including shareholders. In this new era, the effectiveness of corporate governance and board oversight can be improved when:

1. There is better diversity in the boardroom regarding the knowledge, experience, and expertise of directors. The board should be composed of directors with adequate experience who can provide sound advice to management and fully understand the company's businesses, industry, and markets—and thus its commitment and responsibility to all of its stakeholders. Furthermore, directors should have the courage, integrity, reputation, and judgment to make difficult decisions on behalf of all stakeholders, particularly shareholders.

2. There is a good understanding that the primary fiduciary duty of the board of directors is to protect stakeholder interests by overseeing managerial function through hiring the most ethical and competent CEO and approving the appointment of other senior executives, approving their compensation, and removing them when they become unethical or incompetent.

3. There is a keen focus by the board of directors on key strategies, issues, and performance indicators. This requires that directors be proactive rather than reactive and pay attention to important business matters rather than micromanaging. Directors should also have a robust reporting system for receiving timely and credible information and conduct effective analysis to make tough decisions for the benefit of all stakeholders.

4. There is an appropriate tone at the top set by the board of directors promoting ethical and competent behavior and performance throughout the company.

5. There is a mechanism for the board of directors to ensure management is disclosing all relevant information regarding all five dimensions of EGSEE sustainability performance to the company's stakeholders. For instance, an increasing number of boards are establishing sustainability committees that either report to the board or consist of board members

themselves. Examples of such companies are Intel, Roche, Ford, JP Morgan, and Bank of America. While an increasing number of large companies are giving their boards' responsibility for oversight of sustainability, there is no current consensus about the best model to apply. In a 2009 Deloitte survey of 220 directors of American companies with more than $1 billion in revenues, 37 percent of respondents said some committee should oversee sustainability responsibilities.[10] When asked which committee is the best fit, 24 percent of respondents chose risk and governance committees; 22 percent chose the strategy committee, and 15 percent chose the audit committee.[11] These figures suggest that the future may deliver not a single model but rather a range of options for companies.

6. Corporate governance reforms are perceived to be cost-efficient, effective, and scalable.
7. Corporate governance measures are globally accepted and effectively implemented.
8. Directors and officers are held personally accountable for defrauding investors if violations are committed.
9. There is a better link between corporate sustainable performance and executive compensation.
10. The primary responsibility of the director is clearly defined to improve performance rather than compliance.
11. Corporate governance focus has shifted from a shareholder perspective to a stakeholder perspective.
12. Organizations focus on business sustainability consisting of the five EGSEE performance dimensions and integrate these dimensions into their strategy, operations, and stakeholder communications.

Further improvements needed in global corporate governance reforms and practices are:

1. The key driver and determinant of effective governance is the appropriate tone set by directors and officers as well as an organization's leaders.
2. Principles-based, stakeholder-driven governance measures offer a stronger likelihood of success than regulatory-lead measures.
3. Effective organization governance mandates more board independence.
4. Professional risk and liability for directors need to be addressed.
5. The primary responsibility of directors is performance rather than compliance.

6. Organizations should focus on business sustainability by improving all dimensions of the organization's performance from social and environmental to economic performance.

7. Executive compensation should be aligned with the organization's competitive sustainable performance.

8. The board of directors should effectively oversee ongoing risk management and control.

9. A globally accepted and coordinated system of governance, regulation, and oversight is needed to prevent future crises.

10. Investors and other stakeholders should be attentive and more actively pursue their responsibilities by voting their proxies on EGSEE issues.[12]

CORPORATE GOVERNANCE FUNCTIONS

The viability and efficacy of corporate governance depends on the effectiveness of its functions. The seven essential corporate governance functions are:

1. Oversight
2. Managerial
3. Compliance
4. Internal audit
5. Advisory
6. External audit
7. Monitoring

Corporate governance performance can be viable when all participants fulfill the responsibilities their roles require and perform a value-added function.

Oversight Function

Oversight of corporate governance is granted to the board of directors with the fiduciary duty of overseeing managerial function in the best interests of the company's stakeholders. The effectiveness of the oversight function is influenced by directors' independence, expertise, authority, resources, composition, qualifications, and accountability. It is ultimately determined by the board of directors' strategic decisions. Sound and effective strategy by the board of directors is becoming more important in the post-crisis era, especially when monitoring executive risk appetite, particularly as it is related to international operation. The board of directors should obtain a complete understanding and knowledge of corporate culture and its operation as it affects the company's risk profile. The board should also challenge management's strategic decisions and information about risk management and compensation. The board should communicate thoroughly and effectively with a wide range of stakeholders to boost confidence and encourage them to share their concerns with the board. In the aftermath of 2007–2009 global financial crises, the board of directors should take the following 12 steps:

1. Appoint the most competent and ethical CEO and approve hiring of other senior executives.
2. Design executive compensation schemes that are linked to sustainable performance by rewarding high-quality performance and reducing incentives for excessive risk-taking.
3. Remove executives when they become incompetent and/or unethical.
4. Understand the business of the company and be familiar and actively engaged in corporate strategic decisions.
5. Keep informed about corporate major activities and related performance.
6. Oversee corporate affairs and compliance with all applicable laws, rules, regulations, standards, and best practices.
7. Understand corporate reporting in all five EGSEE dimensions of business sustainability.
8. Oversee the reliability and usefulness of financial reports.
9. Oversee business risk assessment and management.
10. Oversee the effectiveness of internal controls.
11. Understand the shareholders' perspectives on the company.
12. Work with management to ensure alignment of management interests with those of shareholders and to protect the interests of other stakeholders (e.g., employees, creditors, customers, suppliers, government, environment, society).

Board Oversight Strategy on Sustainability

The best board strategy is the one that effectively represents and protects the interests of all stakeholders from investors to employees, customers, and society. On July 13, 2011, the Lead Director Network (LDN) invited a select group of independent directors from Fortune 500 companies to discuss ways to improve board governance. Participants discussed four important aspects of board strategy as follow:[13]

1. **The board's role in corporate strategy:** Participating directors were in common agreement that board oversight strategy is the most important duty of the board of directors. The board involvement in strategic oversight should be promoted.

2. **International opportunities and risks are front of mind:** A high majority of participating directors believe that companies should find ways to capitalize on globalization, expand their operation and customer base internationally, and participate in the global capital markets while paying attention to global market risks, political instability, bribery, and corruption, money blundering, human rights, threats to intellectual property rights, and scarce resources.

3. **Improving strategic oversight of international opportunities and risks:** The board of directors should broaden their knowledge, expertise, and experience in the international aspects of their business and/or hire advisors who possess adequate knowledge of globalization and are experts in different geographies.

4. **The lead director's unique role in strategy:** Lead directors play an important role in setting agenda and directions for the board and thus they should focus their attention on corporate strategy, including strategic opportunities and risks.

A study conducted by the Conference Board in 2010 indicates that many boards of directors do not adequately address business sustainability, as many companies do not have an effective structural framework to properly facilitate director oversight of a sustainability program.[14] Directors do not obtain credible and timely information on KPIs and measures of EGSEE sustainability performance. Findings of the 2010 Conference Board survey regarding sustainability in the boardroom are highlighted as follow:

1. Stakeholder interest and influence in corporate sustainability performance (EGSEE) is increasing. There is more demand by regulatory bodies, enforcement agencies, and activist investors for sustainability disclosures, which has encouraged the board of directors to pay more attention to corporate sustainability.

2. Many corporate boards do not receive adequate information on many dimensions of EGSEE sustainability performance.

3. Many companies do not use the available business sustainability standards when developing uniform and consistent sustainability disclosures.
4. Many companies do not evaluate the impacts of sustainability activities (e.g., social, environmental) in their financial performance.
5. Some of the emerging sustainability issues (e.g., climate change, political spending, board diversity) are gaining the attention of investors, and thus the board of directors, which acts as their representative.

BOARD COMMITTEES

Listed public companies in the United States are required to establish three mandatory board committees for audit, compensation, and nominating/governance. These three mandatory board committees should be composed of at least three independent directors. Normally, board committees are provided with sufficient resources and authority to function independently from one another and they are separately evaluated by the board of directors. The establishment of board committees can bring more focus to the board's oversight function by giving it proper authority and by demanding accountability. In addition to these three mandatory committees, public companies often have governance and other committees dealing with topics such as finance, sustainability or CSR, IT, and disclosure. Dodd-Frank Act of 2010 requires a separate board risk committee (BRC) for nonbank financial companies and certain bank holding companies (assets over $10 billion). BRC should be responsible for the oversight of the enterprise-wide risk management policies and practices. BRC should identify, manage, and monitor critical risks, risk appetite process, and oversee execution of that process.

Managerial Function

The managerial function of corporate governance is assumed by the management team, appointed by the board of directors, and led by the CEO. Support to manage the company for the benefits of its stakeholders comes from the CFO, controller, treasurer, and other senior executives. The effectiveness of management is determined by the alignment of its interests with those of shareholders and other stakeholders. Management's primary responsibilities are to achieve all five EGSEE dimensions of sustainability performance. Many companies have established the position of chief sustainability officer (CSO) to ensure effective achievement of EGSEE sustainability performance. The effectiveness of the managerial function also depends on the CEO independence (as opposed to duality) and proper executive compensation, which is tied to sustainable performance and sound whistle-blowing policies and programs.

Compliance Function

Compliance functions of corporate governance are composed of a set of laws, regulations, rules, standards, and best practices established with the intent to create a compliance framework for public companies in which to operate and achieve their goals of sustainable performance. Policymakers, regulators, and standard-setters are being criticized for their reactive rather than proactive approach in establishing and enforcing cost-effective, efficient, and scalable rules and regulations. Regulations should establish a framework within which public companies can achieve sustainable performance while complying with regulations and also exercising a culture of honesty, integrity, and accountability.

Internal Audit Function

Internal audit function of corporate governance is assumed by internal auditors who provide both assurance and consulting services to the company in the areas of operational efficiency, risk management, internal controls, financial reporting, and governance processes. Assurance reports provided by internal auditors are currently intended for internal use by management. Internal auditors are well trained and positioned to provide numerous assurance services but most require additional EGSEE and sustainability training to serve in an effective control function.

Internal auditors assist with compliance of Sections 302 and 404 of SOX by reviewing management's financial statement certifications and internal control over financial reporting and providing some type of assurance on their accuracy. Internal auditors can also provide opinions on their organization's risk management process, internal control systems, and governance measures for internal as well as regulatory purposes.

Legal and Financial Advisory Function

The legal and financial advisory function of corporate governance is assumed by professional advisors, internal legal counsel, financial analysts, and investment bankers. These professionals normally assist companies in evaluating the legal and financial consequences of business transactions. Legal counsel provides legal advice and assists the company in complying with applicable laws, regulations, rules, and other legal requirements. SOX makes legal counsel an integral component of the internal corporate governance structure, where they ensure lawful corporate conduct. Financial advisors provide financial advice and planning to the company, while financial analysts and investment bankers advise corporations, their directors, officers, and other key personnel about coverage and stock recommendations, which can influence corporate governance.

External Audit Function

The external audit function of corporate governance is conducted by outside auditors who express an opinion on the presentation of financial statements in conformity with generally accepted accounting principles. In the United States, external auditors lend credibility to a company's financial statements and thus add value to its corporate governance. External auditors usually perform an integrated audit that examines the company's internal control over financial reporting and financial statements, as required by SOX. External auditors are well qualified to provide assurance on all five EGSEE dimensions of sustainability performance, as discussed in detail in Chapter 11.

Monitoring Function

The monitoring function of corporate governance is the direct responsibility of shareholders and other stakeholders and it can be achieved through direct investor engagement in the business and financial affairs of corporations. Shareholders play an important role in monitoring public companies to ensure the effectiveness of their corporate governance and strengthen shareholder rights by demanding timely access to information, enhancing shareholders' rights, and promoting shareholder democracy. The monitoring function of corporate governance requires that investors be attentive in looking after their investments by participating in the election of the directors and engaging in the proxy voting process. Institutional investors play an important role in corporate governance through monitoring the governance and financial reporting of the companies they invest in. This is most likely to occur in the case of institutional investors who generally hold investments for a decade or more and whose interest is aligned with the long-term economic and comprehensive sustainability of the company.

Institutional investors are distinct from individual investors and consist of pension funds, hedge funds, mutual funds, insurance companies, and endowments of not-for-profit entities like foundations and universities. Institutional investors are also important due to the size of their holdings. They are often market makers because other investors track them for indications of performance, meaning they often play a role that goes beyond their individual holdings.

As major shareholders, institutional investors are more often engaged in the election of directors who focus more on sustainability, the oversight of governance function, and assurance of the achievements of long-term performance. To effectively monitor corporations, institutional investors should promote the goals of the individual investors who fund them. They should also focus on long-term, sustainable performance by acting as stewards that guide publicly held corporations away from unsustainable short-termist behavior. Institutional investors can play an important role in reducing information asymmetry by obtaining private information from management and conveying that to shareholders and, thus, to the capital markets. Institutional investors influence the governance of the public companies they invest in by putting forth proposals intended to improve corporate governance effectiveness. Investors' demand for and interest in EGSEE sustainability performance as well as the transparent disclosure of related information is crucial. This is further discussed in the following section on investors' proxy voting.

PROXY VOTING FOR SUSTAINABILITY

Some companies are providing guidance for proxy voting for sustainability as it has been gradually integrated into business strategies. For example, in 2011 Ceres developed its guidance on proxy voting sustainability principles, which covers all dimensions of sustainability performance including governance, environmental, and social responsibility issues.[15] This sustainability guidance provides ways to cast votes on a variety of sustainability issues of governance, such as proposals that promote directors' loyalty to shareholders or strengthen the link between executive compensation and sustainable performance. The Proxy Voting Sustainability Principles enable investors to better position themselves to vote responsibly and consistently and on the 700-plus sustainability resolutions that were filed with U.S. companies in 2011.[16] The 2012 proxy season survey conducted by Ernst & Young showed that 45 percent of all shareholder proposals up for a vote in 2012 addressed environmental or social issues. Investors and consumers are placing strong pressure on companies to consider the triple bottom line, both within the specific company and across its supply chain. In the survey, 66 percent of companies reported an increase in sustainability-related inquiries from investors in the past year alone. Of the respondents, 83 percent either already work directly with their suppliers on measuring sustainability impacts or are in the process of doing so. Investors can also adopt sustainability principles as a policy to guide their proxy voting consultants to vote on sustainability issues on their behalf.

Corporate Governance KPIs

The effectiveness of corporate governance is influenced by the existence and functioning of its internal and external mechanisms, as designed to achieve corporate objectives of creating shareholder value while accounting for the interests of other stakeholders such as creditors, employees, customers, suppliers, government, the environment, and society. Thus, corporate governance KPIs measure the effectiveness of internal mechanisms—such as the board of directors and its board committees, management, internal controls, and internal audit functions—as well as external mechanisms, including the market for corporate control, the capital market, the labor market, federal and state statutes, court decisions, shareholders' proposals, and best practices of investors' activists. Furthermore, KPIs for each of the seven functions of corporate governance discussed in the previous sections should be identified, measured, assessed, and disclosed. Exhibit 6.1 provides a list of corporate governance KPIs.

EXHIBIT 6.1 Corporate Governance KPIs

Oversight Function

1. Number of board committees
2. Percentage of board independence
3. Full independence of board committees
4. Board diversity in terms of ethnicity, sex, expertise, etc.
5. Staggered board
6. Separation of the position of the chair of the board and the CEO
7. Board accountability and liability
8. Number of board meetings
9. Number of members on the board

(continued)

EXHIBIT 6.1 (Continued)

10. Percentage of insider directors on the board
11. Number of members in the audit committee
12. Number of audit committee meetings
13. Number of audit committee financial experts
14. Value of stock options awarded to the directors

Managerial Function

1. Risk management
2. Codes of conduct and ethics
3. Executive compensation
4. Stock-based compensation
5. Dividend policy
6. Budget and performance evaluation
7. Earnings releases
8. Non-GAAP financial measures
9. Operational information
10. Quantitative analysis
11. Forward-looking data
12. Financial statements
13. Internal control over financial reporting
14. Executive pay-for-performance
15. Ratio of executive compensation to average employee compensation
16. Number of risk events
17. Risk trends
18. Total risk exposure
19. Percentage of strategic objectives achieved
20. Number of internal control improvement initiatives
21. Number of regulatory or legal noncompliance events
22. Frequency of compliance reviews
23. Cost of noncompliance
24. Management's description of its long-term vision
25. Management's perspective on strengths and weaknesses
26. Management's perspective on the opportunities and threats
27. Management's financial and nonfinancial goals
28. Management's description of overall corporate strategy

Compliance Function

1. Existence of compliance board committee
2. Executive compliance officer
3. Number of instances of noncompliance with applicable rules, laws, regulations, and standards
4. Cost of compliance with applicable rules, laws, regulations, and standards

(continued)

EXHIBIT 6.1 (Continued)

5. Whistle-blowing policies, programs, and procedures
6. Restatement of financial and nonfinancial reports

Internal Audit Function

1. Existence of internal audit function
2. Audit committee oversight of internal audit department
3. Independence of internal audit function
4. Appointment of the chief audit executive (CAE) by the audit committee
5. Internal audit reports to audit committee
6. Adequate resources for the internal audit department
7. Internal audit charter

External Audit Function

1. The ratio of non-audit fee to total audit fee
2. Audit quality
3. Auditor independence
4. PCAOB inspection reports
5. Compliance with professional auditing, ethics, and quality-control standards.
6. Audit firm rotation

Legal and Financial Advisors Function

1. Existence of in-house legal counsel
2. Quality of legal services
3. Analyst followings
4. Analyst forecast dispersion
5. Analyst forecast accuracy

Monitoring Function

1. Say-on-pay
2. Majority voting system
3. Shareholders' democracy
4. Institutional investors' ownership
5. Poison pills
6. Proxy-statement issues
7. Online voting by shareholders
8. Ability to nominate directors
9. Approval of major business transactions (mergers and acquisitions)
10. Ratifications of the external auditors

EMERGING CORPORATE GOVERNANCE ISSUES AND CHALLENGES

The five emerging corporate governance issues in 2012 are: (1) compliance with applicable rules, regulations, and standards; (2) board leadership; (3) CEO succession planning; (4) risk assessment and management; and (5) executive compensation.

Compliance

Effective compliance with implementation rules of provisions of both SOX and Dodd-Frank Act of 2010 (DOF) as related to whistle-blowing is a major challenge for public companies. The SEC whistle-blower bounty program under the Dodd-Frank Act of 2012 makes the whistle-blower process external, bringing it to a new level by providing a bounty to employees whose information to the SEC leads to a successful conviction. The final rules for the whistle-blower bounty program enable whistle-blowers to report violations externally to regulators (the SEC) rather than internally through companies' compliance programs as required by SOX. Whistle-blowers are also incentivized to report wrongdoings and violations of laws internally through internal compliance and reporting systems when appropriate. Compliance with provisions of the Foreign Corrupt Practices Act (FCPA) is also receiving the attention of audit committees as the U.S. Department of Justice and the SEC ratchet up efforts to ensure compliance with FCPA in cracking down on money-laundering.

Board Leadership

Success in separating the roles of the chairman of the board and the CEO is gaining new attention as DOF promotes such separation between the leadership of management oversight and management function. Successful separation of the chairman and CEO roles requires both positions to understand and recognize their respective roles. They must candidly and openly communicate challenges and opportunities facing the company and bring collegiality and professional consensus to the board by agreeing on a consistent vision of company strategy and key drivers of success. The separate roles must also avoid sending mixed messages that may undermine the achievement of the company's objectives.

CEO Succession Planning

CEO succession planning is one of the most important and challenging responsibilities of the board of directors in the aftermath of the 2007–2009 global financial crisis. The board of directors should plan for the short-term CEO succession emergencies (e.g., death, departure) as well as long-term strategy and sustainability of the position. During the emergency succession the chairman of the board and/or the lead director should be ready to step in as an acting CEO while the board deliberates on the permanent successor. The primary job of the elected board of directors is to appoint the most ethical and competent CEO and have a succession plan for when she/he becomes unethical or incompetent or departs from the company.

Risk Assessment and Management

Effective risk assessment and management continue to be important issues facing public companies in the aftermath of financial scandals and crises. The Dodd-Frank Act underscores the importance of these issues by promoting the establishment of a risk compliance office and/or board committee and designing compensation schemes that discourage executives from taking imprudent risk at the expense of shareholders. IT risk assessment and management is becoming more important as more companies move toward the use of XBRL in their financial reporting.

Executive Compensation

Executive compensation has been and will be an important agenda for the board of directors, particularly the compensation committee, as long as such pay is perceived to be excessive. Corporations that fail to implement say-on-pay votes, nonbinding shareholder votes to approve executive pay, will face even more challenges regarding this issue. The Dodd-Frank Act of 2010 requires the establishment of a board risk committee (BRC) to review executive compensation plans to ensure such plans do not provide incentives and opportunities for executives to take excessive risk at the expense of investors.

CORPORATE GOVERNANCE REPORTING AND ASSURANCE

Several corporate governance reforms in the United States have been established to restore investors' confidence (e.g., SOX in 2002, Dodd-Frank in 2010).

Corporate governance reporting is intended to present reliable, useful, timely, relevant, and transparent information about how the organization is managed and run. Such reporting covers information ranging from the independence and effectiveness of the board of directors to executive compensation, risk management, and democratic investor election. In a systematic and standardized format, effective corporate governance reporting should disclose all KPIs presented in the previous section of this chapter and listed in Exhibit 6.1. The content and format of such reports should be tailored to the company's organizational culture, applicable regulatory measures, and corporate governance structure, consisting of principles, mechanisms, functions, and roles and responsibilities of all corporate gatekeepers.

Corporate governance reporting (CGR) entails assessing the quality and effectiveness of the organization's corporate governance and reporting findings to interested stakeholders, including the board of directors, executives, auditors, regulatory agencies, and shareholders.

CGR should:

1. Disclose all relevant information about the effectiveness of the company's corporate governance.
2. Focus on the company's EGSEE sustainability performance.
3. Provide transparent information about the company's performance and its impact on all stakeholders.
4. Assess the company's responsiveness to the needs of its stakeholders.

Corporate governance reports should not only ensure effective compliance with all applicable corporate governance measures, reforms, and best practices but also provide adequate information on corporate governance effectiveness and increased transparency for all stakeholders. Eight primary drivers of corporate governance reporting are:

1. Increasing attention on corporate governance in the aftermath of financial scandals at the turn of the 21st century and recent financial crises.
2. Widening demand by regulators and investors for information on how public companies are run and managed.
3. Market-driven interests in companies' business models and KPIs.
4. Changes in balance of power between investors, the board of directors, and management resulting from new governance measures imposed by recent regulatory reforms.

5. More interest by stakeholders in understanding the roles and responsibilities of all corporate gatekeepers including the board of directors, legal counsel, internal auditors, and external auditors.
6. The market demand for better alignment between management compensation, corporate risk-taking, and sustainable performance.
7. Ever-increasing corporate governance regulatory reforms and best practices.
8. Ongoing debate over how to improve the effectiveness of corporate governance, either through principles-based and market-driven best practices or rules-based and regulatory-driven reforms—or maybe combination of both.

It is expected that regulatory reforms will continue to advance and best practices in corporate governance will evolve. The expected progress in corporate governance necessitates better uniform and standardized corporate governance reporting. Nonetheless, the establishment of globally accepted governance reporting presents many challenges regarding the format, content, structure, and frequency of reporting. The eight prevailing challenges are:[17]

1. Corporate governance reporting is a sensitive issue addressing roles, responsibilities, activities, and accountability of directors, which may have some business and legal percussions.
2. There is a wide range of audiences for corporate governance with no clear reporting purposes. This growing diversity of audiences and their needs makes standardized corporate governance reporting difficult.
3. Corporate governance disclosures are often isolated from the story in the sense that major initiatives, developments, and challenges are typically not mentioned in the governance report.
4. Inadequate focus on the effectiveness of corporate governance and the excessive use of the report as a compliance exercise reflecting the process and procedures rather than performance.
5. Investors lack of confidence in the value-relevance of corporate governance reports and their ability to provide useful information about the quality and performance of the board and management.

Corporate governance determines the way an organization is run and managed to create shareholder value while protecting interests of all other stakeholders including employees, customers, suppliers, the environment, society, and government. Effective corporate governance facilitates achievement of sustainable performance and compliance. Thus, corporate governance reporting should provide information about an organization's performance regarding enhanced investor value as well as compliance with applicable laws, regulations, standards, and best practices, which protect the interest of stakeholders. A group of professionals consisting of the Chartered Institute of Management Accountants (CIMA), PricewaterhouseCoopers (PwC), and Radley Yeldar has developed a corporate governance report structure that is flexible enough to be adopted gradually and also align with the best practices of many high-profile companies. The report structure can also be adapted to future changes and reforms. The proposed corporate governance reporting structure consists of two overarching strategies:[18]

1. Telling a governance story that is reliable, useful, and relevant to investors.
2. Demonstrating compliance by reflecting how effectively governance measures, reforms, and best practices are complied with.

Five elements of the proposed corporate governance report are:[19]

1. **Chairman's message:** Personal reporting on governance including the chairman's views on good governance and the culture of the board.
2. **Narrative governance report:** Detailed reporting on governance activities in key areas including characteristics of effective governance (skills, experience, knowledge, and personality traits).
3. **Compliance report:** Details of key activities of the board and its committees (e.g., audit, compensation, nominating) as well as compliance reports from each board committee.
4. **Accountability report:** Detailed report on the effectiveness of the board and its committees, their performance evaluations, and accountability.
5. **Communication report with shareholders:** Reflecting how the information needs of investors are met.

CONCLUSION

The role of corporate governance is to align management incentives with investor interests. Good corporate governance is committed to transparency, which should lead to an increase in capital inflows from domestic and foreign investors. Good corporate governance also implies the need for a network of monitoring and incentives set up by a company to ensure accountability of the board and management to shareholders and other stakeholders. The strongest form of defense against governance failure comes from an organization's culture and behaviors. Effectiveness depends on employees' integrity and begins with the tone management sets at the top. In addition, boards should routinely oversee their own actions against the acceptable governance principles. Organizations should ensure their boards have the qualifications and experience to approve an organization's strategy and to evaluate how it is executed and reported on.

Beyond the organization, the corporate governance system of a country and its standards is determined by factors such as political beliefs, culture, legal system, accounting systems, transparency, ownership structures, market environments, level of economic development, and its ethical standards.

Corporate governance participants must structure the process to ensure the goals of both shareholder value creation and stakeholder value protection for public companies. The corporate governance structure is shaped by internal and external governance mechanisms, as well as policy interventions through regulations. Corporate governance mechanisms are viewed as a nexus of contracts that is designed to align the interests of management with those of the shareholders. The effectiveness of both internal and external corporate governance depends on the trade-offs among its mechanisms and is related to their availability, the extent to which they are being used, whether their marginal benefits exceed their marginal costs, and the company's corporate governance structure.

ACTION**ITEMS**

1. Make sure sustainability is on the agenda for your board of directors and top-level management team.
2. Increase your commitments to business sustainability in terms of board and management attention and sound investment.
3. Reconsider and reevaluate roles and responsibilities of your board of directors, management, internal and external auditors, and legal counsel to ensure they are in compliance with regulatory reforms.
4. Link executive compensation to long-term, enduring, and sustainable performance.
5. Integrate say-on-pay into your corporate governance processes.

6. Pay attention to product innovation and quality, customer retention and attraction, employee satisfaction and productivity, socially responsible citizenship, and environmentally conscious operation.

7. Sufficiently disclose to all stakeholders that you are taking proper initiatives to further social good above and beyond your own interests and compliance and legal obligations.

8. Describe your CSR activities and practices in response to stakeholder expectations including minimizing negative impacts of your operations on society or the environment, while maximizing positive impacts on the community, customers, employees, suppliers, and society.

9. Ensure vigilant oversight function by the board of directors on internal control over financial reporting.

10. Improve board oversight of management in achieving sustainable EGSEE performance.

11. Encourage and enable all stakeholders, particularly shareholders, to take a more proactive role in corporate governance.

NOTES

1. Much of this writing is extracted from the introductory chapter of: Rezaee, Zabihollah. 2008. *Corporate Governance and Ethics* (Hoboken, NJ: John Wiley & Sons).

2. International Federation of Accountants (IFAC). 2009. "International Good Practice Guidance: Evaluating and Improving Governance in Organizations." Available at: https://www.ifac.org/publications-resources/evaluating-and-improving-governance-organizations.

3. Rezaee, Zabihollah. 2007. *Corporate Governance Post Sarbanes-Oxley, Regulations, Requirements, and Integrated Processes* (Hoboken, NJ: John Wiley & Sons).

4. 111th U.S. Congress. 2010. Dodd-Frank Wall Street Reform and Consumer Protection Act of 2010. Pub. L. No. 111-203 (Jul. 21, 2010). Available at: www.sec.gov/about/laws/wallstreetreform-cpa.pdf.

5. International Corporate Governance Network, www.icgn.org/.

6. 111th U.S. Congress. 2010. Dodd-Frank Wall Street Reform and Consumer Protection Act of 2010. Pub. L. No. 111-203 (Jul. 21, 2010). Available at: www.sec.gov/about/laws/wallstreetreform-cpa.pdf.

7. Shearman and Sterling, LLP. 2011. "Reforming the Framework for Financial Regulation in the UK." Available at: http://www.shearman.com/reforming-the-framework-for-financial-regulation-in-the-uk-04-05-2011/.

8. New York Stock Exchange (NYSE)/NYSE Euronext. 2010. "Report of the New York Stock Exchange Commission on Corporate Governance." Available at: http://www.nyse.com/about/listed/1265973393069.html.

9. International Federation of Accountants (IFAC). 2010. Corporate Governance in the Wake of the Financial Crisis. Available at www.ifac.org.

10. Cramer, A. 2011. "Giving Sustainability a Seat in the Boardroom," GreenBiz .com. Available at: http://www.greenbiz.com/blog/2011/04/20/giving-sustainability-seat-boardroom.

11. Cramer, A. 2011. "CSR in the Boardroom: The Board's Role in Advancing Sustainability," BSR, *BSR Insight*. Available at: http://www.bsr.org/en/our-insights/bsr-insight-article/csr-in-the-boardroom-the-boards-role-in-advancing-sustainability.

12. International Federation of Accountants (IFAC). 2011. "Integrating the Business Reporting Supply Chain." Available at: http://www.ifac.org/publications-resources/integrating-business-reporting-supply-chain-summary-key-recommendations.

13. Lead Director Network (LDN). 2011. Engaging with Strategy after the Financial Crisis. Lead Director Network ViewPoints, Issue 11, August 4, 2011. Available at http://www.kslaw.com/imageserver/KSPublic/library/publication/2011articles/8-11LDNViewPoints.pdf.

14. Tonello. M. 2010. The conference Board: Sustainability in the Boardroom, June 2010, Available at http://www.conference-board.org/publications/publicationdetail.cfm?publicationid=1812.

15. Fleming, P. 2011. "Proxy Voting for Sustainability," The Harvard Law School Forum on Corporate Governance and Financial Regulation. October 16, 2011.

16. Ibid.

17. Report Leadership. 2012. "Corporate Governance: Simple, Practical Proposals for Better Report of Corporate Governance." March 2012. Available at www.reportleadership.com.

18. Ibid.

19. Ibid.

CHAPTER SEVEN

The Social Dimension of Corporate Sustainability

EXECUTIVE**SUMMARY**

C orporations have shifted their primary goals from profit maximization to creating value for all stakeholders, including shareholders, while fulfilling their social responsibilities. Corporate social responsibility (CSR) as either ethical or ideological theory suggests that entities, regardless of type and size, have a responsibility to protect the society that they operate in. Social performance measures how well an institution has translated its social goals into practice. It is measured through the principles, actions, and corrective measures implemented. Social performance (SP), or the social bottom line, is about making an organization's social mission a reality, aligned with the interests of society by adding accepted social values and fulfilling social responsibility.

Not all companies present meaningful reports to shareholders and the general public on their social performance. A governing body providing regulations or standards for disclosures on social responsibility will enhance the transparency, accuracy, and usefulness of such reports. This chapter presents the social dimension of sustainability performance.

INTRODUCTION

The true measure of success for corporations should be determined not only by reported earnings but also by their governance, social responsibility, ethical behavior, and environmental initiatives. Social responsibility is the concept that all entities must conduct themselves responsibly, with consideration for the society in which they operate. Yet, a minority of companies present meaningful reports to shareholders and the general public on their social performance. CSR is not just about charities, rather is responsibility to all stakeholders—from shareholders to creditors, customers, suppliers, employees, governments, the environment, and society. CSR demands corporate transition from business-as-usual, as required by law, to true corporate citizenship by "doing good and no harm." CSR is a process of aligning an organization's values, interests, decisions, and activities with those of its stakeholders. CSR encourages business entities to take initiatives to advance some social good beyond their own interests and beyond compliance with applicable laws, rules and regulations through increasing their positive impacts and reducing negative impacts of their activities. As Rosabeth Moss Kanter describes in her book *Supercorp*, companies should think of CSR as:

> embedding a wider look at society into every aspect of operations and using that to drive the business strategy. That's a way companies can find new opportunities for growth and for innovation—which always stems from unmet needs and unsolved problems in underserved markets.[1]

Engagement in CSR initiatives and practices is no longer merely desirable but essential in establishing improved relationships with various stakeholders to maintain long-term sustainability. Some of the perceived benefits of CSR discussed throughout this chapter are:

- Alignment of an organization's interests with those of all stakeholders.
- Development of better relationships with all stakeholders and better understanding of their needs.
- Establishment of good relations with society, government, and communities.
- Utilization of improved risk and crisis management.
- Fostering reputation and brand value.
- Enhancing philanthropy commitments and activities.
- Improving capability and capacity to innovate.
- Ensuring sustainability.
- Improving operational effectiveness and efficiency.
- Enhancing profitability and financial performance.

SOCIAL PERFORMANCE

Social performance obligations to respond effectively to societal and stakeholder concerns can be met by integrating social considerations into business strategic decisions, activities, and operations through voluntary initiatives that go above and beyond regulatory requirements and philanthropic activities. Many factors have encouraged companies to engage in corporate social responsibility activities including:

- Consumer activism
- Corporate malfeasances and unethical behavior (e.g., Enron, WorldCom, Parmalat)
- Socially responsible investing (SRI)

Social performance involves three components:

1. Identification of an organization's social responsibility domains.
2. Development of processes to evaluate stakeholder demands.
3. Implementation of programs to manage social issues.[2]

An organization's social responsibility can be classified into four categories: economic, legal, ethical, and discretionary responsibilities.[3]

1. **Economic responsibilities:** Entities of all types and sizes must produce goods and services that society wants and needs. Unless businesses fulfill their economic function, they will neither have the resources to perform other roles nor will they survive long enough to be an agent for any form of social change.
2. **Legal responsibilities:** Society grants business entities the right to pursue their economic goals, but explicitly requires companies to fulfill these goals within the framework of legal requirements.
3. **Ethical responsibilities:** Society also has expectations for business entities over and above legal requirements. Ethical responsibilities require corporations to engage in business practices in a manner consistent with societal values in such matters as fair employment and the environmental impact of production.
4. **Discretionary responsibilities:** Socially desirable actions taken by business entities that are beyond their economic, legal, and ethical obligations. Corporations have control over the type, timing, and extent of their involvement in discretionary social performance, which may include activities such as philanthropy and community leadership.

Organizations can no longer isolate their operations from the wider society and environment in which they operate, and thus they should effectively measure their social performance to maintain their sustainability. Measuring social performance implies the evaluation of principles, actions, outputs, some elements of outcome, and corrective measures. Social activities include improving reputation, brand value, employee satisfaction, crisis management, environmental preservation, and philanthropy activities. Placing emphasis on the end results and their impact, social performance reporting includes an analysis of the declared objectives of institutions, the effectiveness of their systems and services in meeting these objectives, related outputs (e.g., reaching larger numbers of very poor households), and success in affecting positive change in the lives of clients.

SOCIAL KPIs

Key performance indicators (KPIs) are quantifiable measurements that reflect the critical success factors of an organization, helping them to define and measure progress toward organizational goals. Whatever KPIs are selected, they must reflect the organization's goals, be key determinants to its success, and be quantifiable (measurable). KPIs are usually long-term considerations. KPIs for social responsibility are playing a key role in evaluating social responsibility initiatives. Social activities can be measured through social contribution, strategic partners, community outreach, and time spent volunteering. Proper measurement of KPIs pertaining to social activities and responsibilities enables organizations to effectively report their social performance and fulfill their social responsibilities.

Commonly used social KPIs include building responsible networks, corporate diversity, supporting the community, and social impact (e.g., social investment, employee voluntarism, strategic partnerships, leadership fellows, reputation, brand value, and good relations with community). Some common examples are:

- The percent of employees who consider their business as acting responsibly.
- The number of full-time employees (FTE) dedicated to social investment projects.
- Amount of funds raised per FTE for nonprofit and humanitarian organizations.
- Philanthropy as a percent of (pretax) profit.
- Percentage of operating income dedicated to social contribution.

EXHIBIT 7.1 Corporate Social Responsibility KPIs

- A reliable social net for the low-income households
- Access to appropriate health care
- Access to education
- Access to information exchange
- Company's total number of injuries and fatalities, including no-lost-time injuries per one million hours worked
- Customer satisfaction, retention, and loyalty
- Description of social and ethic activities and projects
- Diversity and equal opportunities
- Donations and other social expenses
- Employee composition by professional category, age, ethnicity, and gender

- Employee satisfaction, competence, and commitment
- Eradication of poverty and justified distribution of national wealth
- Full employment
- Improved purchasing power
- Number of employees, rate of turnover, and hiring/firing procedures
- Payroll for the entire company
- Political freedom and well-protected human rights
- Preservation of cultural heritage
- Productivity (volumes/sales/value added by employee)
- Protected consumers' rights
- Training and internal education
- Wages, contracts, and benefits other than stock options
- Well-maintained national security

- Percent of suppliers that affirmed business code of conduct.
- Social contributions spent per employee.
- Percent of eligible employees who signed the Code of Conduct and Ethics Policy.
- Number of initiatives to promote greater environmental responsibility.
- Total investment in the community.

Exhibit 7.1 presents a list of social KPIs.

CORPORATE SOCIAL RESPONSIBILITY (CSR)

CSR demonstrates corporate conscience, citizenship, and social performance that are integrated into the business model. The World Business Council for Sustainable Development (WBCSD) defines CSR as "the ethical behavior of a company towards society."[4] Internal and external governance mechanisms that monitor and ensure the organization's compliance with applicable laws, rules, regulations, and best practices are intended to benefit all stakeholders beyond profit maximization. As such they may consider the integrated components of the organization's CSR program. The goal of CSR is to embrace responsibility for the organization's actions and encourage a positive impact through its activities on society, the environment, consumers, employees, communities, shareholders, and all other members of the public sphere. Furthermore, CSR-focused businesses proactively promote the public interest by encouraging community growth and development, and voluntarily eliminating practices that are harmful.

The term *corporate social responsibility* is a doctrine that claims that an entity has a responsibility to society. CSR enables an organization's mission and acts as a guide to what the company stands for and will uphold for its consumers. International Organization of Standardization (ISO) 26000 is the recognized international standard for CSR. It is widely accepted that CSR adheres to similar principles but with no formal act of legislation. Community recognition of CSR is important to corporations perhaps most so at the local community level and it is particularly vital for state-owned corporations to maintain legitimacy with the public. Governments and communities can also exert social and national pressure on corporations to donate money and resources to community events, social relief, infrastructure, disease control, and natural disaster relief. These efforts work to enhance their standing as good corporate citizens. Many companies disclose details of their donations on their website, which helps them publicize and build their reputation. Donations should be viewed as corporate social investment with business value, rather than corporate giving with negative cash flow consequences. The bottom line is that these activities create goodwill with local communities and authorities, and this makes doing business easier.

Corporations' primary goals have evolved from pure profit maximization to increasing shareholder wealth, and now, in light of recent corporate governance reforms worldwide, to create shareholder value while fulfilling their social responsibilities. Yet the question being frequently asked is, "Do corporations have social responsibility to stakeholders other than shareholders (e.g., employees, customers, government, society, and environment)?" The answer is definitely yes. For example, tobacco companies may increase their shareholder wealth by selling products that are toxic, but this tarnishes their reputation in society. Another example is that while Wal-Mart saves their customers money by offering more affordable prices, its employment policies and compensation have raised concerns that have been used to prevent access to some markets such as New York City.[5]

Corporate social responsibility is an integral component of corporate governance, particularly when there is a conflict between the corporate goals of maximizing profits and social goals. The existence and persistence of such a conflict requires corporations to establish CSR policies and programs to ensure their boards of directors and senior executives set an appropriate tone at the top, taking the social interest seriously. As corporations choose supply-chain partners in developing countries to maximize cost-effectiveness, the business practices of these partners can impact the program's overall CSR commitment and reputation. For example, Nike is making progress to reduce harmful labor practices and waste throughout its global supply chain, which currently has over 800,000 employees in 46 countries.[6] Thus, emerging issues of CSR should be integrated into all facets of business—from operation to investment—by engaging in noneconomic activities to meet societal demands above and beyond legal duties.

The companies that make it into socially responsible investment (SRI) portfolios chose to be responsible for a variety of profit-oriented reasons including: increased sales, greater innovation, decreased production inefficiencies, decreased future risks, and greater access to capital. The model in Exhibit 7.2 represents the contribution of various predictors of the CSR

EXHIBIT 7.2 Corporate Social Responsibility Model

Source: Adapted from http://anzmac.info/conference/2008/_Proceedings/Index.html.

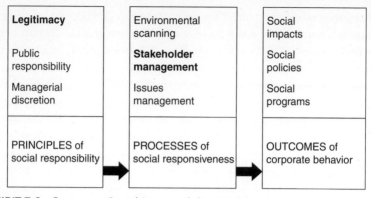

EXHIBIT 7.3 Corporate Social Responsibility Model

Source: Wood, D. J. (1991). "Corporate Social Performance Revisited," *Academy of Management Review*, 16(4): 691–718.

construct that may assist in measuring its association with business performance indicators.

Another model of corporate social responsibility is offered by Donna J. Wood, as depicted in Exhibit 7.3.[7] This CSR model suggests corporations might undertake corporate social behavior because:

1. Their CSR activities relate to the primary business goal of creating value for their stakeholders (e.g., return on investment).
2. They are considered part of corporate philanthropy.
3. They attempt and desire to influence particular stakeholder groups.

International Organization for Standardization (ISO) 26000

The International Organization for Standardization (ISO) 26000 is a globally accepted guidance document for social responsibility, relevant to all types and sizes of entities from governmental to nongovernmental organizations, private businesses to public companies, and from small to large multinational companies.[8] ISO 26000 also covers a broad range of an organization's activity, from economic to social, governance, ethical, and environmental issues. ISO 26000 goes beyond profit-maximization and social performance to cover all dimensions of sustainability performance.

ISO 26000 provides a framework for organizations to contribute to sustainable development (e.g., the health and welfare of society). The subject areas of ISO 26000's social standards are organizational governance, fair operating practices, human rights, labor practices, consumer issues, community involvement and development, and the environment. It is important that companies hold themselves to these standards but it is equally important that they hold their suppliers to these standards. ISO 26000 contains voluntary guidance, not requirements, and therefore is not used as a certification standard like ISO 9001 (quality control) and ISO 14001 (environmental performance).

Profit

The primary objective of business entities is to create shareholder value by generating adequate and sustainable profit. The company should develop, maintain, and enforce fair operating practices in all regions of the world it operates in. It is critical that the company operates fairly and does not tolerate bribery and corruption practices.

People

Corporate global expansion has underscored the importance of human rights in recent years. ISO 26000 seeks to ensure that companies recognize human rights as a critical aspect of social responsibility by ensuring the countries in which they operate respect the political, civil, social, and cultural rights of the citizens. If a company is operating in a country that has as record of violating these rights, it is important to enforce more vigorous CSR programs to prevent such practices and to pressure the government to change these practices or lose business.

ISO 26000 is focused on an organization's labor practices. Labor standards promote consistent, fair employment practices regardless of the region of the world in which the company operates. In addition, the standard lays out guidelines for the company to ensure the health and safety of the employees at the forefront. As with any sound organization, a solid employee development program should be implemented to ensure future success. This not only benefits the organization, but it also benefits that community as a whole by improving workplace performance and labor practices.

Companies have a responsibility to conduct their business in a way that secures the safety and health of their consumer. The ISO 26000 guidance document states that companies should promote fair business, marketing, and information practices by having mechanisms in place to ensure the consumer is protected with respect to product safety, recalls, and private consumer data. Additionally, companies should promote sustainable consumption to ensure the end product is discarded properly with little impact to the environment.

The company should promote social and economic development in the countries in which they operate. These practices can be through community service, donating money to local governments, or sitting on development boards to promote positive change in the community. Companies should give back to promote positive change and develop these areas for the future.

Planet

ISO 26000 goes beyond just having an effective environmental management system as described under ISO 14001. ISO 26000 gives guidance on ensuring the consumption of natural resources and production practices are sustainable, as renewable resource management is becoming more important. ISO promotes sustainable resource management to ensure companies are not exploiting the environment in which they are operating.

In summary, ISO 26000 is designed to help organizations operate in a socially responsible manner by providing guidance on:

- Concepts, terms, and definitions pertaining to social responsibility.
- Background, trends, and characteristics of social responsibility.
- Principles and practices relevant to social responsibility.
- Core subjects and issues related to social responsibility.
- Policies, procedures, and practices for integrating, implementing, and promoting socially responsible behavior throughout the organization.
- Ways to identify and engage stakeholders in socially responsible activities.
- Disclosure of commitments, performance, and other information related to social responsibility.[9]

CSR Issues

There is significant debate on the degree to which CSR constitutes a legitimate activity for a corporation when the cost of CSR activities is immediate and tangible and the related benefit may not materialize in the short term. Some of the challenging issues involve:

- Competition (e.g., the use of advertising, the arrival of new types of CSR risk with new technology)
- The environment (e.g., climate change, regulatory change for hazardous substances and waste)
- Human rights (e.g., labor rights)
- Product responsibility (e.g., access, safety, risk, disclosure labeling, and packaging)
- Bribery and corruption (e.g., financial reporting fraud, financial scandals, and money laundering)
- Respect for privacy
- Ensuring transparency and accountability
- Institutionalization of CSR
- Stakeholder engagement
- Battle for talent
- Community investment
- Supply chain and product safety
- Social enterprises
- Poverty alleviation

Globalization-Related CSR

CSR has emerged as an arena of challenges and opportunities for the business community and accounting profession worldwide. Particularly, multinational corporations are facing challenges on how to respond while balancing local and global realities in determining CSR policies for their headquarters and, more important, for their subsidiaries abroad with different political and cultural norms.

In the globalized world, the long-term value and success of businesses are inextricably linked to the integration of economic, social, environmental, and governance issues into corporate management and operations. The main drivers for implementing CSR strategies have been risk management on the one hand and ethical considerations on the other. For instance, the Global Head of KPMG Sustainability Services, Wim Bartels, stated in a 2008 survey that "In a world of changing expectations, companies must account for the way they impact the communities and environments where they operate."[10] Corporate social responsibility is the key condition for a continued global market economy, and companies will need to accept and implement this concept if they are to keep their license to operate. If every company and business did their part by refusing to pay bribes; implemented fair labor practices; and adopted environmentally, economically, and socially responsible local practices, then the world could be transformed to be more balanced, more just, and more sustainable.[11]

Employee-Related CSR

Employee-related CSR initiatives are derived from and directed toward improving social, political, and economic opportunities for existing and potential employees, contract workers, society, and other stakeholders. Initiatives include empowering employee participation in strategic decisions; improving employee benefits, wages, and work conditions; and being a good citizen. These initiatives also address specific issues of diversity regarding the participation and treatment of employees based on ethnicity, gender, or linguistic capabilities.

Product- and Marketing-Related CSR

Product- and marketing-related CSR initiatives and activities are gaining attention from customers, suppliers, manufacturers, government, and society. Consumer-driven CSR includes product and process innovations; life cycle and footprint assessments; and promotion, advertising, and distribution policies and practices. Implementing a CSR initiative can improve product quality, functionality, transparency, and corporate philanthropy as well as offer the potential to build brand loyalty. Timberland, Interface, and Patagonia are just three brands that have succeeded with CSR strategies.

Supply-Chain-Related CSR

Supply chain CSR covers the entire input, output, and process of buying raw materials from socially responsible suppliers, designing and producing products that are not detrimental to society or harmful to customers, and marketing and selling products that minimize the use of scarce resources (e.g., smaller and environmentally conscious packaging). CSR processing and production activities, including permits to operate (e.g., licenses for mine sites), are becoming integral components of supply chains. Organizations that undertake CSR programs not only integrate them into their own production process but also influence CSR initiatives for a variety of stakeholders in the supply chain, including suppliers and customers.

Stakeholder-Related CSR

Corporations are no longer isolated from their stakeholders, particularly in the wider society in which they operate. They affect the welfare of stakeholders and, in turn, they are affected by their stakeholders' interests and demands. Social responsibility doesn't refer to any responsibility *to* stakeholders but designates a responsibility *by* stakeholders. Ethical investing, the green consumer movement, and the growth of vigilante consumerism are examples of how such conscientious stakeholding can influence the way a business operates. Hence, social responsibility is fully compatible with corporate governance and culture.

CSR AND FINANCIAL PERFORMANCE

Companies worldwide have created their own CSR programs that aim to balance their operations with the concerns of external stakeholders such as customers, unions, local communities, nongovernmental organizations (NGOs), and governments. Social and environmental consequences are weighed against economic gains. Although the field of corporate social responsibility (CSR) has grown exponentially, the debate still exists about the legitimacy and value of corporate responses to CSR concerns. The relationship between corporate social responsibility and financial performance is generally positive, varying between highly positive and moderately positive.[12] Socially responsible practices such as minority hiring and managerial principles have a greater effect on financial performance than environmental responsibility. Social responsibility and financial performance affect each other in a virtuous cycle, wherein successful firms spend more because they can, but such spending helps them to become more successful. Because markets do not penalize companies for being socially responsible, it is compatible with maximizing shareholder value and thus can be pursued by managers.

Corporate decision-makers must consider a range of social and environmental matters if they are to maximize long-term financial returns rather than short-term profits. An initial challenge in testing the relationship between CSR and financial performance is identifying those companies/services that have adopted CSR by issuing a sustainability report. This is effective because corporate social responsibility reflects an approach to internal decision-making, the presence or absence of which may not easily be determined by external observers. Also, a sustainability report provides information to external stakeholders about conduct, allowing consumers, employees, investors, and others to make informed decisions when dealing with the company. Importantly, the preparation of a sustainability report also provides company management with information about social and environmental performance, facilitating improved decision-making.

In summary, there are two differing views regarding the relationship between CSR and a firm's financial performance:

1. Socially responsible behavior is costly due to increased expenses, but no increase in benefits.
2. A positive association between CSR and firm performance will:
   - Enhance employee morale and productivity.
   - Attract and retain high-quality employees.
   - Generate a positive corporate image.
   - Enhance product evaluation via an overall evaluation of the firm.
   - Improve a firm's access to sources of capital.
   - Promote reputation and trust.
   - Attract and motivate talent.
   - Create new business opportunities.
   - Provide a more secure and sustainable working environment.

CSR PERFORMANCE MEASUREMENT

The evaluation of CSR performance is a significant issue both for business and society.[13] By measuring CSR performance, companies can identify their strengths and weaknesses, modify their strategies, and define opportunities for improvement. The development of valid and reliable indicators is an important factor of the measurement process. The major limitation of expert evaluations and single indicators is that they represent only one dimension of the multiple aspects of CSR.

Stakeholder engagement around online CSR/sustainability reporting can take many forms. At the very least, stakeholders should be able to easily contact the company and provide feedback by e-mail, social media, or through online feedback forms. Online tools such as surveys, discussion forums, and web chats have introduced the potential for stakeholder engagement, not only for collecting feedback on reports but also for the ongoing process that companies undertake to identify issues of concern and understand stakeholders' opinions. Some companies use features such as interactive surveys to gather stakeholder views on key CSR issues. Many companies also gather comments and questions that users post and provide answers on a dedicated FAQ page or give space to stakeholder voices in their CSR/sustainability websites by publishing stakeholder views on related performance or reporting. Topical blogs written on behalf of companies may offer an opportunity to connect with stakeholders on CSR issues in a potentially more personalized, transparent, and interactive way than reports, press releases, and other more formalized communication vehicles. Over the last couple of years, pioneering companies have started exploring the use of Web 2.0 communication tools, such as online communities, social networking sites, crowdsourcing, and wikis, which aim to facilitate creativity and collaboration between users (e.g. Pepsi, Campbell Soup, and Unilever have all recently used the Web for crowdsourcing sustainability ideas in addition to social websites like Wikipedia, Facebook, YouTube, and organizations incorporating such technologies). Companies often prepare and distribute CSR information either on their website, in management discussion and analysis (MD&A), or through mandatory filings such as the 10K.

CSR PROGRAMS

An effective CSR program starts at the top of the organization with the board of directors' and senior executives' commitment. They must publicly embrace the CSR program and engage in maintenance through a continuous monitoring system. Once a CSR program has been established, management should take ownership of it. Individual performance reviews should be tied to responsibilities to ensure the objectives are being met. For example, BP tracks emissions targets on a group-wide basis to ensure compliance and maintain assurance standards audited by a third party (Ernest & Young) under ISAE 3000.[14] CSR issues can affect the company's performance, supply chain management, and investment portfolios, and thus should be considered in assessing operating and investment decisions.

The CSR program is designed to minimize the conflicts between corporations and society that are caused by differences between private and social costs and benefits. Examples of such conflicts are related to environmental issues (e.g., pollution, acid rain, global warming), wages paid by multinational corporations in poor countries, and child labor in developing countries. Corporate governance measures, including rules, regulations, and best practices of CSR programs, can raise companies' awareness of the social costs and benefits of their business activities. The Organization of Economic Cooperation and Development (OECD) defines the purpose of a CSR program as "to encourage the positive contributions that multinational enterprises can make to economics, environmental and social progress and to minimize the difficulties to which their various operations may give rise."[15] This definition focuses on two important aspects of a CSR program, namely creation of social value through corporate activities (social value-added activities) and avoidance of conflicts between corporate goals and societal goals (societal consensus).

The benefits of a CSR program include addressing environmental matters, reducing waste, reducing risk, improving relations with society, and discouraging regulatory actions. CSR programs enable corporations to take proper actions to promote social good and advance social goals above and beyond creating shareholder value or complying with applicable laws and regulations. CSR programs should promote a set of voluntary actions to advance the social good, which goes beyond the company's obligation to its various stakeholders. CSR activities should be measured and transparent the same way in which financial activities are measured and disclosed.

Proper CSR metrics, the CSR KPIs discussed in the previous sections, must be established to manage the progress of a CSR program. To manage the programs effectively, management must know what the desired outcome is to ensure they are being met. CSR KPIs must be appropriate and consistent to ensure the correct objectives are being monitored. For example, Cisco uses a CSR business process to measure and report performance on all KPIs associated with their CSR program.[16] Once these metrics are established and programs are implemented, they should be measured and reported and audited to ensure the effectiveness of the programs. Audits of CSR programs should be effective and objective to ensure compliance and achievement of the intended goals. Organizations can create value through their CSR programs by demonstrating that they are committed to generating profit while protecting the interests of the people they employ and interactions with and the environment in which they operate. Organizations are normally trying to develop strategies to differentiate themselves from their competitors by adding value to products or services that are delivered to their customer. In the current global business environment, it is challenging to convince customers to switch brands or services. Successful and well-publicized CSR can tip the scales in a company's favor.

COMPONENTS OF CSR

A 2005 survey conducted by KPMG identifies four key CSR topics including core labor standards, working conditions, community involvement, and philanthropy:[17]

1. **Core labor standards:** Core labor standards are composed of a general commitment to human rights, the right to equality of opportunity and treatment, the right to freedom of association and collective bargaining, the prohibition of forced labor, the abolition of child labor, and commitments to diversity.
2. **Working conditions:** Working conditions address the general working condition of corporate facilities, including working time and organization, work and family, wages and income, occupational safety and health, stress and violence, harassment, and maternity protection.
3. **Community involvement:** Community involvement addresses the extent to which the company fulfills its social concern related to its operations. It also addresses how a company initiates and supports community programs, such as those aimed at improved health and education services.
4. **Philanthropic programs:** Philanthropy is often the primary source of funding for operations run by not-for-profit organizations (e.g., universities, charities). Traditionally, corporations, foundations, and individuals have donated money to not-for-profit organizations to support local, national, and international goodwill and good causes (e.g., The United Way of America, Habitat for Humanity International). These philanthropic programs have traditionally been less strategic than other forms of social involvement in terms of adding social and business value. In many instances, this has built goodwill in the local community by sponsoring and supporting local exhibits, music, and art. Conventional philanthropic programs have contributed to the advancement of many social, community development, and environmental activities without adequate transparency about how donations are spent and what impact they have on the greatest social good.

In recent years, new forms of philanthropic programs have been introduced and promoted through private equity and venture capital (VC) investing, as well as so-called social venture capital (SVC). SVC is a form of VC investing that provides capital to businesses engaged in both conventional philanthropy programs (social, community and environmental activities) and new investment-return social activities. The primary purpose of SVC is to provide market-based capital for social activities while generating attractive investors. SVC engages in a variety of activities, from financing charities to promoting socially driven businesses and revenue-generating social organizations. Some high-profile entities (e.g., Google, Goldman Sachs, Abbott, and Paul Allen's Vulcan) have established SVC foundations that support philanthropic CSR initiatives that ultimately will lead into potential investment opportunities.

Many of these SVC foundations treat philanthropy as a way to promote business growth opportunities and conduct their giving in a manner more consistent with VCs with rigor and oversight rather than traditional philanthropic giving. These foundations measure their performance through the achievement of social return on investment (SROI) such as investment opportunities in capacity building, business growth, workforce training, and advanced education and training for employees. For example, in 2008 Goldman Sachs initiated its 10,000, $100 million philanthropic program to provide business and management education to 10,000 women worldwide. A more recent approach used by companies such as Google through its foundation, Google.org, aims to have the foundation serve as a supporter of long-term projects that may, in many instances, offer business opportunities to the parent company going forward.

CSR REPORTING

Most companies issue CSR/sustainability reports on an annual basis, which enables them to integrate CSR/sustainability reporting with the annual financial reporting process and/or report. The demand for both environmental awareness and corporate accountability compels organizations to expand their concept of success to include ecological and social accomplishments in addition to financial performance. Companies are finding innovative ways of improving the "triple bottom line" of people, planet, and profit to satisfy society and shareholders alike.

CSR reporting on social performance is a key to building stakeholder buy-in and support for the goals and ongoing social achievements. External reporting of social performance in corporate annual reports is becoming widespread, largely because of public and regulatory pressures. There are many ways to report on social performance, though there are no standard methods and the companies can choose from among several generally accepted alternatives. Instead, they must formulate, from scratch, a theory of social performance disclosure, determine the method of annual report presentation, and decide upon the annual activities for disclosure that can vary widely among companies. An important goal of CSR is to exhibit commitment to social performance and to embrace responsibility for the company's actions. Taking responsibility for its impact on society necessitates that a company account for its actions. Social accounting, a concept describing the communication of social activities and actions to particular interest groups within society and to society at large, is an integral element of CSR.

Social accounting emphasizes the notion of corporate accountability. A number of reporting guidelines or standards have been developed to serve as frameworks for social accounting, auditing, and reporting. Exhibit 7.4 presents a list of organizations currently providing guidelines for CRS reporting.

In some nations, legal requirements for social accounting, auditing, and reporting exist despite some difficulties in meaningful measurements of EGSEE performance. Many companies worldwide disclose audited annual reports that cover sustainable development and CSR issues ("Triple Bottom Line Reports"), but the reports vary widely in format, style, and content. In South Africa, as of June 2010, all companies listed on the Johannesburg Stock Exchange (JSE) were required to produce an integrated report in place of an annual financial report and sustainability report. An Integrated Reporting Committee (IRC) was established to issue best practices for integrated reporting as discussed in Chapters 2 and 3. When CSR reporting is integrated into financial reporting, it presents a holistic approach to corporate reporting.

Combining financial and CSR reporting into one report enables organizations to disclose their initiatives in integrating good corporate citizenship into their business. In some parts of Europe, CSR reporting has become mandatory for public companies and, at the same time, investors have come to want and expect greater accountability. The majority of companies there responded by creating annual integrated financial and CSR reports.

Unfortunately, CSR reporting continues to be all over the map. Some companies are making solid progress in reporting but some perceive their reports as extensions of their marketing efforts. Many companies fail to present a balanced picture and want to report only on the good deeds. Today's investors and consumers require a high level of transparency, so anything less can do more harm than good to corporate reputation. If CSR reporting is integrated into financial reporting, it moves it out of the realm of

EXHIBIT 7.4 Corporate Social Responsibility Reporting Guidelines

Organization	CRS reporting guidelines	website
Accountability	• Accountability's AA1000 standard, based on John Elkington's triple-bottom-line reporting.	http://www.accountability.org/
The Prince of Wales's Accounting for Sustainability	• The Prince's Accounting for Sustainability Project's Connected Reporting Framework.	http://www.accountingforsustainability.org
Fair Labor Association	• The Fair Labor Association conducts audits based on its Workplace Code of Conduct and posts audit results on the FLA website.	http://www.fairlabor.org/fla/
Fair Wear Foundation	• The Fair Wear Foundation takes a unique approach to verifying labor conditions in companies' supply chains, using interdisciplinary audit ng teams.	http://fairwear.org/
Global Reporting Initiative	• Global Reporting Initiative's Sustainability Reporting Guidelines.	http://www.globalreporting.org
Institute of Business Ethics	• Good Corporation's Standard developed in association with the Institute of Business Ethics.	http://www.ibe.org.uk/
EarthCheck	• Certification.	
Social Accountability International	• Social Accountability International's SA8000 standard.	http://www.sa-intl.org/
America Enterprise Institute (AEI)	• Standard Ethics AEI guidelines.	http://www.aei.org/
International Standard Organization (ISO)	• The ISO 14000 environmental management standard.	http://www.iso.iso/iso/iso_catalogue.htm
United Nations Global Compact	• The United Nations Global Compact promotes companies reporting in the format of a Communication on Progress (COP). A COP report describes the company's implementation of the Compact's ten universal principles.	http://www.unglobalcompact.org/
United Nations	• The United Nations Intergovernmental Working Group of Experts on International Standards of Accounting and Reporting (ISAR) provides voluntary technical guidance on eco-efficiency indicators, corporate responsibility reporting, and corporate governance disclosure.	http://www.un.org/en/
Verite	• Verite's Monitoring Guidelines.	http://www.verite.org/

marketing and back into its rightful place as solid, straightforward, honest reporting on accomplishments and mistakes. More companies should adopt this method because it forces them to approach all of their reporting from a more holistic point of view.

CONCLUSION

After two decades of rapid globalization beginning in the 1990s, the global business community has become more conscious than ever of the importance of sustainability and social responsibility as they relate to the environment, human rights, and the economy. Contemporaneously, attitudes and commitments toward the importance of sustainability and social responsibility have also progressed among individuals, organizations, and businesses. Nonetheless, every organization has its own unique impact on global sustainability, perspective on what it means to be socially responsible, idea of how important social responsibility is, and finally how to measure and report its efforts to the public. Corporate social responsibility (CSR) promotes a vision of business accountability to a wide range of stakeholders, besides shareholders and investors. Some of the drivers pushing business toward CSR include:

- Shrinking role of the government
- Demands for greater disclosure
- Increased customer interest
- Growing investor pressure
- Competitive labor markets
- Supplier relations

Business is socially responsible only if it pursues some socially responsible objective. Effective CSR programs require organizations to provide social good above and beyond their own interests and legal obligations. The way for a business to be ethical is by pursuing some social welfare, environmental, or religious end in addition to profits. Adequate corporate social responsibility disclosure has important implications for the credibility of the capital markets in transition economies. The goal of CSR is to embrace responsibility for the company's actions and encourage a positive impact through its activities on the environment, consumers, employees, communities, and stakeholders. Ideally, CSR reporting should be integrated into financial reporting. The integrated sustainability reporting enables organizations worldwide to approach their reporting CSR.

ACTION**ITEMS**

1. Pay attention to product innovation and quality, customer retention, and attraction, employee satisfaction and productivity, socially responsible citizenship, and environmentally consciences operation.

2. Sufficiently disclose to all stakeholders that you are taking proper initiatives to further social good above and beyond your compliance and legal obligations.

3. Describe your CSR activities and practices in responding to stakeholder expectations, including minimizing negative impacts of your operations on society or the environment, while maximizing positive impacts on the community, customers, employees, suppliers, and society.

4. Advance some social good beyond your own financial interests, beyond compliance, and exceeding legal obligations.

5. Demonstrate corporate conscience, citizenship, and social performance.

6. Enhance corporations' positive impacts and minimizing negative effects on society.

7. Make your organization's social mission a reality by adding accepted social values and fulfilling social responsibility.

 **NOTES**

1. Kanter. R. M. 2009. *Supercorp: How Vanguard Companies Create Innovation Profits, Growth, and Social Good* (New York: Crown Business).
2. Carroll, Archie B. 1979. "A Three-Dimensional Conceptual Model of Corporate Performance," *The Academy of Management Review*, 4(4): 497–505.
3. Ibid.
4. World Business Council for Sustainable Development. Availabile at: www .wbcsd.org/work-program/business-role/previous-work/corporate-social-responsibility.aspx.
5. http://legistar.council.nyc.gov/LegislationDetail.aspx?ID=452397&GUID= 8A51EFBB-14AD-4794-918B-5ED6D55D3703&Options=ID|Text|&Search =Wal-Mart.
6. Nike. 2012. "Workers and Factories." Nike.com. Available at: http://www .nikebiz.com/crreport/content/workers-and-factories/3-1-0-overview.php? cat=overview.

7. Wood, D. J. 1991. "Corporate Social Performance Revisited," *Academy of Management Review*, 16(4): 691–718.
8. International Organization for Standardization (ISO). 2010. "ISO 26000 – Social Responsibility." Available at: http://www.iso.org/iso/iso_catalogue/ management_and_leadership_standards/social_responsibility/sr_iso26000_ overview.htm#sr-1.
9. Ibid.
10. KPMG International. "KPMG International Survey of Corporate Responsibility Reporting 2008." Available at: www.kpmg.com/EU/en/Documents/ KPMG_International_survey_Corporate_responsibility_Survey_Reporting_ 2008.pdf.
11. Njoroge, J. 2009. "Effects of the global financial crisis on corporate social responsibility in multinational companies in Kenya," Africa Nazarene University (Kenya) Ethical Information Analyst Intern, Covalence SA, Geneva, (June 26, 2009).
12. McKnight, L. 2011. "Companies that do good also do well," *MarketWatch*, March 23. Available at: http://www.marketwatch.com/story/companies-that-do-good-also-do-well-2011-03-23.
13. Igalens, J., and J.P. Gond. 2005. "Measuring Corporate Social Performance in France: A Critical and Empirical Analysis of ARESE Data," *Journal of Business Ethics*, 56(2): 131–48.
14. BP. 2012. "E&Y Assurance Statement" (London: BP.com). Available at: http:// www.bp.com/sectiongenericarticle800.do?categoryId=9036168&contentId= 7066877.
15. The Organization of Economic Cooperation and Development (OECD). 2003. "Guidelines for Multinational Enterprises." Available at: www.oecd.org/data-oecd/56/36/1922428.pdf.
16. Cisco. 2011. "2011 Corporate Social Responsibility Report," B4. Available at: http://www.cisco.com/web/about/ac227/csr2011/docs/CSR2011_full_ report.pdf.
17. KPMG. 2005. "Survey of Corporate Responsibility Reporting 2005." Available at: www.kpmg.com.au/Portals/0/KPMG%2520Survey%25202005_3 .pdf.

CHAPTER EIGHT

The Ethical Dimension of Sustainability

EXECUTIVE**SUMMARY**

E thics can be defined as "a philosophical term derived from the Greek word 'ethos' meaning character or custom."[1] Ethics in the generic term is driven from a combination of the individual and/or family values, moral principles, religious beliefs, cultural norms, and best practices. An individual's values are derived from moral principles that a person was instilled with as being right or wrong, whereas an individual's choices are the actions taken to do what is right or wrong. The current financial crisis was partially caused by a number of ethical lapses made by both organizations and individuals involved in the mortgage markets including: mortgage originators, financial intermediaries, and mortgage borrowers. These lapses collectively contributed to the financial crisis and resulting global economic meltdown and have threatened the sustainability of individuals, businesses, and governments. The crisis and related financial scandals have policymakers, regulators, and ethics advocates questioning what have been considered normal business practices, to what extent ethics and corporate culture affect the business process, and whether ethics performance should be reflected in overall corporate reporting. This chapter addresses these and other ethics-related questions in the context of the ethical dimension of economic, governance, social, ethical, and environmental (EGSEE) sustainability performance.

BUSINESS ETHICS

Business ethics encompasses a set of moral principles, best practices, and standards that guide business behavior. It refers to an organization's collective values, which can be used to evaluate whether the behavior of the collective members of the organization is appropriate, and whether the business is held accountable for its openness, integrity, and behavior.

Organization ethics is a set of formal and informal standards of conduct that people use to guide their behavior at work. These standards are partly based on core values such as honesty, mutual respect, openness, fairness, and trust, but they also can be learned directly from the actions of others, including colleagues and superiors.

Ethics programs are a set of formal policies, practices, and processes that organizations develop to deal internally with issues such as the adoption and dissemination of ethics from top management to the organization; a corporate culture of honesty and integrity, mutual respect, transparency, and accountability; business codes of conduct; and whistle-blowing policies and procedures.

ETHICS AND LAW

Government laws and regulations are often misinterpreted or used by society as a guide for ethical norms and treatments. Laws and regulations are intended to foster ethical treatment to society, however in many cases what is allowed by law may not be viewed as ethical and what is ethical may not be allowed by law. Nonetheless, there is some common ground that provides provisions for both ethical and lawful activity, but conflicts of interest can arise if there is no guidance on what the correct choice may be. Exhibit 8.1 presents the interaction between ethics and law.

Generally speaking, laws are written, approved, and enforced by the level of government where they were written. For example, state laws are enforced by the state and federal laws are enforced by the federal government. However, ethics are simply codes of conduct with no official guidance or disciplinary action. Different people have different ethical standards and an individual may have different opinions about what is right and wrong in different situations. However, there are some areas where there is more universal agreement. For example, almost everybody would be of the view that lying is generally not good, ethical behavior. In addition, ethics are often not written down; they are unspoken rules of conduct that people adhere to. For example, the ethical

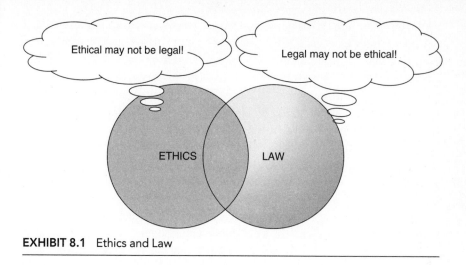

EXHIBIT 8.1   Ethics and Law

responsibility of an electrician is to repair the house wiring properly, correctly, and safely for a reasonable fee, whereas the legal responsibility is to conduct the job according to the provisions of the contract and local codes. Simply put: ethics guides behavior whereas law controls behavior. Laws and regulations are intended to foster ethical behavior of society. However, in some cases what is allowed by law may not be viewed as ethical and what is ethical may not be allowed by law. Nonetheless, ethics and law are interrelated and can influence each other. As rightfully stated by Martin Luther King, Jr., "Morality cannot be legislated, but behavior can be regulated. Judicial decrees may not change the heart, but they can restrain the heartless."[2]

Business ethics is often interpreted as having four primary components:

1. Complying with all applicable laws, rules, regulations, and standards.
2. Refraining from breaking the criminal law relevant to all business activities.
3. Avoiding any actions that may result in civil lawsuits against the company.
4. Refraining from actions that are bad for the company's image and reputation.

Businesses are especially concerned with all actual and perceived unethical activities that may involve loss of money and reputation. Public companies are required by the SEC to have business codes of conduct that address these and other ethical issues. Public companies also retain corporate attorneys and public relations experts to monitor employees on their daily activities to observe the established codes of conduct. Alternatively, public companies can hire philosophers to instruct employees on moral and ethical behavior. Philosophers can teach employees a basic understanding of morality, keep them out of trouble, and systematically address the issue of right and wrong conduct.

Although being moral may prevent a company from some legal and public relations challenges, morality in business is not without cost. A morally responsible company should invest in employee satisfaction, product safety, environmental impact, truthful advertising, and scrupulous marketing. For example, Subaru has established the first auto assembly plant that has zero waste to a landfill and manufactures partial-zero emission vehicles, which emit fewer emissions than a hybrid or alternative fuel vehicles.[3]

There is not always a conflict between the ethical interests of the money-minded businessperson and the ideal-minded philosopher. A business-oriented individual may argue that there is a symbiotic relationship between ethics and business, in which ethical behavior naturally emerges from a profit-oriented business. In this context, good ethics results in good business, which simply means that moral business practices are profitable and sustainable. For example, it is profitable to make safe products since this will reduce product liability lawsuits. Similarly, it may be in the best financial interests of businesses to respect employee privacy, since this will improve morale and thus improve work efficiency. At the same time, some ethical business practices may not be economically viable, even in the long run. For example, this might be the case with retaining older workers who are inefficient, as opposed to replacing them with younger and more efficient workers.

It could be argued that, in a competitive and free market, the profit motive is not inconsistent with a morally proper environment. That is, when customers demand safe products, or workers demand privacy, they will buy from or work for only those businesses that meet their expectations. Businesses that do not meet these demands will not be sustainable.

Ideal business ethics will foster ethical aspirations consisting of: adherence to moral principles, trust, and integrity; promotion of ethics education and practice; and managing and acting with openness, mutual respect, and accountability. Another approach to business ethics is promotion and enforcement of moral obligations of compliance with all applicable laws, rules, and regulations. Corporations that assume an obligation beyond merely compliance with the law, either in their corporate codes or in practice, take on responsibilities that are normally considered optional. Strictly following a legal approach to business ethics may indeed prompt businesses to do the right thing, as prescribed by law. There are, however, overriding challenges with restricting morality solely to what the law requires. First, even in the best legal context, the law will lag behind our moral condemnation of certain unscrupulous, yet legal business practices. For example, drug companies could previously exaggerate the miraculous curative properties of their products; now government regulations prohibit such misleading claims. Similarly, green attributes that were later proved false and/or misleading (called *green-washing*) had been given to products in order to capitalize on the trend towards eco-conscience. Exhibit 8.2 offers a closer look at green-washing attributes as well as the Federal Trade Commission's environmental marketing guidelines.

Thus, prior to the enactment of a law, there will be a period of time when a business practice will be deemed immoral, yet the practice will be legal. This will be a continuing problem since changes in products, technology, and marketing strategies will present new questionable practices that cannot be addressed by

---

EXHIBIT 8.2   Green-Washing Attributes[1]

- Colorful language
- Green products made by a dirty company
- Suggestive pictures
- Irrelevant claims
- Best-in-class identification (even if this is only marginally better than peers)
- No credibility (e.g., green labeling on harmful products)
- Phrasing only scientists can understand
- False labeling
- No proof
- Misinformation

The Federal Trade Commission (FTC) has also created green guides for environmental marketing claims. The FTC offers the following guides on environmental claims:[2]

- General environmental benefit claims
- Degradable/biodegradable/photodegradable
- Compostable
- Recyclable
- Recycled content
- Source reduction
- Refillable
- Ozone-safe and ozone-friendly

Source: Futerra Sustainability Communications; FTC.

[1]Futerra Sustainability Communications. 2008. "The Greenwash Guide," 5. Available at: http://www.futerra.co.uk/downloads/Greenwash_Guide.pdf.
[2]Federal Trade Commission. 1992. "Guides for the Use of Environmental Marketing Claims." Available at: http://www.ftc.gov/bcp/grnrule/guides980427.htm.

existing legislation. A second problem with the law-based approach is that, at best, it applies only to countries such as the United States whose business-related laws are morally conscientious. The situation may be different for developing countries that lack sophisticated laws and regulatory agencies.

ETHICS KPIs

Ethics key performance indicators (KPIs) enable an organization to measure its success in reaching its ethical goals or objectives. KPIs can be very useful as a means of assessing an organization's compliance with its internal established codes of ethical conduct and external laws, rules, regulations, and standards as well as best practices and norms. Proper use of KPIs enables an organization to define its ethical culture and goals and establish metrics to measure related performance. Exhibit 8.3 presents a list of ethics KPIs.

EXHIBIT 8.3   Ethics KPIs

1. Donations and other social expenses.
2. Description of social and ethical activities and projects.
3. Diversity and equal opportunities.
4. Fair wages, contracts, and benefits for employees.
5. Training and internal continuing education.
6. Employee diversity based on, age, specialization, gender, ethnicity, and so on.
7. Number of employees, turnover, and hiring/firing procedures
8. Whistleblowing policies, programs, and procedures
9. Employee productivity.
10. Employee satisfaction, competence, and commitment.
11. Customer satisfaction, retention, loyalty.
12. Fair competition.
13. Truthful advertising.
14. Fair suppliers, contractual relationships, and bargaining.
15. Supplier satisfaction, retention, commitment.
16. Political activities.
17. Business codes of conduct.
18. Uniform and fair enforcement of business codes of conduct.
19. Certification of compliance with business codes of conduct.
20. Resolution of conflicts of interest.
21. Compliance with applicable laws, rules, regulations, and standards.
22. Compliance with best practices and norms.
23. Promotion of core values of mutual respect, fairness, openness, honesty, and trust.
24. Enforcement of responsibility and accountability.
25. Promotion of tolerance, acceptance, caring, and compassion.

The 25 ethics KPIs listed in Exhibit 8.3 can be classified into: corporate culture and its ethics values, ethics codes of conduct and enforcement, ethics performance, and the process of promoting ethical behavior. Values are important and often interpreted in relation to the organization's vision and ethical culture. An organization's vision must be based on and consistent with their core values of integrity, honesty, transparency, integrity, loyalty, mutual respect, tolerance, acceptance, caring, compassion, and fairness. These are not the only values that should determine business culture and character but also the ones that are central to the sustainability of an organization. Values are the embodiment of what an organization stands for, and thus guide the behavior of its members. Any disconnect between individual and organizational values or differences between stated values and practiced values will be dysfunctional. Values are directly related to ethics because values that guide people and organizations to do right or wrong will also cause them to be viewed as being generally ethical or unethical.

Corporate codes of ethics are often viewed as attempts to foster good public relations or to reduce legal liability. Such codes also provide a reasonable model for understanding how moral principles can be articulated and introduced into business practice. The practical advantage of this approach is that it directly stipulates the morality of certain action types, without becoming ensnared in the problem of deriving particular actions from more abstract principles. However, the limitation of the corporate code model is that the principles offered will appear to be merely rules of prudence or good manners without proper enforcement.

Ethics performance and the process of promoting ethical behavior in an organization can be influenced by the organization's norms. Norms are also important for a discussion of ethics and values as they may allow or even encourage certain behavior as "appropriate" that is not in compliance with society's or an organization's stated values. When there is a discrepancy between stated and operating values, it may be difficult to determine what is "right." For example, a company that has among its stated values to treat everyone with dignity and respect, but whose norms have permitted a pattern of sexual harassment over a number of years reveals a disconnect between their proposed and actual ethical performance.

WORKPLACE ETHICS

Workplace ethics is receiving a considerable amount of attention, as the emerging corporate governance reforms require setting an appropriate tone at the top, promoting ethical conduct throughout the organization. A review of the recent financial scandals proves that most ethical dilemmas have financial consequences. Establishment of formal ethics programs is becoming increasingly common in organizations across the nonprofit, for-profit, and government sectors. The 2009 National Business Ethics Survey (NBES) provides valuable information about ethics in the workplace in the aftermath of the 2007–2009 global financial crises.[4] The 2009 NBES suggests many improvements in workplace ethics in the post-financial-crisis era in all key measures of ethical culture, whistle-blowing, openness, accountability, and doing the right thing. Four highlights from the 2009 NBES include:

1. Employees reporting that they observed ethical misconduct in workplace went down to about 49 percent in 2009 compared to 56 percent in 2007.
2. Whistle-blowing reporting was up to more than 63 percent in 2009 compared with 58 percent in 2007.
3. Improvements in key measures (integrity, openness, responsibility, and accountability) of ethical culture in the workplace reported by employees also increased (62 percent in 2009 compared with 53 percent in 2007).
4. Perceived pressure to commit unethical actions, cut corners, or violate ethical standards declined from 10 percent in 2007 to less than 8 percent in 2009.[5]

Nonetheless, about 22 percent of surveyed employees agreed that the financial crisis and related economic meltdown has negatively affected the ethical culture in their company, with more than 10 percent reporting their company has lowered its ethical standards in the post-2007 recession. Additionally, retaliations against employee whistle-blowers have increased.[6] On the one hand, this may suggest that during tough times people behave less ethically; on the other hand, about 80 percent of surveyed employees believed that they work in a company that holds them accountable for their ethical conduct and more than 70 percent reported that their corporate leaders are transparent regarding their ethical decisions and well-being of employees. These results suggest that many executives see value in actively promoting ethics within their organizations.

Organizations of all types and sizes can benefit significantly from the establishment and enforcement of effective workplace ethics standards. The list of potential benefits linked to an effective ethics program includes the following:

- Ability to hire the most ethical senior executives, including chief executive officer (CEO) and chief financial officer (CFO).
- Recruiting and retaining ethical and top-quality employees.
- Promoting a more satisfying, rewarding, and productive working environment.
- Establishing and maintaining a good reputation within communities.
- Securing the trust of all stakeholders to ensure continued self-regulation and prevent intervention by regulators.
- Aligning the work efforts of employees with the organization's mission and vision to enable them to work toward the organization's goals.[7]

Established workplace ethics programs are intended to guide and influence how employees tackle and resolve work-related ethical issues. Some actions toward developing the establishment and enforcement of effective workplace ethics standards include:

- Promoting open and candid discussion of ethical issues.
- Presenting ethical guidance and resources for employees to make appropriate ethical decisions.
- Establishing incentives and opportunities for employees in the workplace to do the right thing and behave ethically.
- Providing fair and prompt mechanisms to internally resolve potential conflicts of interest.

By providing employees with ethics standards, training, and resources, organizations seek to establish a work environment that demonstrates the following four characteristics:

1. There are internal mechanisms for employees to address unethical situations.
2. Employees are encouraged and enabled to acknowledge that they have an ethical dilemma.
3. Resources are readily available to guide employees in working through such dilemmas before making decisions.
4. Employees are rewarded for doing the right thing.

Ethics programs cannot prevent all misconduct from occurring. Even in the most ethical and efficient organizations, there are always a few employees who willfully disregard the rules. In such cases, there is no substitute for clear procedures and sanctions. A good ethics program promotes employees to do the right thing and succeed. Employees need to be sensitive and responsive to workplace ethical issues and be open to addressing them internally rather than resorting to external resolution. External disposition and exposure of unethical workplace issues is generally neither in the best interest of the organization nor its employees.

Employees typically have high ethical expectations and expect their organizations to do what is right, not just what is profitable. Most executives realize that the success of any ethics program requires the active support and participation of employees. Employees who consider their workplace to be ethical, as modeled by their leaders and supervisors promoting honesty, mutual respect, fairness, and trust, generally report more positive experiences regarding a range of outcomes. Some of these outcomes include more ethical workplace culture, less observed misconduct at work, less pressure on employees to compromise ethics standards, more incentives and opportunities to do the right thing, greater willingness to report misconduct, greater satisfaction with their organization's response to reported misconduct, greater overall satisfaction with the workplace, greater loyalty to the organization, and more reasons for feeling valued by the organization.

Directors and executives should set an appropriate tone at the top by promoting ethical culture throughout the organization with a keen focus on ethics programs and adherence to ethical principles and codes of conduct. Some of the potential benefits of ethics programs include attracting and retaining the best and brightest individuals and establishing an ethical workplace. Maintaining a good workplace reputation with key stakeholders is an immeasurable asset that executives should naturally protect. Executives generally recognize that employees can influence the company's reputation through their daily decisions but often fail to fully appreciate how an ethics program can give employees the tools to enhance that reputation.

Enron, in 2001, had gone from being considered one of the most innovative companies of the late 20th century to being the most corrupt and unethical. Its investors lost billions of dollars, executives were convicted, employees lost their jobs and pension investments, and the auditor was derided.

Enron is a classic example of a failure of ethics in the workplace. The primary failure of Enron's directors and executives was the violation of their fiduciary duty to protect the interests of its stakeholders (investors, employees, suppliers, creditors, customers, government, and society). The Enron board waived the companies own ethics code requirements to allow the company's executives to serve as general partner and act as a conduit for much of its business, which created conflicts of interest. The main objective of Enron's directors and officers was to be the financial leader in the industry, rather doing the right thing and conducting their business ethically. Enron was the seventh-largest public company in the United States in the beginning of 2001 but by 2002 it was the largest company to ever declare bankruptcy in U.S. history. The consequences of compromising ethical conduct are extremely costly and can cause the demise of the company and its reputation and loss investment for all stakeholders. What is more, it will affect public trust and investor confidence in the financial markets.

A survey of ethics in the workplace conducted by Deloitte & Touche in 2007 found a strong link between ethics and work-life balance (job satisfaction and flexibility). Ninety-one percent of respondents believed that workers are more likely to behave ethically when they have a work-life balance.[8] Survey results suggest that providing a balance between work and life through a more flexible work schedule provides incentives and opportunities for job satisfaction, fostering an ethical workplace culture. For example, Nestle Purina allows flexible hours and even lets employees bring their dogs to work; FactSet provides free lunches and flexibility regarding employees' time.[9] The survey identifies the following five key factors in promoting an ethical workplace: (1) behavior of management (42 percent); (2) behavior of direct supervisor (35 percent); (3) positive reinforcement for ethical behavior (32 percent); (4) compensation, including salary and bonus (29 percent); and (5) behavior of peers (23 percent).[10] These results suggest increased interaction between the board of directors, audit committees, internal auditors, external auditors, executives, and employees regarding ethical conduct in the workplace.

The National Association of States Board of Accountancy (NASBA) Center for the Public Trust (CPT) addresses the issue of ethics in the workplace, business world, academic community, and society.[11] The CPT has adopted two important guiding documents of core commitments and aspirations to promote ethical behavior in the workplace. Core commitments consist of dedication to specific ethical behaviors as well as passionate commitment to ethical practice and education. Ethics aspirations consist of strengthening trust and integrity; promoting ethics practice and education; and governing and acting with openness, transparency, mutual respect, and accountability. An effective workplace ethics program requires integration of the following ethics principles into the program, communication of these ethics principles to all employees, and enforcement of employees' compliance with these ethical principles:

■ **Fiduciary:** Directors, officers, and employees have a fiduciary duty to act in the best interests of the organization. This implies that every employee should act in a way that generates positive values for the organization.

- **Ethical Culture:** Directors and officers should establish an appropriate tone at the top, promoting ethical and competent behavior throughout the organization.
- **Property:** Everybody in the organization including directors, officers, and employees should respect property as well as the rights of the owners.
- **Reliability:** Employees should be reliable in doing their jobs as specified and expected.
- **Responsibility:** Employees are responsible for honoring their commitments to the organization.
- **Accountability:** Established codes of conduct and related ethics standards should be communicated and enforced; individuals should be held accountable for their compliance with the codes.
- **Transparency:** Employees should conduct business in a truthful and open manner.
- **Dignity:** Employees should respect the dignity of all individuals within the organization.
- **Fairness:** Employees should be treated fairly and with respect while respecting the rights of others.
- **Citizenship:** Employees should act as responsible citizens in the community by respecting all applicable laws of criminal, competition, environmental, and corporate social responsibility.
- **Mutual Respect:** Employees should respect established ethics policies and procedures; employers should enable employees to come forward in reporting unethical behavior.
- **Responsiveness:** Employees have a responsibility to respond to requests for information about the operations and react in a timely and diligent manner.

TRAINING AND ETHICS EDUCATION

Some companies are incorporating ethics into their training to improve business. When employees understand ethical drivers of behavior, the community and customers will take note of the ethical nature of a business. In addition, periodic reevaluations are suggested in ethics training because as times change, so do expectations. For example, when the first computer hacker sent a worm into a university computer system and crippled the entire network, it was considered a prank more than an unethical act. At that time, computers were new things for people and no one had ever been able to do such a thing before. Thus, periodic reevaluations are really important to keep up in a fast-changing world.

Ethics education is a kind of training for people before they begin their careers. Many university curricula are now heavily applying ethics programs. Some people think that ethics is hard to teach because of its inborn characteristics, while others think that ethics can be taught through acquired knowledge and education. For instance, some groups, including the Association to Advance Collegiate Schools of Business (AACSB international), and relevant professional organizations (e.g., Academy of Management), assume that such things can be trained. They recommend ethical decision-making strategies and values to be taught to students to prepare them for making well-considered business decisions.[12] Through ethics education, students can gain knowledge of applicable laws and internal rules and policies; an understanding of underlying values and ethical principles; and the ability to apply rules, standards, guidelines, and values to specific decision-making situations. They also develop positive ethical attitudes, including a sense of personal accountability and individual moral autonomy. A better understanding of all the above knowledge and skills will greatly help to improve the ethical performance in companies.

CORPORATE CULTURE

The delegation of authority, assignment of responsibilities, and the process of accountability influence corporate culture. Proper company-wide communication of corporate culture such as codes of conduct and job descriptions are essential in promoting and enforcing ethical behavior.

Ethics in business has an important underlying postulate: that the majority of business leaders, managers, and other personnel are honest and ethical in conducting their business, and the minority who engage in unethical conduct will not prevail in the long term. Thus, corporate culture and compliance rules should provide incentives and opportunities for ethical individuals to maintain their honesty and integrity, and also provide measures for the minority of unethical individuals to be monitored, punished, and corrected for their unethical conduct. Companies should promote a spirit of integrity that goes beyond compliance with the established code of business ethics or the letter of the law by creating a business culture of doing what is right.[13]

Business ethics are guidelines a company follows to ensure its actions are in accordance with ethical standards. All members of an organization should follow these ethics from leaders, to managers, to the employees.[14] Three factors are most important to affect people's behavior: incentives, opportunity, and choices. Incentives are perhaps the most essential determinant of business ethics. Individuals within the company (managers and employees) tend to act according to incentives provided to them in terms of rewards and the performance evaluation process. Corporate culture and incentives can encourage individuals to behave in the desired ethical manner. However, if opportunities exist, wrongdoers will take advantage and behave in an opportunistic manner. Thus, effective corporate governance, internal controls, and enterprise risk management can reduce the opportunity for unethical conduct.

Individuals, in general, are given the freedom to make choices and usually choose that which will maximize their well-being. Managers and employees make decisions, take actions, and exercise their choices on behalf of the company as agents of their company. Enron, WorldCom, Tyco, and Adelphia, to name a few, had incentives that encouraged their employees to practice unethical behavior, pursuing personal benefits rather than those of shareholders. A corporate culture of promoting ethical and competent behavior throughout an organization, along with strengthening incentives for doing the right thing and reducing opportunities for unethical actions, can improve ethics performance. Exhibit 8.4 presents several high-profile cases of unethical behavior.

EXHIBIT 8.4 Unethical Corporate Practices

Unethical Practices	Company/ Industry	Year	Company/ Industry	Year
Fictitious revenue, documentation forgery, and theft of corporate assets	ZZZZ Best	1987	Enron	2001
Personal use of assets, false documentation, and financial statement fraud	PharMor	1992	Adelphia	2002
Capitalizing expenses, among other issues	Waste Management	1997	WorldCom	2002
Abuse of accounting standards	Savings and Loan Crisis	1982	Stock Options Backdating	2006

CORPORATE CODES OF ETHICS: RULES AND BEST PRACTICES

The SEC rule in implementing Sections 406 and 407 of Sarbanes Oxley (SOX) describes the term "code of ethics" as written standards designed to deter wrongdoing and to promote:[15]

1. Full, fair, accurate, timely, and transparent disclosures in reports and documents filed or submitted to the SEC and in other public communications.
2. Honest and ethical conduct throughout the company, including the ethical handling of apparent or actual conflicts of interest between personal and professional activities and relationships.
3. Accountability for compliance with the established code of ethics.
4. Compliance with applicable regulations and professional standards.
5. The timely and effective internal reporting of noncompliance and any violations of the established code of ethics to an appropriate person or persons designated in the code.

The listing standards of the New York Stock Exchange (NYSE) further expanded on the SEC rules by requiring listed companies to:

1. Adopt and disclose a code of business conduct and ethics for directors, officers, and employees.
2. Promptly disclose any waivers of the adopted code for directors and executive officers.

For example, the NYSE listing standards recommend that each company determine its own business conduct and ethics policies but provide an extensive list of matters that should be addressed by the company's code. Adopted ethics rules for Nasdaq-listed companies are similar to those of the NYSE and also require the company's adopted code to provide for an enforcement mechanism and any waivers for directors or executive officers to be approved by the board and disclosed no later than the next periodic report.

FINANCIAL REPORTING INTEGRITY

Financial reporting integrity is vital in rebuilding investor confidence in corporate America, its financial reports, and the capital markets. Integrity is also important to individuals and society in providing a basis for establishing trust, relying on information, developing markets, achieving desired outcomes, and inspiring public policy.[16]

When the company is running well, retaining the integrity of corporate reporting is relatively easy, but when there is pressure or temptation, "creativity" in financial and nonfinancial reporting emerges. For example, when there are pressures to survive, secure continued employment, fight against the internal politics and whistle-blowers, or satisfy the accounting standards, companies are more likely to stray from ethical reporting practices.

KEY**GUIDANCE**

The six key aspects of integrity are moral values, motives, communication, qualities, achievements, and accountability.

1. **Moral values:** All financial reporting participants should embrace honesty, trustworthiness, and fairness, and observe moral values in fulfilling their reporting responsibilities with a keen focus on substance over form reporting attributes.

2. **Motives:** Reporting should be motivated by a desire to provide relevant, useful, reliable, and transparent information to enable users of reports to make informed decisions rather than a preference for self-interested goals of focusing on maximizing personal wealth through bonuses, stock options backdating, or saving face.

3. **Commitments:** All participants in the financial reporting process should be committed to and accountable for creating shareholder value while protecting the interests of other stakeholders.

4. **Qualities:** All participants in the financial reporting process should be competent, possessing the knowledge and experience needed to discharge their reporting responsibilities. They should also be courageous and capable enough to resist pressure, report both good and bad news, and exercise independent judgment.

5. **Achievements:** Participants in the financial reporting process should strive to achieve the stated financial reporting goals.

6. **Accountability:** Participants in the financial reporting process should be individually and collectively held accountable in achieving the established financial reporting objectives.[17]

The five organizational drivers of integrity in reporting are:

1. **Leadership:** An appropriate tone at the top set by senior executives in promoting ethical behavior and commitment to high-quality financial reporting is vital in ensuring the integrity of financial reports.
2. **Strategy:** A proper strategy should be established for achieving the stated financial reporting goals of providing high-quality financial information with a keen focus on assisting users to make informed decisions. This strategy should identify users' information needs and financial reporting goals as well as recruit competent and ethical senior executives and other professionals (e.g., accountants, auditors) to achieve these goals.
3. **Policies:** Proper policies should be established to support the stated strategy, and these policies should be reviewed periodically and on an ongoing basis for their adequacy, appropriateness, and effectiveness. Reporting policies and procedures are normally concerned with accounting policies, internal control procedures, and risk assessment policies and procedures. Effective implementation of these policies substantially reduces the risk of misleading financial information.
4. **Information:** An organization's policies and procedures should ensure the production of relevant, useful, reliable, and high-quality financial information to assist users in making informed decisions.
5. **Culture:** A culture of ethical behavior and financial reporting integrity should be promoted throughout the organization by linking rewards systems to high-quality reporting and sustainable performance rather than short-term performance or pressure to make the numbers.[18]

ETHICS REPORTING

Ethics reporting is emerging and could be prepared to disclose an organization's ethics performance and related assurance. Section 406 of SOX requires public companies to disclose in their annual financial statements the establishment (or lack of) a corporate code of conduct. Nevertheless, public companies may choose to report their business ethics and submit a separate report to their shareholders or with their regular filings with the SEC. A stand-alone ethics reporting and assurance practice is yet to receive common acceptance in corporate reporting. The process of external ethics reporting needs to be standardized and guidelines need to be established for such reporting. Thus, the existing ethics reporting guidance such as the AA

1000 Accountability Principles should be used for determining the structure and content of ethics reporting.[19] These three principles are: the foundation principle of inclusivity, the principle of materiality, and the principle of responsiveness. The principle of inclusivity is the starting point for determining materiality. The materiality process determines the most relevant and significant issues for an organization and its stakeholders. Responsiveness encompasses the decisions, actions, and performance related to those material issues. When preparing ethics reports, all three principles should be used for guidance and reference.

In the absence of authoritative standards for ethics reporting, an ethics report could contain the following information:

- Existence of an ethics-related board committee or chief ethics executive position (e.g., chief ethics and compliance officer) to oversee the organization's codes of ethical conduct and its effectiveness.
- Establishment, maintenance, and enforcement of codes of ethical conduct.
- An ethics training program that outlines ethics policies and procedures.
- Establishment of incentives and opportunities for ethical leadership and ethical behavior throughout the organization.
- Communication, implementation, and certification of compliance with the established ethics policies and procedures.
- Adoption of internal mechanisms for resolution of unethical dilemmas to minimize their existence and persistence.
- Integration of ethics management with other managerial functions.
- Development of grievance policies and procedures to internally resolve any disagreements and disputes with supervisors and staff, including the integration of whistle-blowing policies into ethics programs and practices to institutionalize ethics in the workplace.
- Establishment of an ethics hotline or an anonymous suggestion box in which personnel are enabled to report suspected unethical activities internally.
- Statement of policy for antidiscrimination based on race, color, ethnicity, gender, religion, and so on.
- Design and implement mechanisms for minimizing pressure, incentives, and opportunities for employees to compromise their professional responsibilities and ethical standards.
- Strengthen customer relations to enhance the company's reputation.
- Implement a control structure that eliminates opportunities for individuals to engage in unethical activities.

Organizations should establish either a board ethics committee of an ethics officer position. The primarily role and responsibilities of the established ethics/compliance officer should be to:

   i. Identify corporate values of the organization.
   ii. Incorporate values into a code of ethics.
   iii. Create training programs to educate directors, officers, and employees regarding their ethics and compliance responsibilities.
   iv. Guide employees in making ethical decision.
   v. Investigate reports of unethical activities.
   vi. Develop a system for reporting ethical breaches.
   vii. Report status of ethical activities to top executives and the board of directors.
   viii. Require certification of compliance with the code of ethics and all applicable laws, rules, regulations, and standards.

Ethics reporting should promote the practice of not only complying with applicable regulations but also committing to doing the right thing and observing ethical principles of professional conduct in avoiding potential conflicts of interest. More specifically, the ethics report should provide relevant, timely, useful, and reliable information pertaining to all established, practiced, and enforced ethics KPIs discussed in this chapter, including the following:

- Contemporary issues in business ethics
- Stakeholders and corporate responsibility
- Corporate governance and compliance
- Ethics and the environment
- Health care ethics
- Ethics and information technology
- Strategic planning and corporate culture
- Ethics and financial reporting
- Establishing a code of ethics and ethical guidelines
- Evaluating corporate ethics
- Integrity
- Objectivity
- Professional competence and due care
- Confidentiality
- Professional behavior
- Ethics aspirations of trust, openness, mutual respect, and accountability.

In order to increase the credibility of the ethics report, assurance should be obtained on the report. The assurance process should gather sufficient and appropriate evidence pertaining to the organization's codes of ethics and compliance with established ethics policies, procedures, and other elements of reported ethics performance. The ethics assurance provider should gather evidence related to, at least, the following questions:

1. Does the company have an ethics committee at the board level or officer position?
2. Does the company maintain effective codes of conduct and ethics standards?
3. Does the company maintain effective whistle-blowing policies and procedures?
4. Do employees' actions comply with the spirit and letter of all applicable laws, rules, regulations, and standards?
5. Is personnel behavior consistent with the company's core values and ethical standards?
6. Are there mechanisms for providing incentives and opportunities to behave ethically and do the right thing?
7. Are there policies and procedures for hiring the most competent and ethical personnel?
8. Are there proper mechanisms for effective resolution of conflicts of interest?

CONCLUSION

The wave of financial scandals, financial crises, and related regulatory responses and best practices has galvanized a demand for and an interest in ethics and compliance training programs. Ethics are broadly described in the literature as moral principles about right and wrong, honorable behavior reflecting values, and standards of conduct. Honesty, openness, responsiveness, accountability, due diligence, and fairness are core ethical principles. Business ethics are a specialized study of right and wrong, using appropriate professional judgment and being accountable for ethical decisions and actions. An appropriate code of ethics that sets the right tone at the top, promoting ethical and professional conduct and establishing the moral structure for the entire organization, is the backbone of effective corporate governance.

Attributes of an ethical corporate culture or an integrity-based culture include a sense of employee responsibility, freedom to raise concerns, managerial modeling of ethical behavior, and expressing the importance of integrity. A company's directors and executives should demonstrate, through their actions as well as their policies, a firm commitment to ethical behavior throughout the company and a culture of trust within the company. Although a right tone at the top is very important in promoting an ethical culture, actions often speak louder than words. Ethics reporting is the effective way to communicate the organization's ethics aspirations and values of trust, integrity, openness, fairness, mutual respect, and professional responsibilities and accountability. Studies by the Institute of Business Ethics (IBE) conclude that conducting business with ethical responsibility and integrity is not only the right thing to do but also is good for the bottom line, as surveyed companies that reflected commitment to ethical conduct and effectively fulfilled their ethical responsibilities consistently outperformed companies with no ethics reporting.[20]

ACTIONITEMS

1. Encourage everybody in the organization to do the right thing.
2. Focus on the corporate culture of promoting ethical values, moral principles, integrity, and competency.
3. Establish an enforceable code of ethics.
4. Require compliance with the established code of ethics and all applicable laws, rules, regulations, and standards.
5. Develop ethics reporting and assurance programs.

NOTES

1. Sims, R.R. 1992. "The Challenge of Ethical Behavior in Organizations," *The Journal of Business Ethics*, 11(7).
2. Martin Luther King, Jr.'s address at Western Michigan University, December 18, 1963.
3. Subaru. 2012. "Subaru and the Environment," Subaru website. Available at: http://www.subaru.com/company/environment-sustainability.html.
4. Ethics Resource Center (ERC). 2009. "The 2009 National Business Ethics Survey (NBES)." Available at: www.ethics.org/nbes/files/FinalNBES-web.pdf.
5. Ibid.
6. Ibid.

7. Joshua Joseph and the Ethics Resource Center. 2000. "Ethics Resource Center's 2000 National Business Ethics Survey." Available at: http://www.asaecenter .org/Resources/articledetail.cfm?ItemNumber=13073.

8. Deloitte & Touche. 2007. "Leadership Counts: Deloitte & Touche USA 2007 Ethics & Workplace." Available at: http://www.deloitte.com/assets/Dcom-UnitedStates/Local%20Assets/Documents/us_2007_ethics_workplace_survey_011009.pdf.

9. Glass Door. 2011. "Top 25 Companies for Work-Life Balance." Available at: http://www.glassdoor.com/Top-Companies-for-Work-Life-Balance-LST_KQ0,35.htm.

10. Rezaee, Z., and Richard Riley. 2009. *Financial Statement Fraud: Prevention and Detection*, (Hoboken, NJ: John Wiley & Sons), 22.

11. National Association of States Board of Accountancy (NASBA) Center for the Public Trust (CPT). 2011. "Board Commitments and aspirations" – Mission and Goals. Available at: Available at: http://www.centerforpublictrust.org/#.

12. Ritter, Barbara A. 2006. "Can Business Ethics Be Trained? A Study of the Ethical Decision-making Process in Business Students," *Journal of Business Ethics* 68: 153–64.

13. Rezaee, Z. 2008. *Corporate Governance and Ethics* (Hoboken, NJ: John Wiley & Sons), 65.

14. Ibid.

15. Securities and Exchange Commission (SEC). 2003. "Disclosure Required by Sections 406 and 407 of the Sarbanes-Oxley Act of 2002." Available at: www .sec.gov/rules/final/33-8177.htm.

16. The Institute of Chartered Accountants in England and Wales (ICAEW). 2007. "Reporting with Integrity: Market Foundation Initiative." Available at: http://www.icaew.com/~/media/Files/Technical/Ethics/reporting-with-integrity-report.ashx.

17. Rezaee, Z. 2008. *Corporate Governance and Ethics* (Hoboken, NJ: John Wiley & Sons), 81.

18. Ibid.

19. AccountAbility (AA). 2008. "AA 1000 Accountability Standard 2008." Available at http://www.accountability.org/images/content/0/7/074/AA1000APS%202008.pdf.

20. Ugoji, K., N. Dando, and L. Moir. 2007. *Does Business Ethics Pay?* (London: The Institute of Business Ethics).

9

The Environmental Dimension of Sustainability Performance: Government Policy, Societal Forces, and Environmental Management

EXECUTIVE**SUMMARY**

Public awareness in companies' environmental performance is growing. To effectively compete in the global market, companies worldwide should integrate environmental sustainability into their business strategies and model. Many of the business calamities that occurred in the past decade prove that corporate environmental responsibilities are vital to economic sustainability, the well-being of society, and future generations. This chapter presents the environmental dimension of economic, governmental, social, ethical, and environmental (EGSEE) sustainability performance including: (1) environmental key performance indicators (KPIs); (2) global environmental initiatives; (3) environmental management systems (EMS); (4) environmental reporting; (6) environmental assurance and auditing; and (7) environmental best practices.

Companies should respond to environmental challenges and turn them into opportunities that change their environmental management, policies, and practices to safeguard the global environment and improve related performance.

INTRODUCTION

Many of the business disasters that occurred in the past decade prove that corporate environmental policies are vital to economic sustainability and the well-being of society. The BP oil spill unleashed an estimated 140 million gallons of crude oil on the Gulf of Mexico, forever affecting the coastal areas around Louisiana, Mississippi, Alabama, and Florida, along with their wildlife and citizens. Organizations should establish an environmental policy framework to address environmental matters and promote policy measures. This means that organizations should create stakeholder value with effective and efficient utilization of scarce resources that mitigates the negative impact on the environment. Environmental sustainability is defined in this chapter as a process of preserving the quality of the environment in the long term and creating a better environment for future generations.

EMERGING ENVIRONMENTAL ISSUES

Several environmental disasters have been bellwethers, particularly because of the impact they have had in setting environmental policy and public opinion, which in turn has altered business's approach to environmental performance. Over the past 25 years, major changes in approaches and attitudes have occurred as a result of the Exxon Valdez spill (1989), disposal of Shell's Brent Spar oil platform, the Union Carbide Bhopal disaster, and the more recent spill from BP's Deepwater Horizon oil rig. Exhibit 9.1 presents these high-profile environmental events and the policy implications they triggered, as well as significant improvements in the environmental risk management and strategy of related companies.

All disaster events presented in Exhibit 9.1 have had profound effects on the environment, wildlife, citizens, local economies, and the welfare of associated companies and their stakeholders. As a result of these events, organizations are now expected to establish an environmental policy framework to address environmental matters and promote policy measures. Society is now expecting organizations to create and preserve stakeholder value with effective and efficient utilization of scarce resources that mitigates the negative impact on the environment.

Emerging environmental issues, including climate change, are affecting the global business landscape; the associated risk assessment and management; and proper measurement, recognition, and disclosure of environmental

EXHIBIT 9.1 Global Environmental Disasters

Company	Year	Event	Description
Hooker Chemical[1]	1940s	Chemical waste dumping	Dumped over 63,000 tons of synthetic chemicals into an industrial landfill, which is currently a superfund site.
Chisso Corporation[2]	1956	Mercury dumping	Dumped mercury from operations into the Minamata Bay in Japan.
Texaco[3]	1964	Oil runoff	Leaked 18 billion gallons of runoff into Ecuador near Lago Agrio.
General Public Utilities	1979	Three Mile Island Nuclear leak	Released radioactive elements into the environment.
Union Carbide (Dow Chemical)[4]	1984	Bhopal chemical leak	Pesticide plant leaked toxic gas, killing thousands; continues to cause health problems for residents.
Exxon[5]	1989	Valdez oil spill	Spilled around 257,000 barrels (10.8 million gallons) into Prince William Sound in Alaska.
British Petroleum	2010	Deepwater Horizon oil spill	Spilled roughly 3.3 million barrels (140 million gallons) into the Gulf of Mexico.
Niger Delta[6]	Ongoing	Oil spill	There have been over 7,000 spills here since 1970 and over 13 million barrels (546 million gallons) released into the environment.
Ok Tedi River Mining ltd.[7]	Ongoing	Waste dumping	Dumped over 90 million tons of waste per year into the Ok Tedi River in Papua New Guinea. (Mine is closing in 2012.)

[1] http://www.epa.gov/region2/superfund/npl/hookerchems/

[2] http://www.env.go.jp/en/chemi/hs/minamata2002/ch2.html.

[3] http://upsidedownworld.org/main/ecuador-archives-49/2907-ecuadorian-court-rules-against-chevron-inhistoric-case.

[4] http://www.bhopal.com/chronology.

[5] http://www.evostc.state.ak.us/facts/qanda.cfm.

[6] http://www.guardian.co.uk/world/2010/may/30/oil-spills-nigeria-niger-delta-shell.

[7] http://www.businesspundit.com/the-worlds-worst-environmental-disasters-caused-by-companies.

Sources: U.S. Environmental Protection Agency; Japan's Ministry of the Environment; Upside Down World; Bhopal Information Center; Alaska's Exxon Valdez Oil Spill Trustees Council; *The Guardian*; Business Pundit.

obligations and performance. Despite ever-increasing environmental rules and regulations and widespread acceptance of climate change and its global impact, many companies have yet to design and implement coherent plans and comprehensive actions to manage risks and opportunities associated with climate change and environmental regulations.

ENVIRONMENTAL KPIs

A general approach to the development of environmental KPIs is to identify relevant factors that could shape or influence an organization's environmental initiatives, programs, and performance. Examples of relevant environmental factors and measures include:

- Efficient utilization of scarce natural resources, including power, energy, and material consumption.
- Continuous monitoring and replacement, where possible, of non-renewable resources, using technological advances for mining unconventional renewable and nonrenewable natural resources.
- Perpetual and progressive use of non-waste technologies.
- Efficient utilization of recycled materials.
- Producing environmentally safer products.
- Minimizing the use of environmentally harmful materials and products.
- Preserving the environment and preventing negative impacts on ecosystems.
- Addressing the number and type of litigations, legal actions, and claims.
- Providing insurance claims for negligent or inappropriate use, disposal, or transport of hazardous materials.
- Environmental profitability and cost accounting (e.g., ratios, trends, indices, value added).

The United Kingdom's Department for Environment, Food and Rural Affairs has developed a set of guidelines for reporting using 22 environmental KPIs, which are based on three simple principles: the quantitative, the relevant, and the comparable.[1] The guidelines are voluntary however; the set of environmental KPIs apply to all UK businesses. Quantitative information should be measurable so management can implement policies that have specific targets and outcomes based on an underlying environmental measure (e.g., carbon dioxide emissions). The information that is collected using

EXHIBIT 9.2 Environmental KPIs

1. Continuous replacement of nonrenewable and scarce resources.
2. Disclosure of ecosystem changes.
3. Disclosure of gigajoules of total energy consumed.
4. Disclosure of metric tons of total carbon dioxide (CO2) emitted.
5. Disclosure of risk exposure and opportunities for climate change.
6. Disclosure of toxic chemical use and disposal.
7. Efficient utilization of unconventional renewable and nonrenewable natural resources.
8. Efficient use of recycled materials.
9. Environmental profitability analysis and assessment.
10. Maximum efficiency in utilization of scarce natural resources.
11. Measurement of resource depletion.
12. Minimizing the use of environmentally harmful materials and products.
13. Preventing negative impacts on ecosystems.
14. Production and use of environmentally safe products.
15. Promoting environmental performance.
16. Proper use of non-waste technologies.
17. Preservation of scarce natural resources of power and energy.
18. Preserving the environment.
19. Promotion of biodiversity.
20. Proper disclosure of environmental litigations, legal actions, and claims and related expenses.
21. Proper disposal and cleanup of hazardous wastes.
22. Proper measurement, disclosure, and reporting of carbon emissions and greenhouse gas emissions.
23. Proper recycling of waste, medical, construction, and hazardous, and non-hazardous materials.
24. Reporting of metric tons of total waste produced.
25. Reporting of total cubic meters of water consumed.
26. Reprocessing and reuse of scarce resources.
27. Use of alternative energy fuel, oil, and gas.
28. Utilization of agriculture/organic foods.
29. Utilization of green cleaning.
30. Utilization of renewable energy.

quantitative measures to build KPIs needs to be relevant to the business and fully transparent, providing a purpose and clear definitions for inter-departmental operations. Progress reports should be developed to track performance on the established KPIs. KPIs that are developed must be comparable and normalized to maintain consistency over time. Exhibit 9.2 presents a list of environmental KPIs.

ENVIRONMENTAL REGULATIONS IN THE UNITED STATES

Reporting environmental performance in the United States in a corporate setting has been built on regulations, societal demand, safety, and transparency through accurate environmental disclosure. Environmental initiatives and regulations have far-reaching consequences for how corporations are viewed in society. Those that fail to comply with societal expectations can be held liable for inadequate environmental consideration. Several environmental regulations in the United Stated are discussed in the following sections.

Environmental Protection Agency (EPA)

The Environmental Protection Agency (EPA) is responsible for identifying and enforcing environmental laws and regulations, and forcing companies to clean up a contaminated site. It can also seek recovery costs for cleaning up a contaminated site. Companies that do not comply will be liable for cleanup costs, remediation of future contamination, degradation to natural resources, societal litigation, and criminal charges. Effective compliance with environmental laws and regulations requires full commitment by companies to initiate environmental management systems and accounting, and auditing practices.[2] On a broad scale, the EPA issues and enforces health and environmental regulations around clean air, clean water, and solid waste, as well as other regulations affecting environmental reporting. In general corporations that are involved in resource-intensive industries are required to follow environmental requirements, laws, and regulations (e.g., the Clean Air Act,[3] the Superfund Amendment and Reauthorization Act [SARA][4]). For specific industries, such as construction, the EPA has developed a set of environmental KPIs for businesses to use as a guideline. The six basic guidelines are as follows: (1) diesel emission reduction strategies, (2) smart energy practices, (3) green remediation, (4) green building/construction practices, (5) water management, and (6) environmentally preferable purchasing.

For contaminated land, the EPA uses a National Priorities List (NPL) to identify hazardous sites that need to be cleaned up. An NPL site is defined as one that releases hazardous materials, pollutants, or contaminants that have negative effects on the environment and human health. At the end of 2009 the NPL consisted of 1,111 seriously contaminated, nonfederal sites.[5] In 2009, the EPA spent over $4 billion on cleanup efforts on sites that were locations of severe human exposure or unknown exposure. From 2010 through 2014 the EPA expects to spend \$335 to \$681 million each year on contaminated sites. As of April 1, 2011, the EPA has identified 1,132 non-federal sites and158 federal sites that are in immediate need of cleanup, with no direct cost estimations.[6] Approximately 70 percent of Superfund cleanup activities historically have been paid for by potentially responsible parties (PRPs) in cases of contamination. The only time cleanup costs are not borne by the responsible party is when that party either cannot be found or is unable to pay for the cleanup. Seeking responsible parties that are jointly and severally liable for cleanup costs at individual sites has spurred a cottage industry of thousands of lawsuits between the PRPs and the EPA, pitting the individual PRPs against themselves and their insurance carriers in an attempt to recover costs paid out to defend, settle, and clean up these sites. On March 27, 2012, the EPA released its proposal for the first Clean Air Act standard for carbon pollution from new power plants.[7] This is an important initiative by the EPA to reduce air pollution and protect the planet. Although the proposed standard is only applicable to power plants built in the future, it is expected to minimize carbon pollution for all power plants.

Climate Risk Disclosure

In June 2009, Ceres and the Environmental Defense Fund (EDF) released a joint report on their analysis of climate risk disclosures of 100 companies in five sectors, based on the 2007 fiscal year's SEC filings. They concluded that investors are not receiving adequate climate information from corporate fillings with the SEC.[8] The report on an examination of climate change disclosures of about 6,400 10-K filings by S&P 500 companies from 1995 to 2009 reveals that there was "an alarming pattern of non-disclosure by corporations regarding climate risks."[9] A survey conducted by Ernst & Young in 2010 suggests the following five global themes regarding climate change:

1. Executive leadership is critical to effective governance of fully understanding and realizing the full potential of the business response to climate change. More than 90 percent of executives surveyed indicated that climate change governance should be addressed at the board and top management level.
2. Business drivers dominated by top-line and bottom-line impacts of climate change initiatives have keen focus on meeting changes in customer demand.

3. Business executives are committed to address the ever-increasing challenges of climate change.
4. Climate change investments have increased despite regulatory uncertainty.
5. Transparent reporting of climate change business strategies, initiatives, and performance are increasing.[10]

In 2010, the SEC released guidance reiterating the relevance and importance of adequate disclosure of material risk associated with climate change by public companies.[11] Items in filing SEC documents S-K or S-X that could trigger climate-related disclosure are items 101, 103, 503(c), and 303. Item 101 pertains to any material capital expenditures on a facility's environmental controls during the company's current fiscal year and previous periods where the company finds it material.[12] Item 103 requires a company or its subsidiaries to describe any material legal proceedings it may be involved in.[13] Item 503(c) gives guidance on what risk factors a company should review and disclose regarding existing or pending regulation on climate change.[14] Item 303 requires public companies to determine the affect any enacted climate change legislation or regulation will have on the company's financial position.[15] For example, pending legislation or regulations on climate change can affect costs of purchasing or improving facilities, as well as demand for products and services. The guidance does not change any existing rules or obligations to disclose and the SEC has stated there will be follow-up action coupled with new rules. The follow-up action will monitor and assess whether additional rules are necessary.[16] Ceres has followed up on company disclosure and found that, "disclosure continues to be highly inconsistent and often inadequate, particularly in mandatory filings, and frequently fails to meet the needs of investors."[17]

In another survey conducted by Ernst & Young in 2010, respondents reported that the top three factors driving their climate change initiatives were: (1) energy costs; (2) changes in customer demand; and (3) new revenue opportunities.[18] Current and future legislation coupled with society's increasing sensitivity to the environment (especially toward pollution, hazardous waste, human health, and other general environmental concerns) necessitate the need for high-level management to pay attention to their companies' environmental practices and obligations. Exhibit 9.3 presents a list of EPA acts relevant to environmental issues.[19]

The EPA has other programs that are voluntary and help drive industry-wide adoption and awareness toward environmental practices. The voluntary programs are: Green Lights, Climate Wise, Waste Wise, and Energy Star.

EXHIBIT 9.3 EPA-Related Acts

EPA Acts	Description
Atomic Energy Act (1954)	Deals with radiation hazards and handling and disposal of radioactive waste. General guidelines are given for the construction and use of nuclear power plants. The law also prohibits citizen law suits and restricts the opportunity for interest groups.
Clean Air Act (1970)	Creates standards for air quality in the United States and is periodically reviewed to ensure the standards are relevant. Amendments in 1990 stressed that market forces control air pollution.
National Environmental Policy Act (1970)	Any project that is funded by the federal government and its agencies must assess the project's environmental impact. The Act was the first environmental statute. Many states have adopted similar laws.
Clean Water Act (1972)	Creates standards for water quality in the United States. The Act has been amended several times to account for the use of different toxic pollutants and address oil spills.
Coastal Zone Management Act (1972)	Allows the federal government and the states to combine forces to protect the U.S. coastlines. The Act also provides funding to states that implement conservation laws.
Endangered Species Act (1973)	Protects endangered species in the United States and abroad by protecting their natural habitats.
Surface Mining Control and Reclamation Act (1977)	Regulates coal mining to ensure local communities and the environment are protected. The Act also enforces the restoration of abandoned mining areas.
Comprehensive Environmental Response, Compensation and Liability Act (1980)	Also referred to as the "Superfund," this Act mandates the cleanup of toxic waste at contaminated sites. An amendment in 1986, which is retroactive, could potentially hold companies liable for contamination incurred before the law was enacted in 1980.
Emergency Planning and Community Right-to-Know Act (1986)	Requires businesses to provide information about the toxic chemicals they emit into the environment (air, water, land).
Oil Pollution Act (1990)	Was created after the Exxon Valdez oil spill in Alaska, and requires associated parties to develop a swift oil-spill response system. The Act also increases the liabilities companies face after a spill (degradation to the natural environment and cleanup costs).

These programs arose out of corporate interest in preparing for future legislation and seeking recognition for early action and uniformity in operating under carbon constraints.

Corporations in the United States are not required to issue environmental reports or follow ISO 14000 environmental accounting standards; however, they are liable for environmental degradation inflicted by their company or subsidies (e.g., the BP oil spill). Many large corporations like IBM, Pfizer, and Apple have developed their own tools in developing environmental KPI reporting variables. The reports are produced annually and include tailored KPIs and goals, which include energy conservation, waste reduction, increased recycling, and use of environmentally friendly materials.

The United Kingdom and the United States both host large corporations or conglomerates that operate throughout the globe. The United Kingdom has developed environmental law that enforces environmental practices, while the United States has regulations that govern industries involved in the use of natural resources. Although both countries have laws and regulations to ensure public safety now and in the future, neither have standards on how to disclose environmental practices. Furthermore, such disclosure is voluntary but increasing in popularity stemming from societal demand. In the United States, the SEC and the Financial Accounting Standards Board (FASB) have given corporations some support in developing reporting standards; however the major increase in reporting is mainly attributed to the increase in social awareness and governmental regulation.[20] The EPA has influenced what type of KPIs are being monitored and used throughout the business world. Moreover, systems have been developed to help report environmental information. The EPA has put through several acts to control and monitor environmental degradation, which enables them to enforce the regulations when companies fail to adhere voluntarily.

The National Association of Insurance Commissions (NAIC) disclosed in 2009 requirements for insurance agencies to provide information on climate change risk. In 2009 insurance companies that have over $500 million in climate-related premiums ($300 million in 2010 and thereafter) have mandatory filings. Insurance companies fall out of this range, so filing is strictly voluntary. Ceres made an attempt to quantify the extent to which insurance companies in America consider climate change in their business models. They found that 88 insurers in 2010 filed responses in six states (New York, New Jersey, California, Oregon, Pennsylvania, and Washington) and that the largest insurers are taking only marginal steps to incorporate climate change into their business models.[21]

GLOBAL ENVIRONMENTAL INITIATIVES AND REGULATIONS

Global environmental initiatives, including the Kyoto Protocol, Copenhagen Accord, World Bank Carbon Finance Unit, Clean Air Initiative, and the International Council for Local Environmental Initiatives (ICLEI), have influenced global awareness of environmental matters and have addressed environmental responsibilities of businesses. These initiatives have had a profound effect on how society and the business world conceptualize environmental impacts. The Climatic Research Unit conducts applied and pure research providing valuable data and information for analyzing climate change. This organization has provided tools and data sets to be used at many conferences to illustrate how the earth is changing and whether it is from human activity or not. Despite some controversy, "global weirding" is happening and countries from around the world are coming together to fix the degradation humanity has caused to the natural environment. Exhibit 9.4 shows a list of global environmental initiatives, some of which are described in the following sections.

Kyoto Protocol

The Kyoto Protocol was established in Kyoto, Japan, on December 11, 1997, and went into effect in February of 2005. The Kyoto Protocol is an international agreement setting targets for 37 industrialized countries to reduce greenhouse gas (GHG) emissions at a rate of five percent per year (based on 1990 levels) until 2012. A total of 191 states have signed and ratified the treaty (the United States signed but has not ratified). Details of the rules, dubbed the "Marrakesh Accords," were adopted in 2001 in Marrakesh, Morocco. The eight main guidelines or rules set by the Kyoto Protocol are as follows:

1. Increase energy efficiency across industry sectors of the national economy.
2. Established sinks and reservoirs of GHGs not controlled by the Montreal Protocol will be increased and protected.
3. Promote the practice of sustainable forest management, afforestation, and reforestation.
4. Promote the use of sustainable forms of agriculture.
5. Conduct research and development on new forms of renewable energy, environmentally sustainable technologies, and carbon dioxide (CO_2) sequestration or reduction technologies, and also reduce methane

EXHIBIT 9.4 Environmental Initiatives

Initiative	Description	Website
Interfaith Center on Corporate Responsibility (ICCR)	Founded in 1971, the (ICCR) is an association of 275 faith-based institutional investors, including national denominations, religious communities, pension funds, foundations, hospital corporations, economic development funds, asset management companies, colleges, and unions.	http://www.iccr.org/
Investor Network on Climate Risk (INCR)	A group of more than 70 leading institutional investors with collective assets of more than $9.8 trillion (as of May 2010).	http://www.ceres.org/incr/
Coalition for Environmentally Responsible Economies (Ceres)	Founded in 1989, in the aftermath of the Exxon Valdez oil spill, Ceres is an association of investors, environmental organizations, and other public interest groups working with companies and investors to address sustainability challenges such as global climate change.	http://www.ceres.org/
The Carbon Disclosure Project (CDP)	A U.K.-based organization promoting standards for the disclosure of greenhouse gas emissions of major corporations. The organization reports that, as of May 2010, 2500, companies in some 60 countries around the world measure and disclose their GHG emissions and climate change strategies through CDP.	
Remarks on climate change by President Obama in the State of the Union Address, The White House, January 27, 2010	President Obama summarized key issues regarding the advancement of clean energy technologies (e.g., nuclear, biofuels, clean coal, wind, etc.), developing offshore oil reserves, and passing legislation that will make clean energy viable.	
SEC Release No. 33-9106; 34-61469, Fed. Reg. 6290 ("Commission Guidance	The document provides that companies should consider the impact of existing and pending climate change legislation, regulation, international treaties, and accords in determining whether disclosure	

(continued)

EXHIBIT 9.4 *(Continued)*

Initiative	Description	Website
Regarding Disclosure Related to Climate Change"), February 8, 2010	is necessary in their business, legal proceedings, risk factors, and management's discussion and analysis (MD&A) of financial condition and results of operations sections.	
Global Reporting Initiative (GRI)	GRI develops a global economy that reports and operates transparently, by providing sustainable development of economic, environmental, social, and governance practices.	http://www.globalreporting.org
U.N. Global Compact	A compact where organizations can join, stating they will follow business practices that will benefit society, involving human rights, labor, environment, and anticorruption.	http://www.unglobalcompact.org/
U.S. Climate Action Partnership	A group of businesses and environmental organizations that formed to bring policy reform to the U.S. through the passage of new legislation on the reduction of greenhouse gases.	http://www.us-cap.org/
U.N. Framework Convention on Climate Change (UNFCCC)	Organized to collaborate on Annex 1 countries that joined the Kyoto Protocol to further develop and discuss climate change policies.	http://unfccc.int/2860.php
OECD Guidelines for Multinational Enterprises (GME)	The mission of OECD is to promote policies and procedures that will benefit the well-being of the global society.	http://www.oecd.org/home/0,2987,en_2649_201185_1_1_1_1,00.html
Kyoto Protocol	The Kyoto Protocol was established in Kyoto, Japan, on December 11, 1997 and went into effect in February of 2005. The Kyoto Protocol is an international agreement setting targets for 37 industrialized countries to reduce greenhouse gas emissions at a rate of five percent per year (of 1990 levels) until 2012.	http://unfccc.int/kyoto_protocol/items/2830.php

(continued)

EXHIBIT 9.4 *(Continued)*

Initiative	Description	Website
Copenhagen Accord	The Copenhagen Accord is an endorsement for the continuation of the Kyoto Protocol and outlines guidelines for preventing anthropogenic interference on the natural environment, combating climate change.	http://unfccc.int/meetings/cop_15/copenhagen_accord/items/5262.php
Montreal Protocol	The Montreal Protocol was established in 1987 addressing issues surrounding the depletion of the Earth's ozone layer by phasing out harmful chemicals such as chlorofluorocarbons (CFCs) and hydrochlorofluorocarbons (HCFCs).	http://ozone.unep.org/new_site/en/montreal_protocol.php
UN Commission on Sustainable Development (CSD)	The Commission on Sustainable Development (CSD) revised its indicators of sustainable development in 2002, with a focus on the development of indicators on a local level and support implementation into developing countries.	http://www.un.org/esa/dsd/csd/csd_aboucsd.shtml
World Bank Carbon Finance Unit(CFU)	The World Bank Carbon Finance Unit enables developing countries to purchase carbon credits from nations that have excess sustainable carbon offset production.	
Clean Air Initiative	The Clean Air Initiative (CAI) was created by the World Bank and USAID as a global initiative to promote higher air quality and reduce pollution and greenhouse gas emissions across all industries.	http://cleanairinitiative.org/portal/index.php

emissions through various recovery, waste, production, transportation, and distribution activities.

6. Reduce and eliminate market inefficiencies and government incentives (tax and subsidies) across all GHG-emitting industries that are apprehensive to the progress of the Protocol.
7. Support the promotion of environmentally sustainable practices to relevant industries that emit GHG and are not influenced by the Montreal Protocol.
8. Limit and/or reduce methane emissions through recovery and use in waste management, as well as in the production, transport, and distribution of energy.[22]

The Kyoto Protocol established standards and committed industrialized nations to stabilize GHG emissions into the future. The protocol recognized that over the past 150 years, nations that went through an industrial revolution were the main culprits of the high level of GHG emissions and would therefore be expected to reduce emissions more than undeveloped countries. The Protocol will bind nations to reduce their emissions of GHG by 5.2 percent (compared to the year 1990) by 2012. The main focus will be to reduce six major GHGs, as follows: carbon dioxide, methane, nitrous oxide, sulfur hexafluoride, HFCs, and PFCs. Total reduction targets are 8 percent reduction for the European Union, 7 percent for the United States, and 6 percent for Japan.[23]

The Kyoto Mechanisms

Nations that adopted the Kyoto Protocol have to meet their GHG emission targets through national measures; however, the protocol offers nations three tools to use to meet the targets. The tools are:

1. **Emission Trading:** Development of a carbon market to trade excess units.
2. **Clean Development Mechanism (CDM):** A program for nations to implement a carbon-reduction project in a developing country to help meet targets.
3. **Joint implementation (JI):** Emission reduction units can be earned from another party's emission-reduction project.[24]

These tools will invigorate green investment and help countries meet their emission targets in a cost-effective way.

Monitoring Emission Targets

Actual emissions have to be monitored and recorded by countries through the development of new programs or existing agencies to carry out the requirements of the Kyoto protocol. For example, the UN Climate Change Secretariat, based in Germany, keeps records of the environmental data in ordinance with the Protocol. Countries agreeing to take part in the Protocol have to submit annual emission and national reports at specific intervals (e.g., quarterly, semiannually, annually, etc.) to ensure compliance. Moreover, the system facilitates a checks-and-balances system, and if countries are having trouble meeting targets the issue can be addressed and resolved.

The adoption and tracking systems established by the Protocol help countries understand the effects their economies or day-to-day activities have on the natural environment. The Protocol also helps countries understand the adverse effects on climate change, which fosters the development of new technologies and social practices to mitigate the effects of its effects in the future. Furthermore, the Protocol was established to help developing countries finance environmental projects and programs—those that are a part of the Protocol—through Clean Development Mechanism (CDM) project activities.[25]

The Kyoto Protocol has made progress in increasing awareness and enabling GHG emissions reductions in some countries since its inception in 1997. In December of 2011, the UNFCCC held a global conference in Durban, South Africa, to amend the Kyoto Protocol and take further action to reduce global GHG emissions. The Durban outcomes are as follows:

1. Extension of the Kyoto Protocol until 2017.
2. Bringing all GHG-emitting nations under the jurisdiction of the UN.
3. Enforcing emissions cuts by those nations by 2020; seeking a 2 degree Celsius change.
4. Funding poor nations by funneling up to $100 billion by 2020.[26]

EUROPEAN UNION EMISSIONS TRADING SYSTEM (EU ETS)

The European Union Emissions Trading System (EU ETS) fights against climate change by reducing GHG emissions from heavy emitters that include power plants and industrial plants in 30 countries. Started in 2005, the EU

ETS is a cap and trade model based off allowances given to companies in a given year, which can be bought or sold in the marketplace. There is a limit to the number of allowances insuring value, with the total number reducing over time to meet a 21 percent reduction of 2005 emission levels by 2020. The program has been successful and is broadening its tracking base in 2013 to include the airline, petrochemical, ammonia, and aluminum industries.[27]

CARBON REDUCTION COMMITMENT (CRC)

The Carbon Reduction Commitment (CRC) Efficient Energy Scheme is a cap and trade model similar to the EU ETS, incorporating allowances and broad market participation. The scheme was started in 2007 and applies to all companies that have a half-hourly electric meter and/or 6,000 megawatt-hours (MWh) of energy consumption (excluding transportation and domestic accommodation). The CRC scheme only applies to emissions not covered under the UK's climate change agreements (CCAs) and the EU ETS.[28]

CALIFORNIA ASSEMBLY BILL 32

The California Assembly Bill 32 was signed into law in 2006 and sets goals of setting an emission cap to reach 1990 levels by 2020. The program is meant to achieve, "[. . .] real, quantifiable, cost-effective reductions of greenhouse gases (GHG)."[29] The program also looks to make progress in five areas:

1. Establish reporting rules for emitters.
2. Meet target emission reductions either through regulations, market forces, or others.
3. Create technologically and efficient ways to reduce GHG emissions.
4. Ensure the public has full disclosure.
5. Create advisory boards to the California Air Resources Board (ARB) (e.g., the Environmental Justice Advisory Committee and the Economic and Technology Advancement Advisory Committee).[30]

GLOBAL PROGRESS

Japan, Canada, the European Union (EU-25), and the United Kingdom gave reports on their national progress in 2005 and 2006.

Japan

Japan projected an increase in 2010 CO_2 emissions by 6 percent or 1.311 million tons over base year 1990. Japan plans to achieve the target 6 percent reduction in GHG emissions by 2010 through by meeting the following objectives:

- A 6.5 percent total emissions reduction composed of:
    - Energy-originated carbon dioxide: 4.8 percent
    - Combination of non-energy-originated carbon dioxide, methane, and nitrous monoxide: 0.4 percent
    - Three fluorinated gases: 1.3 percent
- A 3.9 percent through the use of forest sinks
- A 1.6 percent by following the Kyoto Mechanisms[31]
    (http://unfccc.int/files/adaptation/cancun_adaptation_framework/loss_and_damage/application/pdf/japan.pdf)

Canada

Canada's total GHG emissions in 2004 were 758 million tons of CO_2 equivalent and represented a 26.6 percent increase over 1990 levels, which were 599 million tons (a 34.6 percent increase over the Kyoto target). The high increase was attributed to high population growth (13.5 percent between 1990 and 2002) and a booming industries sector, particularly in the energy sector, where oil exports increase 449 percent (between 1990 and 2002). Despite this, Canada has invested heavily in developing technologies and programs to reduce GHG emissions and kept total output below business-as-usual trends by investing $3.7 billion.[32]

(http://unfccc.int/files/bodies/awg-lca/application/pdf/20120517_canada_1749.pdf)

The European Union

The European Union is projected to reduce GHG emissions by 1.6 percent below 1990 levels. This is despite the fact that 25 EU member states do not benefit from land use, land-use change and forestry (LULUCF) provisions. Additional policies and measures being implemented by the EU-15 (the group of 15 EU countries on track to meet Kyoto targets) will result in total reductions of 6.8 percent. The inclusion of Kyoto mechanisms will lower

GHG emissions to 9.3 percent below 1990 levels. In aggregate, with the use of LULUCF and Kyoto mechanisms, the EU-25 is projected to reduce GHG emissions by 11.3 percent by 2010. The EU-25 is only responsible for 14 percent of the world's GHG emissions, and through various policies and programs, such as the European Climate Change Program (ECCP), it is leading by example across many industries. This role goes beyond demonstrating how to reduce GHG to include environmental sustainability plans.[33]

(http://unfccc.int/files/kyoto_protocol/application/pdf/brochure_on_eu_post_2012_action.pdf)

The United Kingdom

The United Kingdom has agreed under the Protocol to reduce GHG emissions by 12.5 percent below base year levels over the first commitment period (2008–2012). Domestically, the UK set 2010 GHG emissions reductions targets at 20 percent below 1990 levels. Between 1990 and 2004 the UK reduced GHG emissions by 14.6 percent, mainly driven by the restructuring of the energy supply industry and implementing energy efficiency programs, pollution control measures, and general policies combating GHG emissions. The UK was on track to meet its 2010 target with an estimated reduction of 19.4 percent below the base year.[34]

These countries are a few examples of how the world is changing its view and implementing various government regulations, programs, and policies on how to meet targets set by the Kyoto Protocol. For a full list of Annex 1 countries' progress reports, visit the United Nations Framework Convention on Climate Change (UNFCCC) website.[35]

(http://www.defra.gov.uk/environment/climate/government/risk-assessment/#evidence)

(Kyoto protocol progress: http://unfccc.int/kyoto_protocol/items/3145.php)

Copenhagen Accord 2009

The Copenhagen Accord is not a binding agreement like the Kyoto Protocol but it outlines climate change as "one of the greatest challenges of our time."[36] The Copenhagen Accord is an endorsement for the continuation of the Kyoto Protocol and outlines guidelines for preventing human interference on the natural environment, combating climate change. There are 10 main guidelines and objectives the Copenhagen accord seeks to address and are as follows:

1. Provide adequate, predictable, and sustainable financial resources, technology, and capacity-building to support the implementation of adaptive action in developing countries.
2. Mobilizing $100 billion to the Copenhagen Green Climate Fund through contributions from public, private, bilateral, and multilateral sources.
3. The development of a high-level panel to study the contribution of potential sources of revenue.
4. Annex I parties commit to implement individually or jointly the quantified economy-wide emissions targets for 2020.
5. Non-Annex I parties will implement emission mitigation actions, and will distribute such information through national communications that will be subject to international measurement, reporting, and verification.
6. Reducing emissions from deforestation and forest degradation by offering positive incentives to nations needing financial resources.
7. Use various approaches (i.e., markets) to ensure the cost-effectiveness of reducing emissions.
8. Establish a technology mechanism to accelerate the development of sustainable technologies and transfer them to nations based on circumstance and priority.
9. Nations will have adoption and mitigation processes to combat emissions by 2020, especially Annex I nations.
10. Ensure that the Copenhagen Accord be implemented by 2015.[37]

The Accord has 141 parties committed or expressed intention to be listed for climate emission controls to be achieved by 2020. With the success of the Kyoto Protocol and others, and supported by 114 committed parties the effort to combat climate change is expanded upon further with the Copenhagen accord.

The Montreal Protocol

The Montreal Protocol was established in 1987 to address issues surrounding the depletion of the Earth's ozone layer by phasing out harmful chemicals such as chlorofluorocarbons (CFCs) and Hydrochlorofluorocarbons (HCFCs). HCFCs were an initial replacement for CFCs in order to reduce ozone depletion; however, HCFCs are harmful GHGs—some 2,000 times more harmful than

CO_2 —and are being phased out by 2040. There are two control steps to help meet this target: one in 2013 that puts a freeze on production and consumption of HCFCs (based on an average between 2009 and 2010), and a 10 percent reduction by 2015.[38] All UN-recognized nations have ratified the treaty and are phasing out the production of chemicals that are harmful to the ozone layer, while seeking safe alternatives. Currently the ozone layer has not grown thinner since 1998 and is recovering in most of the world. The Antarctic ozone hole is projected to return to pre-1980 levels by 2060 to 2075.[39] The Montreal Protocol has been a success over the past 20 years and has helped innovate and develop effective approaches to solving the ozone depletion protecting human health and the global environment.

The United Nations

The United Nations has long advocated preservation of the global environment. The United Nations Environmental Program (UNEP) was established in 1972 and has been facilitating leadership in nations around the world, enabling environmental care while increasing the quality of life and preserving the planet for future generations.

The Commission on Sustainable Development (CSD) was established in 1992. In 2002, it revised its indicators of sustainable development, focusing on the local development and implementation support in developing countries. In 1996 the CSD piloted an indicator program with 22 countries to look at the effectiveness of the indicators and the integration into national systems. The results from the test were reviewed in 2000 after a three-year trial period with successful results. However, there were some challenges, mainly with creating established programs to ensure success, along with difficulties with human resources and implementing effective policy fluidity throughout the entity. In 2005, a second review of the sustainable indicators was implemented, focusing on such indicators and perspectives in the evolving world. The revised set of indicators includes a core of 50, which is among the larger set of 97 environmental indicators. The entire list can be found in the United Nations report: *Indicators of Sustainable Development: Guidelines and Methodologies*. The main themes of the CSD's sustainable indicators are as follows: poverty; governance; health care; education; demographics; natural hazards; atmosphere; land; oceans, seas, and coasts; freshwater; biodiversity; economic development; global economic partnership; and consumption and production.[40,41] The new focus illustrates the multidimensional approach that is necessary to sustainable development. The multidimensional approach shows that sustainability is complex and needs careful review during the development of action plans and indicator programs if they will be able to measure reliable, accurate, transparent, and consistent information. The CSD has presented and implemented a comprehensive plan and system to track sustainable development in an evolving world and will be a critical tool for nations and organizations to follow in the future.

Over the last 25 years the United Nations has held numerous international meetings aimed at reaching a global consensus to tackle vexing environmental problems. Some examples from the outcome of these meetings have been:

- The Montreal Protocol (on substances that deplete the ozone layer).
- The Kyoto Protocol.
- The Millennium Development Goals (MDGs) (eight international development goals that all 193 United Nations member states and at least 23 international organizations have agreed to achieve by the year 2015. These include eradicating extreme poverty, reducing child mortality rates, fighting disease epidemics, and developing a global partnership for development).

The World Bank Carbon Finance Units (CFU)

As part of the UN system, the World Bank created its Carbon Finance Unit (CFU) to enable developing countries to purchase carbon credits from nations that have excess sustainable carbon-offset production. The CFU is also part of the global effort to combat climate change, improve living standards, and reduce poverty in developing nations. The CFU has a carbon fund, which is financed through contributions from governments and companies globally. The funds are used to purchase emission reduction projects focused on reducing GHG emissions in developing countries. The funds follow the framework laid out by the Kyoto Protocol's CDM or JI tools. The fund grew from $145 million in 2000 to over $2.3 billion in 2009. The increase is staggering and shows that market instruments can play an important role in reducing the costs associated with environmentally sustainable projects in developing countries. In 2009 the CFU signed 15 emission reduction purchase agreements (ERPAs) focused on the waste management, forestry, and renewable energy industries. The CFU had many firsts, including Africa's first forestry project, which was registered by the UNFCCC when ERPA signed a contract with the Democratic Republic of Congo for reforestation. ERPA also initiated repurchase agreements with Thailand and has projects in Pakistan.

The CFU fund is composed of carbon finance units in China and the East Asia and Pacific region and accounts for 72 percent of carbon emission reductions. With Africa, Europe and Central Asia, and Latin America and the Caribbean contributing 21 percent of the portfolio, the South Asia and the Middle East and North Africa regions make up the remaining seven percent. The fund invests mainly in projects to reduce trifluoromethane (HFC-23) by 57 percent, but it also invests in renewable energy, energy efficiency, waste management, and land use and forestry.

The CFU has developed a robust trading platform for trading and investing in environmentally relevant projects in developing nations to foster the sustainable development of economies while preserving human health and the natural environment.

SOCIETAL ACTORS INFLUENCING CORPORATE ENVIRONMENTAL BEHAVIOR

Numerous environmental nonprofits and advocates have arisen in the last quarter century to influence and police corporate environmental behavior. The following are some examples of the most influential:

Advocacy Groups with Corporate Membership Partnerships

- Environmental Defense Fund (EDF)
- Center for Climate and Energy Solutions (formerly the Pew Center on Global Climate Change)
- The Climate Group
- World Wildlife Fund (WWF)

Business to Business Information Sharing Organizations

- Global Compact
- Business for Social Responsibility
- World Business Council for Sustainable Development

Investors groups

- Ceres (Coalition for Environmentally Responsible Economies)
- Interfaith Center on Corporate Responsibility (ICCR)
- Investors Network on Climate Risk (INCR)
- Institutional Investors Group on Climate Change (IIGCC)

World Wildlife Fund (WWF)

The World Wildlife Fund (WWF) was founded in 1961 by a group of scientists, environmentalists, and business and political leaders and it is currently the largest independent conservation company. WWF has more than 6.2 million members globally and works in over 100 different countries. WWF has grown from $120 million in operational revenue in 2001 to over $230 million, of which roughly 85 percent goes to conservation field and policy programs and public education.[42] The WWF continues to allocate operational revenue to species conservation, water pollution management, sustainable forest control, and general climate change efforts. Moreover, WWF continues to research and advocate sustainable development to stop the destruction of the environment around the world. Recently, the WWF launched "Destination Gigaton" in the US to inspire companies to increase action to combat climate change through more ambitious GHG emissions reductions activities.

UN Global Compact

The UN Global Compact is an initiative for corporations wishing to streamline global operations and strategies with 10 universally accepted principals.[43] The principles are structured around four main points: human rights, labor, the environment, and anticorruption.[44] The compact has over 8,700 corporate participants in over 130 different countries. The objective of the compact is to streamline global operating principals for all corporations to follow and support related UN goals such as the Millennium Development Goals.[45]

The compact Global Compact has stringent reporting requirements, which fall under the Communication on Progress (COP). The COP is an annual report produced by the company to ensure commitment to the Global Compact. Failure to comply will result in a company receiving a change in status or elimination from the Compact. Currently the UN Global Compact is strictly voluntary, however as more corporations adopt it, it is likely that industry peers will follow.

Clean Air Initiative (CAI)

The Clean Air Initiative (CAI) was created by the World Bank and USAID as a global initiative to promote higher air quality through the reduction of pollution and GHG emissions across all industries. The CAI was started in Asian cities to help promote clean air and reduce harmful pollutants and GHG emissions through knowledge, policies, and procedures. The CAI has expanded to Latin America and Sub-Saharan Africa in efforts to create awareness and eliminate GHG and pollutant emissions and they also have undertaken strong efforts in Asia. Every year 500,000 people in Asia die prematurely due to poor air quality.[46] The threat of climate change not only impacts the environment but also influences the stability of people's livelihood, creating a double-edged sword. The need to mitigate and eliminate air pollution and GHG emissions is imperative to a healthy, breathable future.

The CAI has registered over 200 organizations, including eight country networks and one nonprofit organization. It is considered by the UN to be a Type II partnership—one that is guided by a partnership council of five members that include cities, governments, NGOs/academia, the private sector, and development agencies.[47] The organization mobilizes action on a local and national level with 1- to 2-year development and implementation plans. The main strategy of the CAI is to reduce air pollution and GHG emissions through coordinated regional and national policies and regulations, and to increase awareness through transference of knowledge, tools, and partners. The CAI also sets goals for cities to scale out by producing real improvements in air quality and integrated activities in urban planning. The program also focuses on scaling up by reaching more Asian cities that do not have programs to improve air quality and avoid business-as-usual practices.[48]

International Council for Local Environmental Initiatives (ICLEI)

ICLEI was founded in 1990, when it initially represented over 200 local governments from 43 countries. ICLEI has grown substantially over the years and it now represents over 1,200 local governments in 70 different countries (this representation equates to almost 600 million people). ICLEI is committed to sustainable development, providing technical consulting, training, and information services. The goal is to transfer knowledge, which supports sustainable development to achieve cost-effective local and global sustainability objectives. ICLEI continues to host conventions and events to promote sustainable development and increase its member base.

Coalition for Environmentally Responsible Economies (Ceres)

The Coalition for Environmentally Responsible Economies (Ceres) was founded in 1989, after the tragic Exxon-Valdez oil spill, to address sustainability challenges and global climate change. Ceres is a group of investors, environmental organizations, and other public interest groups. Currently Ceres has over 130 members with over a dozen Fortune 500 companies endorsing Ceres's 10 principles. The 10 principles are an environmental code of conduct, which member companies have to follow and report on. The 10 principles are as follows:

1. **Protection of the biosphere:** Strives to reduce or eliminate harmful substances that cause environmental damage in the natural environment, preserving biodiversity.
2. **Sustainable use of natural resources:** Efficiently uses nonrenewable resources (e.g., water, soil, forests, air) and materials in a sustainable way.
3. **Reduction and disposal of wastes:** Reduce or eliminate waste through resource reduction or recycling.
4. **Energy conservation:** Use renewable energy sources, while improving internal energy efficiency and reduce energy use.
5. **Risk reduction:** Minimize environmental risks to employees in places of operation through sound policies and procedures.
6. **Safe products and services:** Eliminate or reduce hazardous products or services and inform customers of the environmental impacts such products have.
7. **Environmental restoration:** Correct damages caused to the environment.
8. **Informing the public:** Inform the public of harmful conditions the company may have caused to the environment. Ceres members will not punish employees for bringing such situations to management's awareness.
9. **Management commitment:** Implement and sustain environmental policy.
10. **Audits and Reports:** Complete an annual Ceres report (available to the public) as well as an annual self-evaluation of the progress made on the above criteria.[49]

Ceres has had several accomplishments since its inception, including launching a global reporting initiative, increasing social and investor awareness about environmental practices, and forming the Business for Innovative Climate and Energy Policy (BICEP). Among its other accomplishments, Ceres has been a driving force in influencing corporate governance awareness on environmental sustainability.

Interfaith Center on Corporate Responsibility (ICCR)

The Interfaith Center on Corporate Responsibility (ICCR) was established in 1971 and has 275 faith-based institutional investors focused on building a global community of justice and sustainability. ICCR's six main goals are:

1. Sponsoring shareholder resolutions.
2. Engaging in dialogue with corporate management.
3. Networking with those who share their concerns.
4. Participating in public hearings.
5. Partnering with community organizations.
6. Organizing letter writing campaigns.[50]

The ICCR has created continuity between social and environmental issues by focusing investment decisions on a long-term basis that goes beyond a reasonable rate of return.

Investor Network on Climate Risk (INCR)

The Investor Network on Climate Risk (INCR), sponsored by Ceres, is a collaboration of more than 100 institutional investors with assets reaching almost $10 trillion. The INCR looks to advance the investment opportunities surrounding global climate change and water scarcity. INCR successes include issuing guidance on climate-change-related disclosure to companies that have to file it with the SEC; strengthening the oversight for deep-water drilling; influencing Fortune 500 companies to improve their environmental standards; and hosting a conference with 500 financial leaders at the UN to discuss opportunities to mitigate global climate change.[51]

The world has become aware of the climate-change and sustainability-development challenges that human civilization faces. The Kyoto Protocol, Copenhagen Accord, World Bank Carbon Finance Unit, CAI, ICLEI, and others have demonstrated tremendous support from global nations with enthusiasm to mitigate and reduce pollution, GHG emissions, and other harmful by-products. Despite some controversy, human-created climate change has had an impact on the natural world and countries from around the world are coming together to fix the degradation to the planet.

INTERNATIONAL ORGANIZATION FOR STANDARDIZATION (ISO)

In 1996, the International Organization for Standardization (ISO) created the ISO 14000 standards to help organizations around the world develop adequate environmental management systems. The ISO was established in 1946 to encourage the development and execution of uniform standards through international trade. ISO 9000 standards on quality assurance and quality management are the best-known, with over 1 million certified members.[52] Globalization is creating competitive pressures throughout all globally competitive companies and is a driving force behind the staggering number of companies being certified in ISO 9000.

ISO 14000 standards are not mandatory; however, they are essential tools and guidelines to help organizations manage, monitor, and comply with external stakeholder demands regarding their environmental actions, as well as government laws and regulations. This certification will ensure organizations meet the forthcoming environmental challenges faced by businesses and societies worldwide by providing set standards globally for EMS. The ISO 14000 standards are being viewed by organizations as a way to improve environmental performance while reducing its impact on the environment and they provide a tool for organizations to use instead of merely reacting to governmental laws and regulations. ISO 14000 certification can also help prevent future government litigation or the passage of laws and regulations, and minimize their exposure to environmental costs enforced by governing bodies (e.g., the EPA). Since the ISO 14000 standards are not strictly voluntary, environmental groups, governments, legal representatives, accountants, and other stakeholders should become aware of ISO 14000 standards and their impact.

ISO 14000 standards have six specific guidance areas that help an organization deal with the environmental revolution; they are as follows:

1. **ISO 14004** - Guidance on implementing an EMS
2. **ISO 14010** - Auditing principles and guidance
3. **ISO 14031** - Performance evaluation guidance
4. **ISO 14020** - Labeling guidance (merchandise)
5. **ISO 14040** - Life-cycle assessment principles and guidance
6. **ISO 14050** - Terms and definitions

KEY**GUIDANCE**

Choose an ISO Environmental Standard

Establish the breadth and depth the organization wishes to become involved with environmental standards. Make sure the management review meets the requirements of the ISO 14000 standards. General guidelines for implementing ISO 14000 are as follows:

1. ISO 14001 - Environmental Management Systems - Specification with Guidance for Use
2. ISO 14004 - Environmental Management Systems - General Guidelines on Principles, Systems, and Supporting Techniques
3. ISO 14010 - Guidelines for Environmental Auditing - General Principles
4. ISO 14011 - Guidelines for Environmental Auditing - Audit Procedures - Auditing of Environmental Management Systems
5. ISO 14012 - Guidelines for Environmental Auditing - Qualification Criteria for Environmental Auditors
6. ISO 14020 - Environmental Labeling - General Principles
7. ISO 14021 - Environmental Labels and Declarations - Self-declaration Environmental Claims - Guidelines and Definition and Usage of Terms
8. ISO 14022 - Environmental Labels and Declarations - Self-declaration Environmental Claims - Symbols
9. ISO 14024 - Environmental Labels and Declarations - Environmental Labeling Type 1 - Guiding Principles and Procedures
10. ISO 14031 - Environmental Management - Environmental Performance Evaluation - Guidelines
11. ISO 14040 - Environmental Management - Life Cycle Assessment - Principles and Framework
12. ISO 14041 - Environmental Management - Life Cycle Assessment - Goal and Scope Definition and Inventory Analysis[53]

ISO 14000 standards are becoming a necessity for competing in the global market and are helping organizations develop environmentally sustainable business plans, missions, and goals. For example Apple has eliminated toxic substances such as arsenic, brominated flame retardants (BFRs), mercury, phthalates, and polyvinyl chloride (PVC) from its products and has reduced the size of packaging for its computers by 40 percent. It also offers complete recycling programs for old computers.[54] Many organizations are becoming more vocal in their environmental achievements and will continue to satisfy the growing concern over environmental sustainability. Globally there are other standards that comply or are compatible with ISO 14000 for developing an environmental management system (EMS). One such system is the British Standard (BS) 7750, which helps describe an EMS in that particular region. EMS will be covered in greater detail in the following section.

However, there are some objections to the efficacy of continued compliance to ISO 14000 after a company or a facility has been certified.[55] Studies have shown that certified organizations or facilities do not have better environmental performance than noncertified organizations or facilities.[56] However, a study conducted by Deepa Aravind and Petra Christmann shows that while there is little difference, on average, between facilities that have or have not been certified, those that have high-quality implementation with the full commitment of management have higher post-environmental performance.[57] This illustrates the need for a regular auditing system that eliminates conflict of interest while implementing proper interim monitoring systems to ensure ISO 14000 compliance and commitment. Despite some technical drawbacks ISO 14001 certification does help organizations comply with government regulations, various waste reduction schemes, and reduce overall emissions.[58]

ISO 50001

ISO 50001 standards were issued in 2011 and establish a framework to assess and manage energy for industrial plants; institutional, commercial, and governmental facilities; or entire organizations.[59] ISO 50001 standards are very broad and expected to affect the majority of the world's energy use.

ENVIRONMENTAL MANAGEMENT SYSTEMS (EMS)

An environmental management system (EMS) is a dynamic tool used to improve the environmental performance of a company. The two main objectives of an EMS are to (1) support the prevention of pollution into an ecosystem and (2) establish proper policies, procedures, and goals to meet stakeholder demands on environmental performance. To achieve these objectives an organization will need to take the following steps:

1. Define a broad environmental mission.
2. Develop proper environmental standards and procedures (e.g., a rulebook).

3. Document and communicate such standards to stakeholders.
4. Enforce compliance with such standards.

The green revolution is the next major transformation the business world will take part in. The concept of environmental sustainability is becoming a reality where social awareness and pressure from government bodies through regulation are holding industries accountable for environmental degradation. One essential tool businesses will have to implement in order to comply with various regulations and reporting guidelines is an EMS. Conventional financial accounting looks at how well the company performs on an economic level, whereas accounting that supports the triple-bottom-line approach (social, environmental, and economical) is more sustainable and less susceptible to erroneous litigation claims.

Adoption of an EMS does not guarantee proficient environmental performance; however, it does provide management with more transparent information regarding environmental performance, including compliance with current and future regulations. From a regulatory and social standpoint, EMS is also intended to mitigate risk associated with poor environmental practices. Ideally, EMS implementation will spur innovation and offer incentives for employees to make sustainable progress on environmental concerns. Companies take advantage of environmental opportunities to ensure sustainable performance. For example, DuPont and its greenhouse gas reduction program has seen significant energy savings.

Exhibit 9.5 describes several objectives of EMS. A more detailed discussion of concepts and construction within an organization are discussed in the following sections.

An EMS's environmental policies enable an organization to maintain fluid environmental performance defined by internal missions and goals, which are set by external stakeholders. These EMS policies and goals should illustrate top management's commitment to the environmental policies and procedures established and form a foundation for implementation of future missions. They should also be relevant, reliable, and transparent, and clearly communicated to stakeholders. All stakeholders should regularly review EMS policies to adapt a company to the dynamic environment.

Creating an Efficient EMS Program

Establishing environmental programs is crucial to the success of an organization's EMS system in the early development stages. A program should:

EXHIBIT 9.5 Environmental Management Concepts Environmental Policies

Concept	Purpose
Environmental Policy	1. Establish environmental policy to ensure compliance with internal and external stakeholders. 2. Continually monitor.
Planning	1. Develop a plan for EMS implementation. 2. Identify effects the organization has on the environment. 3. Document relevant, reliable, and transparent environnemental information. 4. Develop a set of KPIs to monitor progress.
Implementation and Operation	1. Incorporate proper resources to implement the necessary policies and procedures. 2. Integrate EMS seamlessly into management systems. 3. Provide employees with proper environmental awareness and training through programs or workshops. 4. Develop a response plan to environmental destruction.
Checking and Corrective Action	1. Objectively measure the ongoing progress of EMS implementation. 2. Implement strategies for corrective actions. 3. Monitor EMS for effectiveness. 4. Implement regular audits of the EMS.
Management Review	1. Implement a managerial process to monitor progress made with the EMS. 2. Evaluate environmental KPIs on a regular basis. 3. Make adjustments to create an optimal EMS.

- Portray how the EMS conditions will be achieved.
- Construct deadlines and responsible employees for developing environmental programs.
- Provide the necessary resources for EMS training and development.
- Establish processes to deal with adverse environmental aspects.

Documentation of the EMS

ISO 14000 standards, specifically ISO 14001, provide precise requirements for documentation of an organization's EMS. EMS documentation should include process information, depicted by charts, and internal operating procedures, which include plans for environmental emergencies. Furthermore, the ISO 1001 standard requires organizations to document the EMS.

Recordkeeping is essential in providing relevant and accurate information so the organization can follow the progress made on implementing and maintaining the goals and missions of the EMS. Specifically, environmental records should include:

- Current and future laws and regulations.
- Process and procedure documents.
- Demonstrated acceptance by employees and stakeholders, through formal compliance and training records.
- General product information.
- Safety reports.
- General or audit reports on environmental progress made by the organization through management (KPI reporting on annual or quarterly reports).

Management Review

ISO 14000 requires executive management to conduct regular evaluations of the EMS to ensure the system is realizing the set goals and missions of the environmental practices. The main goal for management's review is to identify deficiencies and successes to improve the organization's environmental practices in the future. The review should include results from internal monitoring of KPIs and environmental audits and measurements of the EMS's effectiveness with regards to changing regulations or social pressures (e.g., that from stakeholders).

To obtain certification for ISO 14001, an organization must comply with all ISO 14000 standards. At minimum, a four-step process is essential for obtaining certification:

1. Choose an appropriate EMS.
2. File appropriate applications for ISO 14000.
3. Provide documentation concerning the firm's relevant, reliable, and transparent environmental information, including employee training and auditing.
4. Assessment by the registrar for compliance with ISO 14000 standards.

When approved the organization will receive certification, be listed in a register, and benefit from all direct and indirect applications of the certification.

Registration Options

The decision to implement an EMS company-wide or for only specific divisions or locations needs to be established before registration. Full implementation throughout the organization will lead to better integration of the EMS, fully developing sound environmental policies and procedures. Before an application is submitted, ensure that the corporate bodies hosting the EMS meet all ISO 14001 requirements. The EMS implementation must also have the full commitment of senior management. Finally, contact the associated registrar to see if the proposed EMS meets the ISO 14001 standards.

Registration to ISO 14001

Environmental standards are not required by law but they provide the tools necessary for building an EMS that is sustainable into the future and will meet both environmental and economic goals. Registration to ISO 14001 requires that the organization's EMS meet all of the requirements and is adequately documented, reviewed, analyzed, and implemented to an applicable field for a time period that accurately shows how the EMS works. Steps to registration are as follows:

1. Filling out and filing an application.
2. Documentation of all relevant and applicable information about the EMS.
3. Having a registration audit.
4. Having a registrar complete periodic assessment of the EMS.

After the application has been accepted and the organization is certified (through a full on-site inspection and audit), annual periodic assessments of the EMS will be conducted by the organization to ensure compliance with ISO 14001 standards.

ENVIRONMENTAL REPORTING

Environmental reporting is often referred to as *green accounting* or *green reporting*. Environmental information can be included in the corporate annual reports, provided in management discussion and analysis (MD&A), included in a company's corporate social responsibility or sustainability report, or presented in a stand-alone environmental report. Basic environmental information has traditionally been disclosed in both annual reports and MD&A. To move beyond the basic level of environmental reporting, companies should look to a more encompassing sustainability-specific accounting guidance, such as can be found in the Global Reporting Initiative (GRI) reporting framework. Exhibit 9.6 presents GRI environmental performance indicators relevant to environmental reporting.[60]

EXHIBIT 9.6 Environmental GRI Performance Indicators

Materials
EN1 – Materials used by weight or volume.
EN2 – Percentage of materials used that are recycled input materials.

Energy
EN3 – Direct energy consumption by primary energy source.
EN4 – Indirect energy consumption by primary source.
EN5 – Energy saved due to conservation and efficiency improvements.
EN6 – Initiatives to provide energy-efficient or renewable energy-based products and services, and reductions in energy requirements as a result of these initiatives.
EN7 – Initiatives to reduce indirect energy consumption and reductions achieved.

Water
EN8 – Total water withdrawal by source.
EN9 – Water sources significantly affected by withdrawal of water.
EN10 – Percentage and total volume of water recycled and reused.

Biodiversity
EN11 – Location and size of land owned, leased, managed in, or adjacent to protected areas and areas of high biodiversity value outside protected areas.
EN12 – Description of significant impacts of activities, products, and services on biodiversity in protected areas and areas of high biodiversity value outside protected areas.
EN13 – Habitats protected or restored.
EN14 – Strategies, current actions, and future plans for managing impacts on biodiversity.
EN15 – Number of IUCN Red List species and national conservation list species with habitats in areas affected by operations, by level of extinction risk.

Emissions, Effluents, and Waste
EN16 – Total direct and indirect GHG emissions by weight.
EN17 – Other relevant indirect GHG emissions by weight.
EN18 – Initiatives to reduce GHG emissions and reductions achieved.
EN19 – Emissions of ozone-depleting substances by weight.
EN20 – Nitric oxide (NO), sulfur oxide (SO), and other significant air emissions.
EN21 – Total water discharge by quality and destination.
EN22 – Total weight of waste by type and disposal method.
EN23 – Total number and volume of significant spills.
EN24 – Weight of transported, imported, exported, or treated waste deemed hazardous under the terms of the Basel Convention (Annex I, II, III, and VIII), and percentage of transported waste shipped internationally.

(continued)

EXHIBIT 9.6 (Continued)

EN25 – Identity, size, protected status, and biodiversity value of water bodies and related habitats significantly affected by the reporting organization's discharges of water and runoff.

Products and Services

EN26 – Initiatives to mitigate environmental impacts of products and services, and the extent of impact mitigation.

EN27 – Percentage of products sold and their packaging materials that are reclaimed by category. (Note: Not relevant to Enbridge.)

Compliance

EN28 – Monetary value of significant fines and total number of non-monetary sanctions for noncompliance with environmental laws and regulations.

Transport

EN29 – Significant environmental impacts of transporting products and other goods and materials used for the organization's operations, and transporting members of the workforce.

Overall

EN30 – Total environmental protection expenditures and investments by type.

Source: GRI. 2011. "G3 Sustainability Reporting Guidelines."

There are a growing number of companies worldwide that are now issuing separate environmental reports. According to GRI and the Carbon Disclosure Project (CDP):

> Over 3,000 organizations in some 60 countries around the world now measure and disclose their greenhouse gas emissions and climate change strategies through CDP, and close to 1,900 organizations published a GRI-based report in 2010.[61]

There are numerous reporting and certification processes and guidelines to develop proper reporting tools for government agencies and other stakeholders. Industry-led initiatives such as ISO 14000, ISO 26000, and Leadership in Energy and Environmental Design (LEED) are all certification processes in the United States and globally that can be used to track sustainable business development. These initiatives require companies to develop environmental management systems, as discussed in the previous section, but do not require mandatory environmental accounting and reporting.

A common argument for encouraging the issuance of separate environmental reports is that current financially focused annual reports are already very complicated and complex, and adding environmental disclosures would complicate them further. More importantly, by producing a separate environmental report, the organization can signal that it considers environmental disclosures to be as important as financial ones.

ENVIRONMENTAL ASSURANCE AND AUDITING

Environmental assurance is a general term that houses a range of activities that include environmental compliance, company environmental sustainability, environmental risk, and environmental audits. ISO 14010 defines an environmental audit as the systematic and documented verification process of objectively obtaining and evaluating audit evidence to determine whether specified environmental activities, events, conditions, management systems, or information about these matters conform with audit criteria, communicating the results of this process to the client.[62] Conducting an environmental audit will show whether the EMS has been effectively implemented and integrated into the organization's business model. Such audits should be conducted by independent and professionally trained auditors (e.g., Certified Professional Environmental Auditors [CPEA]). ISO 14001 requires the audit to include what is being audited and how often, management and communication of audit results, and how the audits will be performed. Benefits of an environmental audit can include but are not limited to proper compliance with environmental regulations; reduced insurance costs; improved societal view; and a reduction in future and current operation environmental liabilities.

As social and governmental pressures grow, organizations will face increased exposure to environmental obligations through a transformed perspective on environmental sustainability as it is fully integrated into everyday business. Environmental risks are uncertain and can induce significant cost; for example, BP has set aside $20 billion to cover the damage caused by the Deepwater Horizon oil spill in the Gulf of Mexico.[63] Developing an EMS that follows the rigorous certification and audit process provided by the ISO 14000 standards significantly improves an organization's environmental performance. Implementing and maintaining an EMS will help meet future stakeholder demands on environmental sustainability and will reduce associated environmental costs and liabilities.

Knowing the true impact your organization has on the environment can harbor sustainable development into the future. Environmental cost reductions can come from increased local and national community goodwill; reduced number of regulatory audits; and a competitive advantage in a global market through increased efficiencies. An EMS is a monumental achievement and will facilitate proper disclosure of environmental liabilities as well as proper reporting to the public and governmental agencies. Environmental assurance and auditing is expected to lend more credibility and objectivity to environmental disclosures presented in reports. Environmental assurance and auditing can be performed by internal or external auditors and assurance providers.

In the 2011 report "How Sustainability Has Expanded the CFO's Role," Ernst & Young noted that:

> the same standards of third-party assurance that have long been used to validate financial information are increasingly being applied to sustainability reporting as well. Many ratings agencies consider the presence of third-party assurance in their scoring systems.[64]

In Ernst & Young's 2012 survey "Six Growing Trends in Corporate Sustainability," 25 percent of the respondents currently have their sustainability report assured, in part or in whole, by a third party, while another 42 percent plan to do so within five years. Overwhelmingly, the top reason for assurance is to "add credibility to information presented to external stakeholders" (47 percent). Nearly half of those using third-party assurers engage accounting firms (48 percent), while 22 percent engage sustainability consulting firms and 15 percent engage certification firms. NGOs and engineering firms provide assurance services to 4 percent of respondents.[65] Exhibit 9.7 shows CFO's role in sustainability reporting.

CONCLUSION

An organization has several ways in which it can become environmentally sustainable. The organization can follow the pace of laws and regulations set by the government and enforced by federal- and state-level EPAs or it can incorporate an EMS through ISO 14000 or other certification systems. The latter solves problems and goes beyond complying with regulations to stay on the forefront of environmental sustainability. As a result, organizations need to choose whether they are comfortable being in a position of only reacting to government regulation or whether they wish to be more proactive and

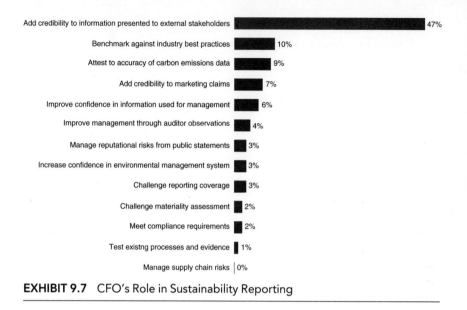

EXHIBIT 9.7 CFO's Role in Sustainability Reporting

anticipatory. Action as opposed to reaction will ease stakeholders' demands on environmental compliance and also reduce audits and litigation from federal regulating bodies. An organization will benefit economically and socially through the implementation and continued use of an EMS that is relevant, accurate, and sustainable in monitoring and developing environmental best practices, missions, and goals.

ACTION**ITEMS**

1. Establish and implement processes for identifying climate-change-related risks and assessing the risks and minimizing their impacts on business operations and financial reports.
2. Be sure to have a climate change policy pertaining to risk assessment and management.
3. Disclose adequate information about the risks posed by climate change and the actions taken in response to understanding of climate change risks.

4. Ensure your organization has a plan to address, assess, reduce, or mitigate its emissions and their impact on operations.

5. Establish and implement compliance processes to keep up with ever-increasing regulatory reforms.

6. Consider the potential high costs of noncompliance with regulatory reforms and related rules, policies, and procedures.

7. Take appropriate steps to engage key constituencies on the topic of climate change and initiatives taken to address its impacts.

8. Address external mandatory compliance initiatives (e.g., Environmental Protection Agency rules and SEC climate change guidance).

9. Address voluntary sustainability initiatives such as GRI reporting framework guidelines.

NOTES

1. Department for Environment, Food and Rural Affairs. 2006. "Environmental Key Performance Indicators Reporting Guidelines for UK Business" (London: Queen's Printer and Controller), 17.

2. Environmental Protection Agency (EPA). 2012. "Introduction: Environmental Enforcement and Compliance," EPA website. Available at: http://www.epa.gov/region9/enforcement/intro.html.

3. U.S. Congress. 1970. The Clean Air Act. Available at: http://www.gpo.gov/fdsys/pkg/USCODE-2008-title42/pdf/USCODE-2008-title42-chap85.pdf.

4. EPA. 2012. "Cleaning Up the Nation's Hazardous Waste Sites," EPA website. Available at: http://www.epa.gov/superfund/index.htm.

5. U.S. Government Accoutability Office. 2010. "Superfund: EPA's Estimated Costs to Remediate Existing Sites Exceed Current Funding Levels, and More Sites Are Expected to Be Added to the National Priorities List." Available at: http://www.gao.gov/products/GAO-10-380.

6. EPA. 2012. "National Priorities List." Available at: http://www.epa.gov/superfund/sites/npl/.

7. EPA. 2012. "Carbon Pollution Standard for New Power Plants," EPA website. Available at: http://epa.gov/carbonpollutionstandard/.

8. Ceres and the Environmental Defense Fund. 2009. "Climate Risk Disclosure in SEC Filing: An Analysis of 10-K Reporting by Oil and Gas, Insurance, Coal, Transportation and Electric Power Companies" June 2009.

9. Ceres, the Environmental Defense Fund, and the Centre for Energy and Environmental, 2009. "Security, Reclaiming Transparency in a Changing Climate: Trends in Climate Risk Disclosure by the S&P 500 from 1995 to the Present."

10. Ernst & Young. 2010. "Action amid Uncertainty: The Business Response to Climate Change." Available at: www.ey.com/GL/en/Services/Specialty-Services/Climate-Change-and-Sustainability-Services/Action-amid-uncertainty--the-business-response-to-climate-change.

11. Securities and Exchange Commission (SEC). 2010. "17 CFR Parts 211, 231 and 241: Commission Guidance Regarding Disclosure Related to Climate Change; Final Rule," *Federal Register* 75(25).

12. Ibid., 6295–96.

13. Ibid., 6293.

14. Ibid., 6296.

15. Ibid., 6296.

16. Fornaro, J.M. 2011. "SEC Guidance on Disclosure Related to Climate Change Overview: Analysis and Consequences for Public Companies, *Journal of Accountancy*. January. Available at: http://www.journalofaccountancy.com/Issues/2011/Jan/20103158.htm.

17. Ceres. 2011. "New Report Outlines What Companies Should Be Disclosing on Climate Change Risks and Opportunities," press release, February 25. Available at: http://www.ceres.org/press/press-releases/new-report-outlines-what-companies-should-be-disclosing-on-climate-change-risks-and-opportunities.

18. Ernst & Young LLP (2010a). Action amid uncertainty: the business response to climate change. (EYG No. DK0054).) (2010, May 21). http://www.ey.com/Publication/vwLUAssets/Action_amid_uncertainty:_the_business_response_to_climate_change/$FILE/Action_amid_uncertainty.pdf.

19. EPA. 2012. "Summaries of Environmental Laws and Eos," EPA website. Available at: http://www.epa.gov/lawsregs/laws/.

20. Holland, L., and Yee Boon Foo. 2003. "Differences in environmental reporting practices in the UK and the US: the legal and regulatory context," Department of Accounting and Finance, De Montfort University: 1–18.

21. Ceres. 2011. "Climate Risk Disclosure by Insurers: Evaluating Insurer Responses to the Naic Climate Disclosure Survey." Available at: http://www.ceres.org/resources/reports/naic-climate-disclosure.

22. United Nations. 1998. "Kyoto Protocol to the United Nations Framework Convention on Climate Change." Available at: http://unfccc.int/resource/docs/convkp/kpeng.pdf.

23. Kyoto Protocol. 2012. Available at: http://www.kyotoprotocol.com/.

24. United Nations Framework Convention on Climate Change (UN FCCC). 2012. "Emissions Trading." Available at: http://unfccc.int/kyoto_protocol/mechanisms/emissions_trading/items/2731.php.

25. United Nations Framework Convention on Climate Change (UNFCC). 2012. "Kyoto Protocol," UNFCC website. Available at: http://unfccc.int/kyoto_protocol/items/2830.php.

26. *Energy and Environmental Management* (EAEM). "'Historic' or 'hollow'? These are the Durban outcomes," December 12, 2011. Available at: http://www.eaem.co.uk/news/historic-or-hollow-these-are-durban-outcomes.

27. European Commission. 2010. "The EU ETS, a system based on the 'cap and trade' principle." Available at: http://ec.europa.eu/clima/policies/ets/index_en.htm.

28. Department of Energy and Climate Change. 2012. "Will the CRC affect my organization?" Available at: http://www.decc.gov.uk/en/content/cms/emissions/crc_efficiency/my_org/my_org.aspx.

29. California Air Resources Board. 2009. "Assembly 32 Fact Sheet." Available at: http://www.arb.ca.gov/cc/factsheets/ab32factsheet.pdf.

30. Ibid.

31. UNFCC. 2006. "Report Indicating Demonstrable Progress toward Achieving the Commitment." Available at: http://unfccc.int/resource/docs/dpr/jpn1.pdf.

32. Government of Canada. 2006. "Canada's Report on Demonstrable Progress Under the Kyoto Protocol—Demonstration of Progress to 2005." Available at: http://unfccc.int/resource/docs/dpr/can1e.pdf.

33. Commission of the European Committees. 2005. "Communication from the Commission—Report on Demonstrable Progress under the Kyoto Protocol." Available at: http://unfccc.int/resource/docs/dpr/eur1.pdf.

34. UK Department for Environment, Food and Rural Affairs. 2006. "Demonstrable Progress: The United Kingdom's Report on Demonstrable Progress under the Kyoto Protocol." Available at: http://unfccc.int/resource/docs/dpr/uk1.pdf.

35. UNFCC website with full list of Annex 1 countries' progress reports. Available at: http://unfccc.int/national_reports/annex_i_natcom/submitted_natcom/items/3625.php.

36. Copenhagen Accord, 7.18. December 2009. "Conference Of The Parties, 15th session Draft Decision-/CP.15."

37. Ibid.

38. United Nations Development Programme. "HCFC phase-out Management Plans." Available at http://www.undp.org/content/undp/en/home/our-work/environmentandenergy/focus_areas/ozone_and_climate/hcfc_phase-out_managementplans.html.

39. Environmental Protection Agency (EPA). 2007. "Achievements in Stratospheric Ozone Protection," *EPA Publication EPA-430-R-07-001*. Available at: http://www.epa.gov/ozone/2007stratozoneprogressreport.html.

40. The United Nations. 2007. "Indicators of Sustainable Development: Guidelines and Methodologies. Third edition." Available at: http://www.un.org/esa/sustdev/natlinfo/indicators/guidelines.pdf.
41. "Indicatiors of Sustainable Development: Guidelines and Methodologies," October 2007, http://www.un.org/esa/sustdev/natlinfo/indicators/guidelines.pdf.
42. World Wildlife Fund (WWF). 2012. "Annual Report 2011." Available at: http://www.worldwildlife.org/who/financialinfo/2011AR/WWFBinaryitem26046.pdf.
43. United Nations Global Compact. 2012. "Overview of the UN Global Compact." Available at: http://www.unglobalcompact.org/AboutTheGC/.
44. United Nations Global Compact. 2012. "The Ten Principles." Available at: http://www.unglobalcompact.org/AboutTheGC/TheTenPrinciples/index.html.
45. United Nations Global Compact. 2012. "Overview of the UN Global Compact." Available at: http://www.unglobalcompact.org/AboutTheGC/.
46. Clean Air Initiative (CAI). 2012. "About Us," The CAI's Clean Air Portal. Available at: http://cleanairinitiative.org/portal/aboutus.
47. Ibid.
48. Clean Air Initiative. 2012. "What We Do," The CAI's Clean Air Portal. Available at: http://cleanairinitiative.org/portal/whatwedo.
49. American Business. 2010. "Coalition for Environmentally Responsible Economies," Available at: http://american-business.org/154-coalition-for-environmentally-responsible-economies.html.
50. The Interfaith Center on Corporate Responsibility (ICCR). 2012. "About ICCR." Available at: http://www.iccr.org/about/.
51. Investor Network on Client Risk (INCR) – Ceres. 2012. "About Us." Available at: http://www.ceres.org/incr/about.
52. International Organization for Standardization (ISO). 2009. "The ISO Survey of Certifications – 2009." Available at: http://www.iso.org/iso/pressrelease.htm?refid=Ref1363.
53. Rezaee, Z., and R. Elam. 2000. "Emerging ISO 14000 environmental standards: a step-by-step implementation guide," *Managerial Auditing Journal* 15 (1/2): 60–67.
54. Apple. 2012. "MacBook Pro and the environment." Available at: http://www.apple.com/macbookpro/environment.html.
55. O'Rourke, D. 2003. "Outsourcing regulation: Analyzing nongovernmental systems of labor standards and monitoring," *Policy Studies Journal* 31: 1–29.
56. Damall, N., and S. Sides. 2008. "Assessing the performance of voluntary environmental programs: Does certification matter?" *Policy Studies Journal* 36: 95–117.

57. Aravind, D., and P. Christmann. 2011. "Decoupling of Standard Implementation from Certification: Does Quality of ISO 14001 Implementation Affect Facilities' Environmental Performance?" *Business Ethics Quarterly* 21(1).

58. Ibid.

59. International Organization for Standardization (ISO). 2011. "ISO 50001." Available at: http://www.iso.org/iso/iso_catalogue/management_and_leadership_standards/specific-applications_energy.htm.

60. Global Reporting Initiative (GRI). 2011. "G3 Sustainability Reporting Guidelines." Available at https://www.globalreporting.org/reporting/latest-guidelines/g3-guidelines/Pages/default.aspx.

61. GRI and CDP. 2011. "Linking GRI and CDP: How are the Global Reporting Initiative and the Carbon Disclosure Project Questions Aligned?" Available at: www.globalreporting.org/resourcelibrary/Linking-GRI-And-CDP.pdf.

62. ISO. 2002. "ISO 14010." Available at: http://www.iso.org/iso/iso_catalogue/catalogue_ics/catalogue_detail_ics.htm?csnumber=23156.

63. BP. 2010. "Update on Gulf of Mexico Oil Spill," press release, June 25, 2010. Available at: http://www.bp.com/genericarticle.do?categoryId=2012968&contentId=7063132.

64. Ernst & Young. 2012. "How Sustainability Has Expanded the CFO's Role," Climate Change and Sustainability Services website. Available at: http://www.ey.com/US/en/Services/Specialty-Services/Climate-Change-and-Sustainability-Services/How-sustainability-has-expanded-the-CFOs-role.

65. Ernst & Young, GreenBiz. 2012. "Six Growing Trends in Corporate Sustainability," 11. Available at: http://www.ey.com/Publication/vwLUAssets/Six_growing/$FILE/SixTrends.pdf.

PART THREE

Emerging Issues in Sustainability Performance, Reporting, and Assurance

CHAPTER TEN

Business Sustainability in Action: Global Initiatives and Emerging Issues

EXECUTIVE**SUMMARY**

Business sustainability has gained a widespread acceptance in the past decade and is now supported by a powerful coalition of forces including senior executives of high-profile global companies and business associations. A number of global initiatives presented in this chapter are relevant to business sustainability and sustainability reporting and assurance. These initiatives provide guidance to organizations in managing the economic, governance, social, ethical, and environmental (EGSEE) dimensions of sustainability standards and are intended to improve product quality, operational effectiveness, and efficiency. They also aim to promote global trade, enhance risk assessment, foster social responsibilities, preserve the environment, strengthen governance, and standardize business sustainability. These initiatives also provide best practices for product quality assurance, risk management, environmental stewardship, governance effectiveness, quality assurance, supply-chain management, socially responsible behavior, balancing trades, strategic decisions, and sustainable performance. This chapter presents practical guidance on business sustainability as well as global initiatives and emerging issues in business sustainability.

INTRODUCTION

Sustainability is gaining momentum and becoming an integral component of corporate strategies. In the third annual "Sustainability & Innovation Global Executive Study" conducted in January 2012, more than 2,800 corporate leaders worldwide indicated that that 31 percent of surveyed companies report that sustainability is contributing to their profits, whereas 70 percent have considered sustainability to be a permanent addition to their management agenda.[1] The survey suggests that business sustainability is gaining momentum in 2012 and onwards, and will continue to be the main theme of corporate boardrooms and executive agendas. Emerging sustainability issues covered in this and coming chapters include:

- The rise of integrated reporting.
- A holistic approach in sustainability reporting on all five EGSEE dimensions of performance.
- Integrated assurance reporting.
- The use of XBRL in sustainability reporting
- The role of continuous auditing in sustainability assurance.
- Success stories in business sustainability developments and strategies.
- The use of sustainability in supply-chain management.
- Best practices of sustainability reporting and assurance.
- The role of corporate gatekeepers in business sustainability.
- Evolving sustainability key performance indicators (KPIs).
- Integrating business sustainability into business education.
- Global development and initiatives in sustainability.

GLOBAL INITIATIVES ON BUSINESS SUSTAINABILITY

Business sustainability is defined in previous chapters as a strategy of designing and implementing business strategies that manage the interests of an organization's stakeholders by generating sustainable performance in all EGSEE dimensions while also sustaining the human and natural resources to be utilized in the future. Business sustainability is affected by many factors including global initiatives and best practices. Corporate sustainability is influenced by participating businesses, which set the bar that others will need to meet or exceed. The benefits of a business sustainability program include: addressing environmental matters, reducing waste, increasing efficiency, reducing risk, improving relations with society, and discouraging regulatory actions. Business sustainability programs provide corporations with the necessary tools to make sustainable products, take proper actions to promote social good, and advance social goals above and beyond creating shareholder value or complying with applicable laws and regulations. Business sustainability programs should also promote a set of actions to advance the social good, going beyond the company's obligation to its various stakeholders.

Business sustainability programs, developments, and activities have evolved and are shaped by many global initiatives, as discussed in the following sections. Numerous global initiatives have developed to enable organizations to establish business sustainability programs to achieve high performance in all EGSEE dimensions.

United Nations Global Compact (UNGC)

The United Nations Global Compact (UNGC) was established on July 26, 2000, in New York.[2] The UNGC is regarded as a global strategic policy initiative for businesses that are committed to aligning their operations and strategies with 10 globally accepted principles in four general categories (i.e., human rights, labor, environment, and anticorruption). The UNGC has grown to include more than 8,000 participants, including over 6,000 businesses in 135 countries around the world. It is a network-based initiative with the Global Compact Office and seven UN agencies at its core.

Exhibit 10.1 presents the four categories of UNGC's initiatives and related principles. All 10 principles of the UNGC are relevant to business sustainability, as they particularly address the social, environmental, and ethical dimensions of sustainability performance.

In addition, the Global Compact serves as the Secretariat for a Climate Change initiative. In 2007 the UNGC initiated Caring for Climate to advance the role businesses have in climate change. The compact provides a framework for organizations, public policy, and social norms related to climate change. It can also support CEOs in developing strategies and practices and to disclose emissions properly.[3]

Organization for Economic Co-operation and Development (OECD)

The Organization for Economic Co-operation and Development (OECD) is a forum of 34 countries, initially founded in 1961 to promote cooperation among member counties and advance democracy and the market economy. OECD's goals include stimulating economic progress and world trade, and establishing a platform to compare policy experiences and best practices.[4]

EXHIBIT 10.1 The United Nations Global Compact (UNGC) Initiatives and Related Principles

Human Rights	
Principle 1	Support and respect the protection of internationally proclaimed human rights.
Principle 2	Make sure that business practices are not complicit in human rights abuses.
Labor	
Principle 3	Uphold the freedom of association and the effective recognition of the right to collective bargaining.
Principle 4	Eliminate all forms of forced and compulsory labor.
Principle 5	Work toward the effective abolition of child labor.
Principle 6	Eliminate discrimination with respect to employment and occupation.
Environment	
Principle 7	Support a precautionary approach to environmental challenges.
Principle 8	Undertake initiatives to promote greater environmental responsibility.
Principle 9	Encourage the development and diffusion of environmentally friendly technologies.
Anti-corruption	
Principle 10	Work against corruption in all its forms, including extortion and bribery.

Source: Adapted from UN Global Compact Principles, available at http://www
.unglobalcompact.org/AboutTheGC/TheTenPrinciples/index.htm.

OECD was originally formed in Europe after World War II as the Organization for European Economic Cooperation (OEEC), but now its member countries extended beyond Europe. The OECD works with the government of its member countries to identify drivers of economic, social, and environmental developments, to assess productivity and global flows of trade and investment, and to examine data to predict future trends. Finally, OECD also suggests best practices and international standards for EGSEE sustainability performance, ranging from governance to environmentally safe use of chemicals and nuclear power plants, to social responsibility, the quality of products, and the well-being of ordinary people.

The OECD contributes to the advancement of business sustainability by assisting its member countries in the following four overriding areas:

1. Improvements in regulation and governance at all levels of political and business life to gain investor confidence and public trust in the global

financial and capital markets that ensure sustainable economic performance worldwide.

2. Establishment of sound and healthy public finances as a basis for future sustainable economic growth.

3. Development of best practices to foster new sources of growth through innovation, economic advances, and environmentally friendly green growth strategies.

4. Development of necessary skills for nations and their citizens to work productively now and meet the job requirements of tomorrow.[5]

Published in 2008, the "OECD Environmental Outlook to 2030" is based on projections of economic and environmental trends to 2030.[6] The key environmental challenges for the future are presented according to a "traffic light" system. The "Outlook" also presents simulations of policy actions to address the key challenges, including their potential environmental, economic, and social impacts.

The 2008 OECD report suggests a list of environmental issues that are considered not be effectively managed including ecosystem fragmentation and quality, water scarcity, urban air quality and hazardous waste management and transportation. The report indicates that much improvement needed in the environmental areas such as road transport emissions, municipal waste generation and GHG emissions Nonetheless, some improvements have been made in environmental initiatives in OECD countries in climate change, water and air quality.

The 2012 Sustainability Practices report published by the Conference Board in July 2012 addressesa total of 72 environmental and social practices such as atmospheric emissions, biodiversity policies water consumption, human rights practices, charitable and political contributions and labor standards.[7] This report indicates that three environmental practices had disclosure rates of more than 50 percent among 3000 U.S and non U.S companies that currently disclose sustainability information. The first most reported environmental practice with a disclosure rate of 64 percent was the adoption of an energy efficiency policy. The implementation of emission-reduction programs was the second most disclosed environmental practice with a disclosure rate of 57 percent. The third most reported environmental practice with a 55 percent disclosure rate was the implementation of a waste reduction policy. Among the least reported environmental practices were the use of the levels of emission of carbon monoxide and recycled water with a disclosure rate of about two percent each. Finally, Companies with less than

$1 billion in annual revenue compared with larger companies had the highestenvironmental footprint score and highest disclosure environmental disclosure rate practices.[8]

Taken together, the major environmental practices most commonly utilized by sustainability disclosing companies addressed in the 2012 Conference Board report are:

1. Energy, electricity, and fuel consumption levels.
2. Water consumption levels and discharge to water.
3. Environmental supply chain and procurement policies.
4. Waste, recycling, and sustainable packaging policies.
5. Reported environmental spills and fines.
6. Atmospheric emissions (e.g., carbon dioxide, nitrogen and sulfuroxides, methane, and other greenhouse gases).[9]

Among all environmental initiatives discussed in the report, management of atmospheric emission, particularly greenhouse gases (GHGs) is considered as the most important priority for government and business worldwide.[10] The risk of GHGs should be assessed effectively and managed properly because GHGs are currently posing significant threats to climate stability that could cause temperature shifts that may change living conditions in many regions of the world. Global companies are taking a range of initiatives to assess and manage theirlevel of emissions including the adoption of production schedule that reduces the need for purchased energy and the use of cutting edge technology that improves the efficient utilization of scarce energy resources.

SOCIAL ACCOUNTABILITY INTERNATIONAL (SAI)

Social Accountability International (SAI) is "a non-governmental, multi-stakeholder organization with the core mission of advancing the human rights of workers around the world."[11] SAI aims to accomplish its goals by promoting ethical workplace practices, fair and equitable employment, and corporate social responsibility (CSR).[12] SAI has developed the SA8000 standard to promote workplace integrity, productivity, and accountability through socially responsible standards and guidance for implementing international labor standards aimed at improving the lives of more than a million workers in 65 countries. SA8000 standards are relevant to business sustainability and address workplace issues by encouraging businesses and consumers to obtain products and services from workplaces that enrich, not denigrate, the livelihoods of people. SA8000 certification covers millions of employees over 2,500 facilities in about 70 countries. AS 8000 standards are voluntary compliance guidelines that assist organizations worldwide to establish locally grounded programs designed to build an enabling environment for labor rights by:[13]

- Fostering local capacity and leadership to encourage worker participation in organization activities and support employer compliance efforts.
- Advancing social dialogue as a foundation for sustainable change.
- Aligning government enforcement with incentive-driven voluntary compliance.

American Society for Quality (ASQ)

American Society for Quality (ASQ) is a global community of experts and the leading authority on quality in all fields, organizations, and industries. ASQ's mission is promoting professional development and improving quality.[14] ASQ activities are intended to:

- Advance professional development, membership community, credentials, knowledge, and information services, as well as advocacy on behalf of its more than 85,000 members throughout the world.
- Strengthen accountability and responsibility to improve quality and productivity, enriching workers' lives, workplaces, and communities to make the world a better place by utilizing quality tools, techniques, and systems.[15]

The International Integrated Reporting Committee (IIRC)

The International Integrated Reporting Committee (IIRC) has brought together world leaders from the fields of investments, corporations, accounting, securities, regulation, standards, academia, civil service, and other professional areas to develop a new approach to sustainability reporting. The IIRC is working to develop a set of globally accepted, uniformed, and standardized sustainability reporting guidelines. The IIRC promotes integrated reporting, aimed at making the link between sustainability and economic value by focusing on interrelationships between all economic, social, environmental, and governance dimensions aspects of sustainability performance. The IIRC has prepared a comprehensive "Discussion Paper on Integrated Reporting (IR)" for public consultation and is planning to release the final version of IR in 2012.[16]

Relevance of ISO Standards to Business Sustainability

The International Organization for Standardization (ISO) is a nongovernmental organization and the world's largest promoter of International Standards, consisting of membership from 162 countries with a Central Secretariat in Geneva, Switzerland.[17] Several ISO standards, from ISO 9000 on quality control to ISO 31000 on risk assessment and management, address business sustainability. These ISO standards collectively offer guidance to organizations in managing all five EGSEE dimensions of sustainability performance. These standards present best practices for quality assurance, supply-chain management, risk assessment and management, balancing trades, strategic decisions, social responsibility fulfillments, and sustainable performance, as described in the following sections.

ISO 9000

The ISO 9000 standards represent an international consensus on good quality management practices designed to improve product quality.[18] ISO 9000 standards are applicable to all organizations—regardless of sizes, type, industry, or location—that are interested to improve the quality of their products and services. ISO 9001 standard is the only standard in the family of ISO 9000 standards against which organizations can be voluntarily certified. The other standards in the family cover vocabulary, performance improvements, documentation, training, and financial and economic aspects.

ISO 14000

The ISO 14000 family addresses various aspects of environmental management, as extensively discussed in Chapter 9.[19] ISO 14001 and 14004 standards specifically address environmental management systems (EMS). The other standards and guidelines in the family discuss specific environmental aspects such as labeling, performance evaluation, life-cycle analysis, communication, and auditing.

ISO 26000

In November of 2010, ISO released its ISO 26000 standards to provide guidelines for social responsibility (SR).[20] ISO 26000 standards are intended to assist organizations to be socially responsible and consist of voluntary guidance, not requirements. Therefore, they are not for use as a certification standard like ISO 9001 and ISO 14000.

ISO 26000 presents globally accepted guidance for social responsibility relevant to all types and sizes of entities, from governmental to non-governmental organizations, private businesses to public companies, and from small to multinational corporations. ISO 26000 also covers a broad range of organizational activities, including economic, social, governance, ethical, and environmental issues. ISO 26000 goes beyond profit-maximization and social performance to cover all EGSEE dimensions of sustainability performance. Social responsibility performance promoted in ISO 26000 is conceptually and practically associated with development of sustainable EGSEE performance because fulfillment of social responsibility necessitates and ensures sustainable development overall.

ISO 26000 standards offer an understanding of what social responsibility is and what organizations need to do to operate in a socially responsible manner by providing guidance on:

- Principles, concepts, definitions, and terms relevant to social responsibility.
- Background, characteristics, trends, and best practices of social responsibility.
- Procedures and practices concerning social responsibility.
- Core issues and subjects pertaining to social responsibility.
- Designing, implementing, promoting, and integrating socially responsible behavior throughout the organization.
- Identifying and engaging with all stakeholders associated with social responsibility.
- Assessing social responsibility performance.
- Communicating commitments, performance, and achievements of social responsibility.[21]

ISO 31000

ISO 31000 was issued in 2009 in response to the perceived lack of risk assessment and management, which is considered a contributing factor to the 2007–2009 global financial crisis. ISO 31000 standards are designed to assist organizations in the development, implementation, assessment, monitoring, and continuous improvement of risk management in all areas of financial, operations, compliance, and reputation.[22] These guidelines, while applicable to all types and sizes of organizations, do not require a one-size-fits-all approach but rather emphasizes the fact that risk assessment and management must be tailored to an organization's risk appetite, structure, and other needs.

ISO 50001

ISO 50001 standards were issued in 2011 and establish a framework to assess and manage energy for industrial plants and institutional, commercial, or governmental, facilities. This framework can also be adapted to an entire organization.[23] ISO 50001 standards are very broad so they are expected to affect the majority of the world's energy use.

MACRO SUSTAINABILITY ISSUES

Today humanity and the businesses we operate are vulnerable to extreme weather and environmental changes driven by the persistently expanding population. (Every day 240,000 more people are born than die.) Changes in the climates in which businesses operate influence business sustainability and they will continue to do so in the future. The following list names just a few of the many challenges that drive the need for sustainability.

- It is likely that the expanding population has increased the loss of free natural resources that businesses rely on (e.g., pollination).[24]
- The world's energy consumption in terms of oil has increased from 76,000 to 87,000 barrels a day between 2000 and 2010.[25]
- The genetic diversity of the world is declining and a large fraction may be lost in the next half century.[26]
- We need to adapt our business practices to mitigate the effects of climate change and reduce the amount of greenhouse gases (GHGs) in the Earth's atmosphere.

Corporations involved in many industries are potentially vulnerable to shortages in natural resources:[27]

- The environment will no longer support businesses that are dependent on increasingly degraded ecosystem services (e.g., where the resource in question cannot be farmed or synthetically manufactured, such as freshwater and tuna).
- Resources that, though associated with agricultural practices, directly contribute to the degradation of ecosystems and species extinction (e.g., palm oil or tropical hardwoods) are becoming increasingly hazardous from a reputation and brand-loyalty perspective.
- Value-added products where the profit obtained in western markets is achieved through levels of production mechanization raise significant

Do you anticipate your company's core business objectives to be affected by natural resource shortages (e.g., water, energy, forest products, rare earth minerals and metals) in the next three to five years?

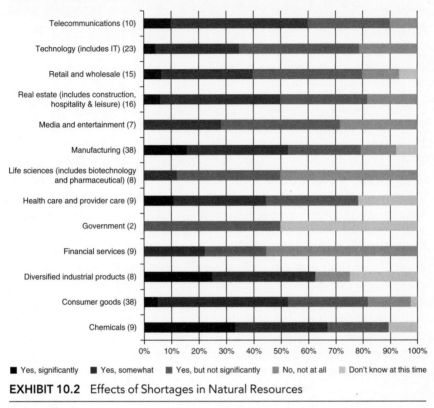

■ Yes, significantly　■ Yes, somewhat　■ Yes, but not significantly　■ No, not at all　▪ Don't know at this time

EXHIBIT 10.2　Effects of Shortages in Natural Resources

ethical concerns (e.g., the manufacture of smartphones and tablet devices or factory-farmed meats).

Exhibit 10.2 presents potential effects of natural resource shortages (e.g., water, energy, forest products, rare earth minerals, and metals) on companies' core business objectives in the next three to five years.

These changes provide incentives and opportunities for local and international governments to intervene and initiate programs and regulations on environmental degradation (e.g., forest controls, mining controls, pollution controls). Specific regulations enacted by the Environmental Protection Agency (EPA) to combat environmental issues are presented in Exhibit 9.3.

Business sustainability coupled with accurate documentation and implementation of voluntary and regulatory environmental practices could potentially mitigate future degradation of the environment while increasing the utility, productivity, and profitability of corporations. Moreover, the single most important problem is that our society is focusing on a single and simple solution to climate change.[28] The earth and its inhabitants are irrevocably intertwined.

CLIMATE CHANGE

Carbon dioxide (CO_2) is the principal greenhouse gas emitted as a result of human activity (e.g., burning of coal, oil, and natural gas) and comprises 9–26 percent of the atmosphere. Other GHGs are: water vapor, excluding clouds (36–70 percent); methane (4–9 percent); and ozone (3–7 percent).[29] Elevated atmospheric CO_2 levels are linked to an increase in atmospheric temperature, which can and will adversely affect weather patterns.[30] Moreover, awareness and subsequent regulations tied to the preservation of the natural environment has begun to influence how corporations perceive and report true economic profits.

Increasing volatility in climate patterns has increased uncertainty about future demand, supply chains, and infrastructure stability. For example, cyclical changes in ocean current and storm propagation have regular and significant impacts on supply-chain and business management.[31] Additionally, the more difficult it is becoming to calculate the costs to productivity as well as demand following storm cycles, which cost the United States roughly $485 billion in 2008 GDP terms.[32] As climate patterns continue to evolve in response to the changing environment, it is critical that business policy and practice evolve with them.

In 2011, the Intergovernmental Panel on Climate Change (IPCC) released its Special Report on Managing the Risks of Extreme Events and Disasters to Advance Climate Change Adaptation (SREX).[33] The SREX addresses many issues, including the relationship between climate change and extreme weather, and the implication of climate events for society and sustainable development. The SREX report suggests that climate extremes, exposure, and vulnerability are affected by many factors including natural climate, variability, anthropogenic climate change, and socioeconomic development. Effective disaster risk management and adaptation to climate change can significantly reduce relevant exposure and vulnerability risks. Disaster risk management is closely related to environmental performance of EGSEE sustainability, which is performed by assessing causes and effects of climate change and how to mitigate risk disaster events and structural inequalities caused by poverty and inefficient uses of natural resources. The focus on disaster risk management can reduce the negative impacts of environmental extremes and thus improve business sustainability performance.

The International Auditing and Assurance Standards Board (IAASB) released its proposed International Standard on Assurance Engagements (ISAE) 3410, "Assurance Engagements on Greenhouse Gas (GHG) Statements," in December of 2010.[34] The proposed ISAE standard allows both *limited* and *reasonable* assurance of GHG engagements. In the case of a *limited* assurance engagement, basic evidence-gathering procedures (e.g., inquiry; analytical procedures) form the basis for reaching conclusions. In the case of a *reasonable* engagement, a much broader range of evidence-gathering procedures, including assessment of risks of material misstatement, are used.

The proposed ISAE 3410 requires the practitioner to choose appropriate evidence-gathering procedures suitable to the circumstances of the engagement based on an assessment of the risk of material misstatement. The timing, extent, and nature of the evidence gathering depend on the type of assurance engagement and, at minimum, should include inquiry and analytical procedures and an assessment of risks of material misstatements in GHG statements. GHG limited assurance engagement requires an understanding and assessment of risk of material misstatement of GHG statements. However, obtaining an understanding of all of the components of the entity's internal control is not required in a limited assurance engagement, although it is required in a reasonable assurance engagement. It should be noted that the skills, knowledge, and experience, as well as the materiality thresholds for misstatements and the preconditions, for a limited assurance engagement are identical to those of a reasonable assurance engagement.

GHG Reporting Trends

Company interest in GHG emissions of their operations and supply chains are driven less by regulatory concern than by three other factors: (1) reputation management, (2) customer expectations, and (3) efficiency goals.

Reputation issues arise when independent organizations rate or rank companies on climate emissions and goals, either separately or as part of a larger corporate rating or ranking scheme. Since the largest part of some companies' carbon footprint can be found in their supply chains, many are pressing suppliers and trading partners to report and reduce their emissions. And many companies recognize that greenhouse gas emissions are a form of waste—a byproduct that has no value to the company or its customers, a proxy for inefficiency. In that vein, reducing greenhouse gas emissions is an efficiency measure. Moreover, emissions are increasingly seen as a risk factor—a liability to a company and

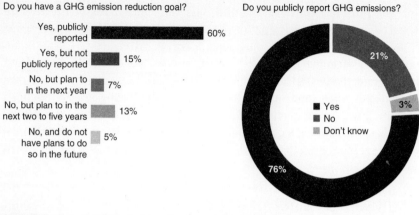

Do you have a GHG emission reduction goal?

Yes, publicly reported — 60%
Yes, but not publicly reported — 15%
No, but plan to in the next year — 7%
No, but plan to in the next two to five years — 13%
No, and do not have plans to do so in the future — 5%

Do you publicly report GHG emissions?

21%
3%
76%

- Yes
- No
- Don't know

EXHIBIT 10.3 GHG Emissions Goals and Reporting

Source: http://www.ey.com/Publication/vwLUAssets/Six_growing/$FILE/SixTrends.pdf, p.18.

its shareholders should public and political climate concerns resurface.[35] Exhibit 10.3 presents GHG emissions goals and reporting.

Water Management

Water management is gaining considerable attention as the 2030 Water Resources Group predicts that the demand for water will outstrip supply by 40 percent by 2030.[36] Deloitte and the Carbon Disclosure Project (CDP) created the 2011 "Water Disclosure Global Report," a study of 354 financial institutions with assets of $43 trillion. The report raised corporate awareness of global water issues and the urgent needs for more effective water management. The study found that:

- About 59 percent of respondents reported water scarcity as a substantial risk to their business.
- More than 69 percent identified opportunities in the efficient use of water and/or revenue from new water-related products or services.
- Water-related issues received less attention (57 percent) than climate-change-related issues (94 percent).
- An increasing number of respondents have been able to provide data regarding their water usage, which suggests more awareness of water issues among respondents.

■ Energy companies reported higher levels of water-related risks and lower levels of broad oversight of water strategies, policies, and procedures.[37]

Interest in reporting on water is also on the rise, especially in water-intensive industries such as metals and mining, oil and gas, chemicals, agriculture, power and utilities, and food and beverage. Sixty-two percent of respondents publicly report their water usage. About one in six of those have had their water footprint verified by an independent third party; 22 percent said they plan to do so within five years.[38] Exhibit 10.4 presents GHG

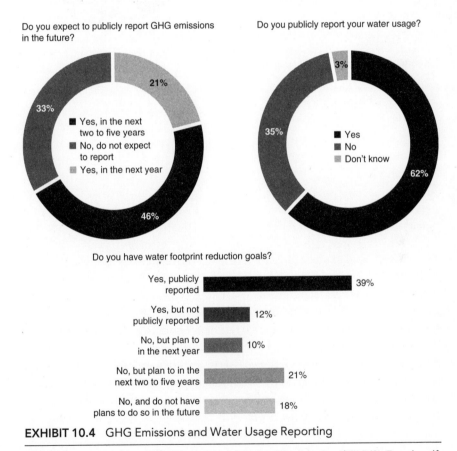

EXHIBIT 10.4   GHG Emissions and Water Usage Reporting

Source: http://www.ey.com/Publication/vwLUAssets/Six_growing/$FILE/SixTrends.pdf, p. 19.

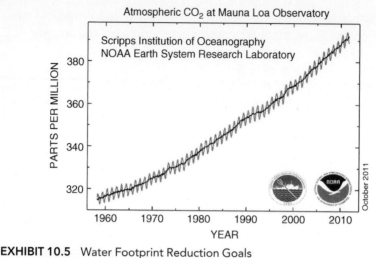

EXHIBIT 10.5 Water Footprint Reduction Goals

Source: "Trends in Atmospheric Carbon Dioxide—Full Mauna Loa CO_2 record," http://www
.esrl.noaa.gov/gmd/ccgg/trends/.

emissions and water usage reporting; Exhibit 10.5 depicts water footprint
reduction goals.

SUSTAINABILITY KPIs

The primary goal of an organization is to operate effectively and efficiently in
generating sustainable performance. Key performance indicators (KPIs) are
measures that are critical to the success of the organization and assessment of
its performance. A key performance indicator (KPI) is a way for an organization to measure its success in reaching its defined goals or objectives. KPIs can
be very useful as a means of assessing an organization's current position and
deciding on new strategies, if necessary. Proper use of KPIs enables an
organization to define its goals, establish metrics to measure its performance,
and track sustainability goals. KPIs are developed to reflect critical success
factors. They typically differ from one organization to another and are
normally classified into financial and nonfinancial KPIs. Financial KPIs
deal with information that can be measured on a monetary basis. Examples
of financial KPIs are sales growth, earnings, return on equity, earnings-per-
share, dividends, and return on assets. Nonfinancial KPIs are relevant

to information that cannot be measured in monetary values. Examples of non-financial KPIs are: information on environmental and social matters, customer satisfaction activities, employee training and turnover, supplier satisfaction, and ethics compliance.

KPIs have traditionally been used to measure progress toward meeting financial goals, such as increasing turnover by 20 percent within six months. Now they are also being used to evaluate activities that are normally difficult to measure. An example would be customer satisfaction, employee participation, waste, efficiency, or CO_2 emissions. KPIs are most effective when used to monitor knowledge-based processes that are measurable. For example, a general goal of increasing the number of returning customers would be hard to measure using KPIs, but a defined goal of increasing the number of returning customers by 15 percent within one year would be measurable. A KPI metric consisting of a defined target, a measurable benchmark, and a specified time frame should be developed to ensure the achievability of the intended goal. KPIs are typically measured in real time, but the results are often assessed continuously so that progress can be measured on a daily, weekly, and yearly basis. KPIs are often derived from raw data. Those that are commonly used by organizations can take one or more of the following forms:

1. *Quantitative indicators* appear in numerical terms, such as the percentage of customers who buy products ever year.
2. *Qualitative indicators* appear in nonnumerical terms such as the effectiveness of corporate governance or corporate reputation.
3. *Practical indicators* interface with existing processes, such as lists of employee capabilities.
4. *Directional indicators* demonstrate improvement or progress (or lack thereof), such as comparing the current month's sales to those of the past several months.
5. *Actionable indicators* reflect an organization's ability to effect change, such as KPIs showing initiatives taken to address climate change.

Checklist for implementing KPIs:

- KPIs should be carefully designed, including all necessary factors to achieve measurable results and effective implementation.
- KPIs should focus on whether an organization is achieving its goals, as stated in its mission.

- KPIs should be linked to each of the five EGSEE dimensions of sustainability performance.
- KPIs should be properly communicated to individuals affected by their implementation.
- KPIs should be focused on meeting the intended goals.
- KPI results should be used as an incentive mechanism to motivate individuals to reach their potentials.
- KPIs should not be used excessively to the points that dilute their effects.
- KPIs should not be used to measure something that is not measurable.

Employees as Key Stakeholders

Employees are an integral part of an organization. They are the laborers and provide the fruits of capitalism. Healthy and happy employees that are deeply established in an organization's cultural norms and support management's goals are crucial for business success. Furthermore, employees with this mindset will tend to stay with their jobs for a longer period of time (reducing turnover), which can help an organization acquire top industry talent. If an organization is not complying with regulations (e.g., environmental) or not staying on the forefront of its business ethics, employees will take their talents elsewhere. Internal regulators and auditors as well as sustainable practices, principles, goals, missions, and visions are essential to maintaining a healthy working environment retaining employees.

Employees are also a part of their local communities. If an organization is doing well, they can commend it, increasing the corporation's public image; however, if an organization is shirking its responsibilities, they can sound the alarms, alerting lobbying parties, lawsuits, and take other actions to retard the growth of the organization in that particular area. With the advent of the Internet, one disgruntled employee can reach far more people than in the past. Organizations are consistently battling with developing a multiple bottom line (MBL) to ensure they are building a sustainable company and keeping a healthy workforce.

A 2012 Ernst & Young survey[39] found that employees are a key driver in a significant number of companies. When asked to rank the top three stakeholder groups driving their company's sustainability initiatives, employees were ranked second (cited by 2 percent of respondents), behind customers (37 percent) and ahead of shareholders (15 percent), policymakers (7 percent) and nongovernmental organizations (7 percent). It's no coincidence that employees have emerged as a key audience for sustainability reports.

Employees can be cheerleaders of their company's sustainability efforts, even when they are cynical of the overall commitment of businesses to reduce their impacts. GreenBiz Group's Green Confidence Index found that in 2009 and 2010 Americans were more than twice as likely to say that the company they worked for was "doing enough" to address environmental issues compared to other companies.[40]

The practice of employee education and engagement on sustainability has spread rapidly and evolved into a more institutionalized element of companies' broad sustainability strategies. This type of engagement isn't the initial driver of most strategies; however, sustainability initiatives can be embraced as an integral part of the company's ethos once employees are involved.

Companies deploy a wide range of tools to increase employee engagement on sustainability issues. Examples include:

- "Treasure hunts" to identify untapped opportunities to reduce waste and energy use.
- Creation of personal sustainability plans.
- Incentives for employees to incorporate sustainability into their everyday lives.
- Earth Day fairs, in which outside organizations set up booths to engage and educate employees.
- Employee awards and recognition programs that provide commendations or cash for employees or teams that make measurable environmental improvements or demonstrate best-in-class practices.[41]

While the tools and techniques for employee engagement vary widely, the benefits are consistently described by companies that implement such programs. Most important, they enhance employee attraction and retention, improve operational efficiencies, strengthen customer relations, increase innovation, and strengthen community ties. Moreover, companies that distribute their sustainability reports broadly with employees find that they often share this information with their families, friends, and neighbors, as well as with customers and suppliers. Employees can become a powerful voice in support of a company sustainability message.

Suppliers

The role of suppliers in business sustainability is important in ensuring the quality and safety of products and services being delivered to customers. The supply chain is arguably one of the most important aspects of an organization's business sustainability. A competent supply-chain management system can yield significant competitive advantages. Wal-Mart, Costco, GE, McDonald's, and others have superior supply chains and therefore have significant influence over their supply chains' sustainability practices, which can be measured through systems such as ISO 14000 or other compliance measures. However, clearly documenting and influencing a whole supply chain to be environmentally sustainable following the same practices as the parent company is difficult. Large organizations wield purchasing power and can influence directly quality control, timing, amounts, and even environmental impact, on a supplier, causing a trickledown effect. Suppliers in industry that is comprised of a few large players, such as the telecom or public utility industries, have to adopt particular environmental standards at higher rates than more fragmented markets.[42] Moreover, direct pressures from stakeholders (regulators, suppliers, industry associations, etc.) have the most influence on an organization's pursuing some form of environmental certification.[43] Other pressures that influence an organization and its supply chain include the industry's general attitude, current position toward environmental sustainability, and other corporate governance issues.

Customers

Customers give direct feedback to organizations and have been demanding products that are recyclable, reliable, user-friendly, environmentally friendly, have a long life expectancy, and are backed up through warranties. This implies that consumers apply more pressure on organizations to conform to an MBL in the short and long term than other market participants, such as commercial customers. As the world's economies flatten out and become one intertwined global market, customers will have more of an impact on international fronts. For example, U.S. customers have been able to influence Chinese companies to adopt and conform to environmental practices like ISO 14000.[44] This is a coercive power, and one that should not be trifled with. Customers have purchasing power; if no one will buy the finished goods, then the business tends to fail. Customers shape the future of products by giving critical feedback to organizations. Social and environmental sustainability has become inherent in many industries such as the automotive industry, where car manufactures have been pressured to engineer more fuel-efficient vehicles and alternative propulsion systems such as pure electric and fuel-cell engines. Some of these changes are coming from regulatory bodies pushed by society's demanding healthy living environments. As the end users of finished goods, customers will have unlimited power through collective establishments (e.g., voting, joining environmental groups, and acting on an individual level) to become environmentally and socially sustainable.

Society

It is the collective efforts of many that can develop voluntary standards such as the ISO series (9000, 14000, and 26000). Leadership in Energy and Environmental Design (LEED), sustainability indicators, and deeper awareness of the intimate relationship humans have with the environment will impact future generations. Global warming is becoming a global issue, and has brought environmental sustainability into the headlines. Nations are being affected by its consequences and have made strides through regulation or voluntary actions to help mitigate the current and long-term effects of climate change. Local communities have the power to put pressure on organizations through voting on local and national ballot measures (elected officials) and involvement with environmental activist groups and non-government organizations (NGOs). Moreover, lawsuits can restrict proposed projects and citizens can attempt to collect damages from unlawful practices. Communities that claim to have an interest in environmental practices tend to use these actions to lobby for compliance with local views and regulations.[45] For example, Portland, Oregon, has a very eco-conscious population and businesses there are urged to build and upgrade to LEED standards; the city also has a comprehensive recycling program. This can be measured using indicators set forth by regulations, local attitudes, demographics, and actions taken to increase the local community's environmental sustainability.[46]

BUSINESS SUSTAINABILITY IN ACTION

Many companies' disclose their financial and nonfinancial information on environmental, social, and governance (ESG) performance. Other names for ESG reports are "financial, social and environmental performance" (Novo Nordisk), "environmental health and safety" (Jardine Engineering Corporation), "corporate social responsibility" (Hitachi Group), "corporate sustainability" (UPS), "corporate responsibility" (UTC), "sustainability" (Duke Energy), and "corporate citizenship" (Novartis). Further adding to the confusion, for some companies a "corporate social responsibility" report is largely about its philanthropic activities (The Boeing Company).

Companies that are considered leaders in promoting business sustainability all have several best practices in common. For example, FedEx in its recent sustainability/CSR reports, indicates that it is committed to sustainably connecting the world, creating shareholder value, serving its customers, assessing its environmental impact, using innovation and technology to improve operations, using natural resources efficiently, and contributing to society. Wal-Mart's business sustainability hinges on "saving people money so they can live better." It focuses on a culture of integrity, respect for individuals, service to customers, and striving for excellence. Exhibit 10.6 presents a sample of business sustainability, assurance, and reporting practices currently employed by some companies worldwide.

LESSONS LEARNED FROM SUSTAINABILITY

There are many ways to develop and implement sustainability practices. A few strategies are:

1. Integrate sustainability strategies in all corporate plans, decisions, actions, and reporting.
2. Obtain commitment to business sustainability from the board of directors and senior executives.
3. Adopt the most suitable business sustainability policies and practices, as there is no one-size-fits-all approach to business sustainability strategies.
4. Incorporate sustainability reporting and assurance into overall corporate reporting, including annual reports filed with regulators or furnished to shareholders.
5. Use a bottom-up approach in promoting business sustainability throughout the organization by providing incentives in achieving EGSEE sustainability performance.
6. Identify and utilize both internal and external drivers of business sustainability.
7. Integrate key sustainability drivers into business sustainability strategies.
8. Communicate sustainability initiatives, policies, and procedures to all employees throughout the organization and require compliance with the policies.
9. Obtain assurance on sustainability reports from an independent, qualified assurance provider.
10. Provide sustainability trainings for executives and employees.

EXHIBIT 10.6 A Sample of Global Companies with 2011 Sustainability Reporting and Assurance

Company	Report Link	Content	Assurance
Brown Forman		KPIs on environmental performance to protect the environment by reducing waste and gas emissions, and energy, ecological resources, and water consumed by 30 percent.	NO
Cabot Corporation		KPIs on environmental, social, and economic performance by taking advantage of the latest technology to improve by 50 percent.	NO
The Campbell Soup Company		KPIs on economic, social, environmental, and governance performance by advancing global wellness and nutrition; developing a more sustainable environment; honoring their social role; improving the approach on how to conduct business, building employee engagement; creating positive social impacts; enabling operational efficiency; reducing costs; fostering innovation; strengthening relationships with customers; and creating a business advantage over the long term.	NO, but going to seek external assurance
Coca-Cola	http://www.thecoca-colacompany .com/sustainabilityreport/ TCCC_2010_2011_GRI_Report.pdf	KPIs on ethics, governance, environment, economic, social, and supply chain performance by improving Coca-Cola System for water stewardship, energy efficiency, climate protection, sustainable packaging, healthy communities, governance and ethics, and stakeholder engagement.	Reasonable Assurance
John Deere	http://www.deere.com/en_US/ docs/html/corporate/ 2011_global_citizenship_report/ index.html	KPIs on environmental, operational, and economic performance by continuing to produce and develop products and solutions according to sustainable standards and practices; reducing water and energy waste and greenhouse gas emission; using LEED criteria in offices and buildings evaluation.	NO
Duke Energy	http://www.duke-energy.com/ sustainability/sustainability-reports .asp	KPIs on environmental, social, economic, and governance performance by managing resources (water, air, energy); minimizing emission, waste, and oil spills; contributing to build strong communities; safe work	NO

(continued)

EXHIBIT 10.6 (Continued)

Company	Report Link	Content	Assurance
		environments for employees; energy saving program; delivering affordable energy for customers; staying profitable; and demonstrating strong governance and transparency.	
FedEx	http://about.van.fedex.com/citizenship_report	KPIs on environmental, social, and economic performance by paying attention to emission; reducing the impact on planet (water waste, using solar energy, planting trees, control emission); charity work; involvement in education; optimized transportation process (less time, quick delivery); switching to electrical machines; maximized recycling; and active involvement in social responsibility.	Reasonable Assurance
Microsoft	http://download.microsoft.com/download/E/8/7/E879B21A-1FB9-4820-98A7-C9978071AF99/Microsoft_2011_Citizenship_Report.pdf	KPIs on supply-chain, environmental, social, and governance performance by strengthened monitoring and managing; promoting human rights; and continuing leadership in corporate governance, compliance, and political involvement.	Reasonable Assurance
Procter & Gamble	http://www.pg.com/en_US/sustainability/reports.shtml	KPIs on environmental, supply-chain, and social performance by replacing petroleum-based materials with sustainably sourced renewable materials; cold water washing; packaging reduction, reducing consumer solid waste; renewable energy powering plants; manufacturing waste to landfill; truck transportation reduction.	Reasonable Assurance
Xerox	http://www.xerox.com/about-xerox/citizenship/enus.html	KPIs on social and environmental performance by creating a healthy and safe environment for their employees; staying focused on how to do high-quality business and how to deliver high-quality services; improving the usage of energy and water; reducing waste and gas emissions; and recycling is their primary methods for ensuring compliance with corporate policies and goals.	NO
Wal-Mart	http://walmartstores.com/download/4887.pdf	KPIs on environmental, social, governance, and ethics performance by designing its own environmental management system (EMS) and monitoring and managing all areas of EGSEE.	Reasonable Assurance

11. Infuse sustainability objectives and accomplishments into the annual evaluation of the performance process for the board of directors, executives, and employees.

12. Continuously monitor and improve sustainability strategies, policies, procedures, and practices.

13. Promote grassroots sustainability initiatives—when customers demand sustainable products and when employees are sustainability-oriented—through executive focus on sustainable and enduring performance.

14. Promote voluntary commitments to business sustainability initiatives rather than mandatory enforcement of sustainability measures.

15. Produce an integrated and comprehensive sustainability report on all five EGSEE dimensions of performance.

16. Obtain assurance of all five EGSEE dimensions of sustainability performance.

17. Constantly communicate commitment to sustainability performance, reporting, and assurance to all stakeholders.

EMERGING ISSUES IN SUSTAINABILITY

Sustainability is evolving and, as such, many of its issues are emerging. A 2012 survey conducted by Ernest & Young shows that:

1. The three key stakeholders who drive sustainability initiatives are customers (37 percent), employees (22 percent); and shareholders (15 percent).

2. More than 66 percent of 269 respondents reported that they have received sustainability-related inquiries from their investors in the past 12 months.

3. The top five ranked sustainability issues by participants are greenhouse gas emissions (GHG) reduction (70 percent), efforts to reduce energy consumption (70 percent), publishing a sustainability report (51 percent), producer responsibility for recycling of products and/or packaging (42 percent), and working conditions/human rights issues (40 percent).

4. The top three means of communicating sustainability performance and initiatives are company website/communications (83 percent), sustainability reports (77 percent), and active response to sustainability ratings agency surveys (55 percent).

5. The majority of respondents (78 percent) considered sustainability rankings/ratings important; the majority of respondents (76 percent) are currently issuing sustainability reporting.

6. The reported top five challenges in producing sustainability reports are access to data (32 percent), budget constraints (18 percent), determining materiality (14 percent), credibility of data (10 percent), and lack of audience interested in sustainability reports (10 percent);

7. The majority of respondents (75 percent) are using the GRI framework for their sustainability reporting; only a small portion (25 percent) of respondents reported that they have their sustainability reports assured by third-party providers (accounting firms, sustainability consulting firms, and certification firms).

8. The top three reasons for obtaining a third-party assurance on sustainability reports are lending credibility to the information presented to external stakeholders (47 percent), benchmarks against industry best practices (10 percent); and attestation to the accuracy of carbon emissions data (9 percent).

9. The top five perceived important audiences of sustainability reports are customers (21 percent), employees (18 percent), shareholders (15 percent), analysts (13 percent); and NGOs (13 percent); the majority of participants reported that their CFO is either somewhat involved in sustainability reporting (52 percent) or is not involved (35 percent).

10. The most important drivers of sustainability agenda in the near future will be cost reduction (74 percent), stakeholders' expectations (68 percent), managing risk (61 percent), revenue generation (56 percent), and government regulation (37 percent); the most important factors driving sustainability agendas are energy costs (93 percent), changes in customer demand (87 percent), brand risk (87 percent), increased stakeholder expectations (86 percent), competitive threats (81 percent), revenue generation opportunities (80 percent), potential regulations (73 percent), and investor engagements (65 percent).

11. The majority of respondents are expecting their future sustainability budgets to either increase (53 percent) or remain the same (39 percent).[47]

A 2012 KPMG study reports 10 emerging megaforces or challenges of sustainability as follows:[48]

1. **Climate Change:** Annual output losses from climate change are predicted to be in the range of 1 to 5 percent.

2. **Energy and Fuel:** An ever-increasing demand for energy and fuel along with growing uncertainty about fuel supply is likely to increase fossil fuel markets' volatility.

3. **Material Resource Scarcity:** Global demand for scarce material resources is expected to increase as industrialization and world population continue to grow.

4. **Water Scarcity:** It is expected that the global demand for freshwater will exceed supply by 40 percent by 2030 which will cause shortages in quality and quantity of water.

5. **Population Growth:** The world population is predicted to grow to 8.4 billion by 2032, which provides businesses with both challenges and opportunities to address the multifaceted needs of the growing population.

6. **Wealth:** The global middle class is expected to grow 172 percent between 2010 and 2030 because of globalization, industrialization, and technological advances.

7. **Urbanization:** The majority of people are expected to live in cities by 2030, which demands access to urban civilizations.

8. **Food Security:** The expected population growth and continuous depletion of scarce resources in the next two decades will contribute to substantial increases in food prices (70 to 90 percent by 2030).

9. **Ecosystem Decline:** The expected substantial decline in ecosystems will make natural resources scarcer, more expensive, and less diverse.

10. **Deforestation:** It is expected that forest areas will decline globally by 13 percent from 2005 to 2030, and thus availability of forests products (i.e., wood) will significantly decrease in the future.

A 2012 report by PWC provides seven reasons why investors should pay attention to sustainability performance and reporting.[49] These reasons are:

1. **Shareholder sustainability resolutions are gaining traction:** There has been a steady growth in shareholder resolutions on environmental and social dimensions of sustainability performance (20 percent in 2011, compared with 18.1 percent in 2010 and 16.3 percent in 2009). This trend of investor interest in climate change is expected to increase as investors better understand and appreciate the risks associated with economic, governance, social, and environmental activities and performance and their impacts on overall business strategies.

2. **Steady growth in sustainability investment:** Sustainable and responsible investing has significantly increased in the United States during the past 15 years, accounting for about 12.2 percent of total $25.2 trillion investment in 2011.

3. **Studies show positive correlation between environmental, social, and governance sustainability performance and financial performance:** Firms that engage in sustainability activities have experienced better stock performance, lower volatility, and higher return on investment and return on equity.

4. **Financial services firms establish sustainability research departments:** The Sustainability Investment Research Analyst Network (SIRAN) covers more than 50 investment firms and supports about 260 financial analysts in providing sustainability information.

5. **Availability of sustainability indices:** Several financial service providers (e.g., Thomson Reuters, MSCI, Bloomberg) supply both financial and sustainability data, as well as comparison analysis and impact monitoring and valuation tools.

6. **Use of EGSEE sustainability performance data:** Investors are now more receptive to use EGSEE sustainability performance data in their investment decisions, according to data provided by Bloomberg Terminal.

7. **Growing interest in sustainability information by institutional investors:** Institutional investors including banks, asset managers, pension funds, foundations, and insurance companies now show more interest in sustainability information, including climate-change risk disclosure.

CONCLUSION

All organizations—regardless of size, industry, or location—can benefit from business sustainability initiatives, strategies, and practices by improving EGSEE performance; creating sustainable shareholder value; and managing interests of other stakeholders, including creditors, employees, suppliers, government, society, and environment. Organizations that effectively manage their business sustainability, improve EGSEE performance, and enhance reputation can also reap other benefits like cost engineering and efficiency, effective utilization of scarce resources, stronger regulatory compliance, fulfilled social responsibility, improved governance, and a corporate culture of integrity and competency.

ACTIONITEMS

1. Make sure internal and external corporate governance mechanisms are in compliance with all applicable laws, rules, regulations, standards, and best practices.
2. Consider changes in your corporate governance in the aftermath of the 2007–2009 global financial crisis.
3. Make sure your sustainability reporting is in compliance with the GRI reporting framework guidelines.
4. Ensure compliance with sustainability rules, regulations, standards, and best practices.
5. Integrate sustainability initiatives into your strategic decisions, actions, and performance measurements.

NOTES

1. Boston Consulting Group (BCG).2012. "Nearly a third of companies say sustainability is contributing to their profits, says MIT Sloan Management Review-Boston Consulting Group report," press release, January 24, 2012. Available at: http://www.bcg.com/media/PressReleaseDetails.aspx?id=tcm:12-96246.
2. United Nations Global Compact (UNGC). 2000. "About Us." http://www.unglobalcompact.org/AboutTheGC/TheTenPrinciples/index.html.
3. UNGC. 2012. "Environment: Caring for Climate."Available at: http://www.unglobalcompact.org/issues/environment/climate_change/.
4. Organization for Economic Co-operation and Development (OECD). 2012. "History." Available at: http://www.oecd.org/document/25/0,3746, en_36734052_36761863_36952473_1_1_1_1,00.html.
5. Ibid.
6. OECD. 2008. "Environmental Outlook to 2030." Available at: http://www.oecd.org/dataoecd/29/33/40200582.pdf.
7. The Conference Board. 2012. Sustainability Practices: 2012 Edition (July 2012). Available at www.conferenceboard.org.
8. Ibid.
9. Ibid.
10. Ibid.
11. Social Accountability International (SAI). 2012. "About SAI." Available at: http://www.sa-intl.org/index.cfm?fuseaction=Page.ViewPage&pageId=472.

12. Ibid.
13. Ibid.
14. American Society for Quality (ASQ). 2012. "About ASQ." Available at: http://asq.org/about-asq/who-we-are/index.html.
15. Ibid.
16. International Integrated Reporting Committee (IIRC). 2010. "Integrated Reporting Academic Network Response to IR Discussion Paper December 2011." Available at: http://www.theiirc.org/wp-content/uploads/2012/02/Global-Integrated-Reporting-Academic-Network-United-Kingdom.pdf.
17. International Organization for Standardization (ISO). n.d. ISO website. Available at: http://www.iso.org/iso/home.html.
18. International Organization for Standardization (ISO). n.d. "ISO 9000 Essentials." Available at: http://www.iso.org/iso/iso_catalogue/management_and_leadership_standards/quality_management/iso_9000_essentials.htm.
19. International Organization for Standardization (ISO). n.d. "ISO 14000 Essentials." http://www.iso.org/iso/iso_catalogue/management_and_leadership_standards/environmental_management/iso_14000_essentials.htm.
20. International Organization for Standardization (ISO). 2010. "ISO 26000 Standards." Available at: http://www.iso.org/iso/iso_catalogue/management_and_leadership_standards/social_responsibility/sr_iso26000_overview.htm#sr-1.
21. Ibid.
22. International Organization for Standardization (ISO). 2009. "ISO 31000: Risk Management–Principles and Guidelines." Available at: http://www.iso.org/iso/iso_catalogue/management_and_leadership_standards/risk_management.htm.
23. International Organization for Standardization (ISO). 2011."ISO 50001: Energy Management." Available at: http://www.iso.org/iso/iso_catalogue/management_and_leadership_standards/specific-applications_energy.htm.
24. Diamond, J. 2005. *Collapse: How Societies Choose to Fail or Succeed* (New York: Viking), 489.
25. BP. 2011. "BP Statistical Review of World Energy: June 2011." Available at: http://www.bp.com/assets/bp_internet/globalbp/globalbp_uk_english/reports_and_publications/statistical_energy_review_2011/STAGING/local_assets/pdf/statistical_review_of_world_energy_full_report_2011.pdf.
26. Diamond, J. 2005. *Collapse: How Societies Choose to Fail or Succeed* (New York: Viking), 488.
27. Ernst & Young, GreenBiz. 2012. "Six Growing Trends in Corporate Sustainability," 18–19. Available at: Available at: http://www.ey.com/Publication/vwLUAssets/Six_growing/$FILE/SixTrends.pdf.
28. Diamond, J. 2005. *Collapse: How Societies Choose to Fail or Succeed* (New York: Viking), 498.

29. Environmental Protection Agency (EPA). n.d. "Atmosphere Changes," EPA website. Available at: http://www.epa.gov/climatechange/science/recentac .html.
30. National Oceanic and Atmospheric Administration (NOAA). n.d. "What Is an El Niño?" NOAA website. Available at: http://www.pmel.noaa.gov/tao/ elnino/el-nino-story.html.
31. Lazo, J.K., M. Lawson, P.H. Larsen, and D.M. Waldman. 2011. "U.S. Economic Sensitiviy to Weather Variability." *Bulletin of the American Meteorological Society* (June): 709. Available at: http://journals.ametsoc.org/doi/pdf/ 10.1175/2011BAMS2928.1.
32. Ibid.
33. Intergovernmental Panel on Climate Change (IPCC). 2011. "Special Report on Managing the Risks of Extreme Events and Disasters to Advance Climate Change Adaptation (SREX)." Available at: http://ipcc-wg2.gov/SREX/report/.
34. International Auditing and Assurance Standards Board (IAASB). 2010. "Proposed International Standard on Assurance Engagements (ISAE) 3410: Assurance Engagements on Greenhouse Gas Statements." Available at: www.ifac.org/sites/default/files/publications/exposure-drafts/20110111-ISAE_3410_GHG_Exposure_Draft-V1-final.pdf.
35. Ernst & Young, GreenBiz. 2012. "Six Growing Trends in Corporate Sustainability," 18–19. Available at: http://www.ey.com/Publication/vwLUAssets/ Six_growing/$FILE/SixTrends.pdf.
36. Deloitte and Carbon Disclosure Project (CDP). 2011. "Water Disclosure Global Report." Available at: http://www.deloitte.com/view/en_US/us/Services/ additional-services/sustainability-climate-change/ 97fc3321602b3310VgnVCM3000001c56f00aRCRD.htm.
37. Ibid.
38. Ernst & Young, GreenBiz. 2012. "Six Growing Trends in Corporate Sustainability," 18–19. Available at: http://www.ey.com/Publication/vwLU Assets/Six_growing/$FILE/SixTrends.pdf.
39. Ibid.
40. Ernst & Young, GreenBiz. 2012. "Six Growing Trends in Corporate Sustainability," 18–19. Available at: http://www.ey.com/Publication/vwLU Assets/Six_growing/$FILE/SixTrends.pdf
41. Ibid.
42. Delmas, M., and M.W. Toffel. 2004. "Stakeholders and Environmental Management Practices: An Institutional Framework," *Business Strategy and the Environment* 13: 209–222. Available at: http://onlinelibrary.wiley .com/journal/10.1002/%28ISSN%291099-0836.
43. Kollman, K., and A. Prakash. 2002. "EMS-based environmental regimes as club goods: examining variations in firm level adoption of ISO 14001 and EMAS in U.K., U.S. and Germany," *Policy Sciences* 35: 43–67.

44. Christmann, P., and G. Taylor. 2001. "Globalization and the environment: Determinants of firm self-regulation in China," *Journal of International Business Studies* 32: 439–58.

45. Maxwell, J.W., T.P. Lyon, and S.C. Hackett, 2000. "Self-regulation and social welfare: The political economy of corporate environmentalism," *The Journal of Law and Economics* 43: 583–619.

46. Delmas, M., and M.W. Toffel. 2004. "Stakeholders and Environmental Management Practices: An Institutional Framework," *Business Strategy and the Environment* 13: 209–22. Available at: http://onlinelibrary.wiley .com/journal/10.1002/%28ISSN%291099-0836.

47. Ernst & Young, GreenBiz. 2012. "Six Growing Trends in Corporate Sustainability," p.6 Available at: http://www.ey.com/Publication/vwLUAssets/ Six_growing/$FILE/SixTrends.pdf.

48. KPMG. 2012. "Sustainability Megaforces Impact on Business Will Accelerate," press release, February 14, 2012. Available at: http://www.kpmg.com/ Global/en/IssuesAndInsights/ArticlesPublications/Press-releases/Pages/ sustainability-megaforces-impact.aspx.

49. PricewaterhouseCoopers (PwC). 2012. "Do investors care about sustainability? Seven trends provide clues." Available at: http://cfodirect.pwc.com/ CFODirectWeb/Controller.jpf?ContentCode=KOCL-8SSLSC&SecNavCode-ASPP-4NHLQD&ContentType=Content.

CHAPTER ELEVEN

The Future of Business Sustainability: Sustainability Reporting and Assurance

EXECUTIVE**SUMMARY**

B usiness sustainability is a process of creating sustainable value for all stakeholders by focusing on profit, planet, and people. Sustainability reporting and assurance is an evolving corporate practice with significant potential to improve the transparency and reliability of information for investors and stakeholders. Many global professional organizations including the Global Reporting Initiative (GRI) and the International Integrated Reporting Committee (IIRC) are working to develop a set of globally accepted, uniform, and standardized sustainability reporting guidelines. The GRI initially focused on a triple bottom line of economic, social, and environmental performance, with version 3.1 (also the third generation or G3) of its sustainability framework. The fourth generation (G4) will cover economic, governance, social, and environmental performance.

INTRODUCTION

The existing sustainability reports are rather complex and unstandardized. They are composed of disclosures of both voluntary and mandatory information on some aspects of economic, global, social, ethical, and environmental (EGSEE) sustainability performance dimensions, and typically encouraged by GRI guidance. The IIRC promotes integrated reporting aimed at solidifying the link between sustainability and economic value by focusing on the interrelationships between the economic, social, environmental, and governance dimensions of business performance. The ever-increasing use of sustainability reporting drives a need for assurance on the disclosed sustainability information. This chapter presents emerging challenges and opportunities in business sustainability and the related sustainability reporting and assurance.

THE EMERGENCE OF BUSINESS SUSTAINABILITY

We define business sustainability in Chapter 1 as the process of moving away from a short-term focus on profitability to a business model based on generating sustainable economic performance while also achieving social, governance, ethical, and environmental performance. This business sustainability model focuses on strategic decisions that create sustainable shareholder value while managing and protecting the interests of a broader range of stakeholders, including creditors, customers, suppliers, employees, environment, government, and society. Business sustainability is a journey intended to provide organizations with the appropriate strategies to offer sustainable products and services; manage the organization's affairs and activities effectively; take proper actions to promote social good; promote ethical culture; and preserve the environment.

Business sustainability is based on the premise that considering the impact of a company's operations on the community, society, and the environment is entirely consistent with the traditional mission of making a profit. A 2011 survey of global executives reports that:

- A majority (over 75 percent) of more than 4,700 executives said sustainability-related strategies are necessary to be competitive
- More than 68 percent of respondents believed that their commitment to sustainability has increased, compared to 59 percent in 2010 and 25 percent in 2009.
- Over 74 percent expected that their sustainability commitments would increase in the future.
- Nearly 50 percent said that their sustainability commitments could influence their employment choices.[1]

Companies can only survive and generate sustainable performance when they continue to be profitable and are able to create shareholder value. Nonetheless, all five sustainability performance (EGSEE) dimensions supplement each other and are not mutually exclusive. Companies that are governed effectively are, by default, conducted ethically, and are socially and environmentally responsible.

The International Integrated Reporting Committee (IIRC) emphasizes the relevance and importance of sustainability and the link between sustainability and economic value by promoting the concept of integrated thinking to the way a company views and manages its business. As result of this integrated thinking, a company is then in a position to create reporting that provides information regarding financial, social, governance, and environmental strategies and performance. This supports the needs of long-term investors by reflecting the broader and longer-term consequences of the decisions corporations make.[2] Sustainability reporting focuses on all five EGSEE dimensions of sustainability performance (affecting long-term firm value); however, other than the financial dimension, these are largely ignored by the current financial reporting process. The interest in business sustainability is growing, as evidenced by a 2010 UN Global Compact/ Accenture CEO study, which finds that over 93 percent of the participants (766 CEO worldwide) reported sustainability as an "important" or "very important" factor for their organizations' future success. The study also found that more than 81 percent said that sustainability issues are now integrated into their organization's strategy and operations.[3] Ioannou and Serafeim have conducted several studies regarding value-relevance of business sustainability to investment decisions and conclude that, in the earlier periods of sustainability disclosures (1993–1997), sustainability was viewed by analysts as value-destroying, whereas in recent periods (1997 onwards), sustainability has been regarded as value-creating.[4]

Sustainable development has become an integral component of business strategies in creating shareholder value and protecting the interests of other stakeholders. Sustainability strategies can assist in improving operational efficiencies and reducing costs, mitigating risks, and identifying future revenue opportunities. Deloitte has established sustainability strategies 1.0 and 2.0 to assist organizations in creating value by embracing opportunities and managing risks from economic, social, and environmental developments, integrating sustainability into their supply-chain management and using sustainability development to drive innovation and long-term strategies.[5]

Deloitte pinpoints the three aspects of innovation as cost leadership, quality/performance, and speed to market; they suggest the following ways that sustainability can drive innovations:

1. Commodity and raw material availability and use: Maximize the utilization of scarce resources.
2. Energy consumption and cost: Minimize the risk of unnecessary energy depletion.
3. Emissions and waste: Reduce waste and minimize the cost of greenhouse gas emission.
4. Water availability and quality: Use water resources efficiently.
5. Demand for sustainable products: Promote sustainable products.[6]

The business sustainability model presented in this section is consistent with the "Sustainability Framework" of the International Federation of Accountants (IFAC), which addresses four perspectives:

1. The business strategy perspective, which focuses on the achievement of long-term strategic decisions, objectives, goals, and performance.
2. The internal management perspective, which focuses on directing and integrating management activities to ensure sustainability performance.
3. The investors' perspective, which focuses on effective communications with shareholders regarding sustainability performance.
4. The stakeholders' perspective, which focuses on presenting both financial and nonfinancial sustainability key performance indicators (KPIs), as well as providing sustainability assurance on disclosed sustainability information.[7]

SUSTAINABILITY REPORTING

The coverage, format, and content of sustainability reporting are evolving. The terms: "environmental, social and governance (ESG) reporting," "risk compliance and governance (RCG)," "corporate social responsibility (CSR) reporting," "integrated reporting," and "sustainability reporting" have historically been used interchangeably to describe corporate and accountability reports. Moreover, these terms have a wide range of coverage on financial and nonfinancial KPIs pertaining to economic, risk, compliance, environmental, social, and governance issues.

The GRI defines sustainability reporting as "the practice of measuring, disclosing, and being accountable to internal and external stakeholders for organizational performance towards the goal of sustainable development."[8] The GRI's sustainability reporting framework consists of reporting principles, guidelines, sector supplements, and technical protocols. In this book we focus on the five EGSEE dimensions of sustainability performance, three of which (economic, social, and environmental) are already covered in G3.1. The governance and ethics sustainability performance dimensions are under consideration and will be developed by the GRI in its G4, which is slated to be implemented in 2013. The fourth generation of GRI guidance will be more comprehensive in covering all five EGSEE dimensions of sustainability performance. The coverage of governance and ethics sustainability performance is as important as the three sustainability dimensions addressed in the G3 for four reasons:

1. The existence and persistence of financial scandals and crises demonstrate lapses in the corporate governance and culture related to ethical behavior and actions.
2. Regulators, policymakers, and standard-setters worldwide are promoting ethical behavior and the establishment of codes of business conduct for public companies.
3. Ethics and compliance is becoming an integral component of corporate reporting.
4. New corporate governance measures and reforms have been designed in the aftermath of the 2007–2009 global financial crisis to improve corporate governance effectiveness in preventing further crises.

Importance of Sustainability Reporting

The widening focus on sustainable performance and long-term value-adding strategies has driven a need for new reporting and accountability structures that extend beyond conventional financial statements into nonfinancial KPIs based on all aspects of the firm. Conventional corporate reporting has traditionally presented KPIs based on historical financial statements. Historical financial KPIs have been used by investors and other users of corporate reports to assess future earnings and cash flows. Recently, corporations are disclosing more forward-looking financial information about their strategic performance and selected nonfinancial KPIs (e.g., social responsibility, governance) through their management discussion and analysis (MD&A) to make corporate reports more relevant to all stakeholders, including shareholders. Nonetheless, diverse stakeholders have demanded more financial and nonfinancial KPIs regarding economic, governance, social, and environmental issues.

In the first decade of the 21st century, significant progress has been made in sustainability reporting. The IIRC was established in August 2010 to develop an integrated reporting framework aimed at making the link between sustainability and economic value by managing sustainability performance and disclosing sustainability information.[9] In July 2011, the Singapore Exchange (SGX) released its sustainability reporting guidance framework, requiring newly listed companies to disclose accountability for their operations and to conduct business in a sustainable manner. This guidance presents principles intended to assist listed companies to evolve their conventional financial reports to include sustainability reporting.[10]

Sustainability reporting is evolving and its adoption has made significant progress during the past decade. In 2000, about 44 companies followed the GRI guidelines to disclose sustainability information, whereas in 2010, the number of sustainability reports grew to 1,973; as of September 2011, more than 3,000 global companies disclosed sustainability information.[11] As business sustainability gains more attention and more organizations worldwide issue sustainability reports, there is an urgent need to converge the various types of sustainability and CSR reports under one globally accepted and uniformly practiced caption preferably "sustainability reporting." Sustainability reporting can be used for internal purposes and external reporting. Internally, it is used for managing and reporting on the achievement of sustainability development, performance benchmarking, and evaluation. Externally, sustainable reporting is used for decision-making purposes by all stakeholders, including investors, and to ensure compliance with all applicable laws, rules, regulations, and standards.

A recent survey sponsored by the Investor Responsibility Research Center (IRRC) Institute in conjunction with the National Association for Environmental Management (NAEM) indicates that:

- Investors, companies, and regulators are increasingly interested in sustainability issues pertaining to governance, social, and environmental performance and their potential impacts on firm value.
- Investors often complain about difficulties in obtaining meaningful sustainability information on EGSEE performance.
- Companies are concerned about survey fatigue and the potential cost of providing sustainability information.[12]

The survey also documents that the following six key points:

1. There is no consistency among companies in capturing, storing, and disclosing sustainability information, which is tracked at different levels and details.
2. The overriding derivers of managing and reporting sustainability disclosures (metrics) are common business-sense fundamentals of feasibility, business reputation, customer satisfaction, and potential impacts.
3. Sustainability reporting should present information on strategic sustainable performance as well as corporate accountability in achieving sustainable performance.
4. Business sustainability should reflect both strengths (social responsibility, customer satisfaction) and concerns (downside, risks, negative attributes, noncompliance with related regulations) regarding achieving performance in all EGSEE dimensions of sustainability.
5. There is a need for more improvements in communicating sustainability information to all stakeholders.
6. Sustainability reporting and assurance guidelines and practices should be advanced and promoted to create consistent and uniform disclosures of sustainability information.[13]

The following nine challenges should be addressed in corporate reporting:

1. **Stakeholder-centric focus:** Corporate reports should be value-relevant to all stakeholders, including shareholders, creditors, suppliers, customers, employees, government, the environment, and society.
2. **Forward-looking information:** Corporate reports should provide forward-looking information about strategic decisions and performance.
3. **Integrated and holistic reports:** Corporate reports should provide financial and nonfinancial information on KPIs relevant to all five EGSEE dimensions of sustainability reporting.
4. **Digital corporate reports:** Future corporate reporting should be in digital form, as explained in the next sections.
5. **Principles-based reporting:** Focus of corporate reporting on the multiple-bottom-line of economic, governance, social, ethical, and environmental performance necessitates the use of a principles-base reporting approach. The principles-based approach should define the conceptual framework for EGSEE sustainability reporting and reflect integrated thinking by organizations.

6. **Simplicity and ease of the preparation:** The unnecessary complexities (measurement and valuation, compliance with rigid rules and standards) in sustainability reporting should be reduced.
7. **Transparency:** Future corporate reporting should be transparent and balanced in disclosing both favorable and unfavorable KPIs.
8. **Assurance:** Assurance should be obtained on the EGSEE information reported. Depending on the nature of the information, different levels of assurance—from reasonable (audit level) to limited or moderate (review level)—could be obtained.
9. **Consistency in sustainability disclosures:** A uniform and standardized sustainability reporting is needed to completely, accurately, and consistently identify, measure, recognize, and disclose sustainability information on all five dimensions of EGSEE sustainability performance.

Guideline on Sustainability Reporting

The Global Reporting Initiative (GRI) has developed a framework for sustainability reporting that is applicable to all EGSEE dimensions of sustainability performance for organizations of all sizes and types.[14] The GRI in its G4 version, which is planned to be published in 2013, presents new concepts, trends, and requirements of best practices of sustainability reports. G4 is designed to improve the content of G3 and G3.1 and to move toward convergence in sustainability reporting.

The emerging move toward sustainability reporting requires management to develop a right balance of managing all EGSEE activities in creating sustainable shareholder value while protecting interests of other stakeholders, including creditors, employees, suppliers, customers, government, environment, and society, based on the global sustainability guidelines developed by the GRI and the International Integrated Reporting Committee (IIRC). The IIRC released a discussion paper entitled "Towards Integrated Reporting: Communicating Value in the 21st Century," in December 2011.[15] This discussion paper is intended to generate dialogues among policymakers, regulators, standard-setters, investors, the business community, the accounting profession, and academics worldwide for the development of an integrated report that encompasses financial, governance, compensation, environmental, and social information alongside managerial commentary. The five guiding principles of integrated reporting are:

1. **Strategic focus:** Defines the strategic objectives of achieving sustainable performance.

2. **Connectivity of information or "integrated thinking":** Represents connections among all aspects of an organization's activities from strategic objectives to performance evaluation.

3. **Future orientation:** Includes management expectations about the future and policies to establish the right balance between short-term and long-term objectives.

4. **Responsiveness and stakeholder inclusiveness:** Defines an organization's relations and interactions with all of its stakeholders, including shareholders, creditors, suppliers, the environment, and society.

5. **Conciseness, reliability, and materiality:** Provide concise and reliable information that is material in assessing sustainable performance.[16]

Materiality and Sustainability Reporting

Materiality is an important issue to ensure disclosure of important financial items while avoiding information overload. Materiality is a matter of professional judgment that can be influenced by a number of factors. The four common thresholds for materiality used historically for financial reporting are:

1. Relevance to an organization's operation, investment, and financing activities.
2. The qualitative importance of the activities.
3. The quantitative significance of activities.
4. The capability of affecting users' decisions.

The same four materiality thresholds used in financial reporting can also be applicable to all four other dimensions (governance, ethics, social, environmental) of sustainability performance. The emerging sustainability issues, along with risks and opportunities associated with all five EGSEE dimensions of sustainability performance, underscore the importance of the materiality concept in sustainability reporting and assurance. The SEC in its disclosure guidance on climate change describes materiality as "information is material if there is a substantial likelihood that a reasonable investor would consider it important in deciding how to vote or make an investment decision, or, put another way, if the information would alter the total mix of available information."[17]

Role of Gatekeepers in Sustainability Reporting

Corporate gatekeepers responsible for overseeing business sustainability and its reporting and assurance are the board of directors, particularly the audit committee, management, internal auditors, legal counsel, and the external auditors.

Management's responsibilities are for the development of business sustainability mission, strategies, actions, performance, and reporting. Management is particularly responsible for the completeness, accuracy, reliability, and quality of the company's sustainability report on all five dimensions of sustainability performance, including financial statements and internal control over financial reporting, establishment, maintenance, and enforcement of corporate codes of conduct, the effectiveness of corporate governance, fulfillment of social responsibilities, and compliance with environmental rules and regulations.

The audit committee should oversee business sustainability developments, strategies, actions, performance, risk assessment, reporting, and assurance on all five EGSEE dimensions of sustainability. Internal auditors should work under the oversight of the board of directors in assisting management in effective discharging of its business sustainability responsibilities. Internal auditors can also work with external auditors to provide assurance on sustainability reports. The legal counsel's responsibility is to ensure that sustainability events and transactions are executed in accordance with applicable rules, regulations, and standards and represent the company in case of violations of applicable laws. Independent auditors should provide appropriate assurance on all EGSEE dimensions of sustainability performance, as discussed in the next section.

The Use of XBRL in Sustainability Reporting

Extensible Business Reporting Language (XBRL) format has recently gained considerable attention and is becoming an integral component of corporate reporting. XBRL is a standardized machine-readable language intended to enable the electronic communication of business information with the main purpose of making business information more accessible, as well as facilitating timely and accurate analysis of both internal and external business information. Companies and the users of corporate reports can electronically search, download, and analyze information that is tagged in the XBRL-format, based on a defined taxonomy. The XBRL tags are processed by XBRL-enabled software applications, which present a standardized structure for the content of information and its contextual attributes.

The SEC has recommended since 2009 that public companies submit, and post on their corporate websites, financial information using XBRL format for their financial reporting purposes. Furthermore, XBRL format can also be applied to all five EGSEE dimensions of sustainability performance, as discussed throughout the book. The largest public companies (top 10 percentile) in all industries are submitting XBRL-formatted financial information to the SEC, which includes their financial statements along with the accompanying foot-notes and schedules. Submitted XBRL-based financial statements are intended to impact only the format of submitted statements not the content and amount of information presented.

The accounting profession in general, and the Big 4 auditing firms in particular, have trained and educated many public companies and their investors about XBRL and its process implications. Taxonomies for XBRL applications have been developed for different industries and are based on United States GAAP as well as IFRS. Public companies and their financial reporting preparers and investors should soon begin their XBRL implementation efforts effectively in advance of any mandatory XBRL submission. The listed companies in Singapore are already required to file their financial statements in XBRL and it is expected that other countries will follow suit. Regulators in other countries are allowing the use of XBRL, including Australia, China, France, Germany, India, Japan, the Netherlands, Sweden, and the United Kingdom.

Organizations worldwide are now able to use the latest in digital reporting technology by publishing their financial statements in XBRL. External auditors can also provide their assurance on XBRL-based financial statements, which make audit reports uniformly available on XBRL reports. It is expected that the preparation of sustainability reports in XBRL will be the next step in fully digitalizing corporate reports. The use of XBRL-based corporate reports necessitates utilization of continuous auditing which takes assurance reports a step closer to electronic auditing. Users of XBRL reports will benefit from assurance on these reports. Companies listed in the United States are now liable for the content of their XBRL reports filed with the SEC. The International Financial Reporting Standards (IFRS) Foundation published its exposure draft of the IFRS Taxonomy 2012 for public comment in January 2012.[18] The proposed IFRS Taxonomy 2012 is the first IFRS Taxonomy to integrate common practice extensions to the IFRS XBRL Taxonomy. These extensions were developed through an analysis of about 200 IFRS financial statements and are intended to assist companies to file IFRS compliant financial statements online.

The XBRL-formatted reporting can advance the use of sustainability reporting. The mandatory use of XBRL-formatted financial reporting is an important step in applying XBRL to all five EGSEE dimensions of sustainability performance as well as effective and efficient analysis by all participants (board of directors, management, auditors, legal counsel, financial analysts, regulators, investors) involved in the corporate reporting process. Sustainability data can be tagged for each of the five EGSEE dimensions with the use of XBRL to be read and processed by computers. Once sustainability data is tagged based on XBRL taxonomies they maintain their attributes when they move from one computer platform to another. The tags describe each of the five EGSEE dimensions of sustainability performance data with both human and machine readable and understandable labels in relation to other sustainability data elements and applied sustainability frameworks (e.g., version 4.1 of GRI). XBRL-tagged sustainability reports can be used by all stakeholders (investors, creditors, employees, customers, suppliers, government, society, and environment) interested in sustainability information. The global acceptance of XBRL-formatted sustainability reports requires a proper development of taxonomies for each of the five EGSEE dimensions of sustainability performance. The challenging issues are who will develop sustainability taxonomies and whether the developed taxonomies will be trusted and effectively used by providers of both sustainability reports and assurance, as well as users of the reports. The developers of sustainability reporting guidance should also consider establishing XBRL-formatted sustainability taxonomies. The global acceptance of XBRL-tagged sustainability reporting depends on the development of taxonomies for all five EGSEE dimensions of sustainability performance and the entire sustainability reporting. In March 2012, the GRI released its taxonomy for tagging sustainability data and the first public comment period on the development of G4 as its future guidelines.[19]

Mandatory Sustainability Reporting

Corporate stakeholders including investors, creditors, governments, employees, suppliers, customers, and civil society demand accurate, reliable, and relevant financial and nonfinancial information on KPIs on all aspects of business. Sustainability reports are expected to provide value-relevant information to both external and internal users of such reports. Stakeholders should have more transparent information about EGSEE performance, which will enable them to make more informed decisions. Sustainability reporting can create more incentives for management to refocus its goals, strategic decisions, and actions from a short-term to a long-term prospect and improve internal management practices, enabling companies to establish better relationships with stakeholders. The absence of EGSEE performance reporting handicaps stakeholders, as they are unable to differentiate between sustainable and unsustainable organizations.

The increasing number of global organizations voluntarily issuing sustainability reports, and the general perception of the related net benefits can provide incentives for organizations worldwide to issue these reports. Organizations that perform better financially are more likely and have more incentives to initiate sustainability reporting. The potential benefits of providing sustainability information are that stakeholders will be able to obtain relevant and useful information regarding long-term financial sustainability performance, as well as performance on ethics, governance, social responsibility, and environmental issues. More sustainability disclosures may also increase firm value by mitigating agency problems and by improving managerial production and investment decisions. Potential costs of sustainability reporting relate to the preparation of sustainability reports, obtaining assurance on these reports and the associated opportunity costs of those involved with the sustainability reporting and assurance process. The potential effects (net benefit) of sustainability reporting should become apparent and should encourage policymakers and regulators worldwide to consider mandatory sustainability reporting and related assurance. Currently, sustainability reports are largely a matter of choice by individual organizations. Policymakers and regulators should be cognizant to the increasing demand by investors for sustainability disclosure and consider mandatory sustainability reporting in their future rule-makings. Corporations should consider the ever-increasing attention to EGSEE sustainability performance and understand the key drivers of business sustainability that will eventually affect their strategic decisions. Global use and popularity of voluntary sustainability reporting is regarded by many as a stepping-stone to a mandatory sustainability reporting in the foreseeable future.

The existing sustainability reports are rather complex and inconsistent. They are composed of disclosures of voluntary information on some aspects of EGSEE sustainability performance dimension—such as ethics, social responsibility, and governance typically encouraged by the GRI guidance—as well as mandatory financial reporting required by financial regulators and standard-setters, and semi-mandatory requirements on environmental matters. Lack of uniformity and diversity of compliance make sustainability less globally applicable, accepted, and enforceable. This complexity in sustainability reporting is further complicated by the different levels of assurance provided on different dimensions of sustainability performance—for example, reasonable assurance on economic performance; limited assurance on other dimensions. Nonetheless, mandatory compliance on economic and environmental sustainability performance and voluntary initiatives on ethical, social, and governance performance is evolving as more companies worldwide are issuing sustainability reports to disclose their business sustainability performance indicators, improvements in sustainability strategies, and compliance requirements. It is the authors' hope that, despite the perceived complexity in the sustainability reporting and assurance process, global organizations continue to disclose sustainability information that reflects their commitment to improve performance in all five EGSEE sustainability dimensions while assessing the challenges and opportunities of business sustainability. As a future state, automation of sustainability reporting and assurance by using the XBRL-formatted reporting and continuous assurance process can significantly reduce the reporting complexity and promote uniformity.

Sustainability information can be disclosed to corporate stakeholders by several means:

■ Annual reports to shareholders and other stakeholders, particularly in the management discussion and analysis (MD&A).
■ A stand-alone voluntary report disclosing all five EGSEE dimensions of sustainability performance.
■ Integration into business and market indices and/or credit rating metrics
■ Mandatory standardized and globally accepted sustainability reports.

Sustainability disclosures as of now are voluntary with less uniformity in content and format. The market-driven and voluntary reporting is effective as long as stakeholders demand it and the majority of companies are willing to issue such reports. Mandatory sustainability reporting can be more uniformly enforced and widely used. Benefits of mandatory sustainability reporting are:

1. Better uniformity and standardized reporting that reduces the potential for purposefully reporting strengths and intentionally omitting concerns.
2. Promotion of comparability in sustainability reporting by using mandated and enforceable sustainability standards.
3. Enable all stakeholders to have access to uniform, standardized, and comparable sustainability information in assessing EGSEE sustainability performance.

4. Encourage management to focus on sustainable financial performance rather than short-term achievement of earnings targets.
5. Stakeholders will be better served in making informed decisions.

However, the argument against mandatory sustainability reporting is twofold: (1) many encourage a check-a-box compliance mentality rather than true presentation of sustainability information; and (2) it may create an unnecessary compliance burden to smaller companies with higher compliance costs. Alternatively, public companies can be given the hybrid option of the "comply or explain" mechanism which allows companies to comply with a set of globally accepted sustainability reporting standards (e.g., G4 of GRI) or choose not to comply as long as their decision is properly explained (e.g., feasibility, scaling, cost effectiveness).

Sustainability reporting is now voluntary even though South Africa, Singapore, and some countries in the European Union (Sweden) require all their listed companies to issue sustainability reports. Many recent initiatives have promoted mandatory sustainability reporting. Global adoption of sustainability reporting through market-driven forces and regulatory-enforceable standards is needed to promote universal and uniformed sustainability disclosures.

Sustainability Reporting in Action

The global issuance of sustainability reports has made significant progress in the past decade, and as of September 2011 more than 3,000 global companies disclosed sustainability information.[20] Many companies worldwide may still be reluctant to release sustainability information on their governance, ethics, social, and environmental performance that may raise expectations and create further accountability for them to improve their performance in these areas. Other companies may face the challenges of finding best practices to disclose complete, concise, accurate, reliable, comparable, and standardized sustainability reports that are transparent, useful, and relevant to all stakeholders. Further evolution is, in many cases, required in the internal reporting systems and process to produce the information with all of the attributes described above.

The European Commission (EC) is recently considering whether to require disclosure of nonfinancial environmental, social, and governance (ESG) information. The EC is considering determining what types of organizations would be required to disclose ESG information, which international framework (e.g.,

GRI) would serve as a standard reporting guideline, and if and to what extent ESG disclosure would be integrated with financial information in one annual report.

A study conducted by the Conference Board shows that during the 2011 proxy season, the number of shareholder proposals on social and environmental policy issues has increased from 28.1 in 2007 to 29.1 percent in 2010.[21] In 2011, 243 proposals related to matters of social and environmental policy were submitted, which constitutes about 35.2 percent of the total number of proposals. This suggests shareholders are now paying closer attention to social and environmental issues as well as the long-term value generation potentials of sustainability strategy.

The environmental dimension of sustainability performance includes reducing an organization's carbon footprint, creating a better environment, and improving the air and water quality of the property and the surrounding community.

The social dimension of sustainability performance ranges from better employee health and well-being to becoming a positive contributor to the sustainability of the planet and improving the quality of life for future generations.

The economic dimension of sustainability performance includes increased focus on long-term sustainability, effectiveness, efficiency, and productivity; cost savings in energy, water, and supplies; attracting new business and building greater customer loyalty and reputation; improved risk management and safety and fostering collaboration with other innovative companies.

The examination of best practices of sustainability reporting as described in Exhibit 10.4 suggests that companies who are planning to issue sustainability reports should take the following steps:

1. Understand and assess the risks of material misstatements in sustainability reports.
2. Address the challenges and opportunities involved with disclosing EGSEE performance in sustainability reports.
3. Design and implement effective and efficient accounting and internal control systems to properly identify, classify, measure, assess, recognize, and disclose all EGSEE dimensions of sustainability performance.
4. Ensure commitment from the board of directors and top-level management to business sustainability and sustainability reporting.
5. Comply with all applicable sustainability laws, rules, regulations, and best practices (labor to environmental initiatives).

6. Obtain assurance on all five EGSEE dimensions of sustainability perform-ance as examined in the next section.
7. Ensure quality and quantity of sustainability disclosure.

SUSTAINABILITY ASSURANCE

The number of companies issuing sustainability reports is growing. These reports should currently include assurance from an external assurance provider (and certainly will in the future). Unlike audit reports on financial statements, assurance reports on sustainability information are neither standardized nor regulated or licensed. A number of professionals including internal auditors, external auditors, and other service providers currently offer assurance on sustainability reports. The Big 4 accounting firms have developed expertise in sustainability reporting and assurance and they are well equipped with a long history in assurance to provide sustainability assurance services.

Sustainability Assurance Guidance

The type and extent of sustainability reporting influences corporate reporting which, in turn, may have implications for audits of EGSEE performance, including historical financial statements, as well as internal control over financial reporting. A number of global professional organizations have estab-lished assurance standards relevant to all dimensions of sustainability perform-ance, as summarized in Exhibit 11.1. The eight risk assessment standards issued by the Public Company Accounting Oversight Board (PCAOB), which are intended to improve the effectiveness of the auditor's assessment of and response to risk of material misstatement in an audit of financial statement, can be applied to the assessment of all five risk components (strategic, operations, financial, reputation, compliance) of business sustainability.[22]

In April of 2011, the International Federation of Accountants (IFAC) released its revised "International Standard on Assurance Engagements Other Than Audits or Reviews of Historical Financial Information," 3000 (ISAE 3000).[23] Specifically, ISAE 3410 deals with assurance engagements for an organization reporting greenhouse gas (GHG) statements. The assurance engagement covers assurance procedures performed surrounding a GHG statement, and any remainder of the statement. ISAE 3410 does not deal with: statements of emission that are not GHG emissions; related GHG emission information (e.g., KPIs based on such data); or offsetting projects used by other entities as emission deductions.[24]

EXHIBIT 11.1 Guide to Sustainability Reporting for Listed Companies

Organization	Link	Mission	Standard
AccountAbility Standards	http://www.accountabilty.org	AccountAbility Standards' mission is to set the standards for Corporate Responsibility and Sustainable Development	The AA1000 AccountAbility Principles Standard (AA1000APS) The AA1000 Assurance Standard (AA1000AS) The AA1000 Stakeholder Engagement Standard (AA1000SES)
AICPA	http://www.aicpa.org	AICPA's mission is to form members using the best resources, information, and leadership in a manner which provides the public, employers, and client's valuable services in the highest standards of professionalism.	Statements on Auditing Standards (SASs) Statements on Standards for Attestation Engagements (SSAEs) Statements on Quality Control Standards (SQCSs) SAS Nos. 122–124 SAS No. 125 AU section 9558A
Canadian Charted Accountant	http://www.cica.ca/	Canadian Charted Accountant's mission is to gain and increase public confidence in CA's professionalism and profession by acting in the public interest and by sustaining their members to excel.	International Standards on Auditing as Canadian Auditing Standards (CASs) Canadian Standards on Quality Control (CSQCs) International Standards on Quality Control (ISQCs) International Standards on Auditing (ISAs) GAAP
Corporate Register .com	http://www.corporateregister .com/	Corporate Register's mission is to provide the content of their work free of charge as a service to the global CR stakeholder community, to provide	AA1000

(continued)

EXHIBIT 11.1 *(Continued)*

Organization	Link	Mission	Standard
		specialist tools for advanced users (some of them may have fees) and maintain the quality of their site and services, in order to advance CR globally.	
Global Reporting Initiative (GRI)	https://www.globalreporting.org/Pages/default.aspx	GRI's mission is to continue to support companies that are involved in sustainability and reporting by answering questions about why and how to report and provide guidance to companies and other organizations worldwide.	G3
International Auditing and Assurance Standards Board (IAASB)	http://www.ifac.org/auditing-assurance	IAASB shaped their mission around public interest: developing a strong and professional accountancy organization and firm by adopting and implementing high-quality international standards and designing high-quality practices for professional accountants; speaking out on public interest issues where the accountancy profession's expertise is most relevant.	International Standards on Auditing (ISAs) International Standards on Quality Control (ISQCs)
International Standard on Assurance Engagements (ISAE) 3000	http://www.ifac.org/sites/default/files/publications/exposure-drafts/IAASB_ISAE_3000_ED.pdf	ISAE standard performs in a limited assurance engagement. Amongst other matters, the practitioner is required to determine the nature, timing, and extent of the procedures to be performed to obtain a level of assurance that is meaningful to intended user.	ISAE 3000 ISAE 3402 ISAE 3410
PCAOB	http://pcaobus.org/Pages/default.aspx	The PCAOB mission is to provide information to prepare informative, accurate, and independent audit reports. They also oversee the audits of public companies in order to protect the interests of investors and further the public interest; the audits of broker-dealers, including compliance reports filed in federal security law.	Rule 3100 AS1-15 AU200, 300

The revised ISAE 3000 is a principles-based standard designed to be applied effectively to a broad range of subject matter engagements relevant to an organization's activities, reports, and related assurance. The revised ISAE 3000 provides a framework based on the principles of assurance level, materiality, completeness, and professional judgment. Consistent with the original ISAE 3000, the revised standard also uses the terms "reasonable assurance" and "limited assurance" to distinguish between the two types of attestation and direct engagements. According to the revised ISAE 3000, the underlying subject matter can take many forms, including financial and nonfinancial performance and conditions, physical characteristics (capacity of facilities and environmental plans), system processes (internal control and IT system), and behavior (governance, ethics, and society). All of these underlying subject matters are applicable and relevant to EGSEE dimensions of sustainability performance presented throughout this book.

The practitioner providing assurance services should measure and evaluate the sustainability against established and predetermined criteria. Criteria are benchmarks, thresholds, standards, rules, regulations, laws, and best practices used in measuring, evaluating, and reporting the underlying subject matters. The selected criteria should be commonly acceptable, relevant, reliable, understandable, transparent, applicable, suitable, enforceable, and consistent. The practitioner should take the following steps:

1. Obtain an understanding of the organization's five EGSEE sustainability performance measures.
2. Obtain an understanding of the organization's current and prospective sustainability initiatives.
3. Perform analytical procedures designed to enhance the understanding of the relations among different components of EGSEE sustainability performance and identifying areas of high risk that might affect reliability of financial statements.
4. Conduct assessment of sustainability risks.
5. Encourage communication among the audit engagement team members regarding EGSEE sustainability dimensions that might affect the risks of material misstatement of financial statements.
6. Rest the effectiveness of internal control systems used to collect, compile, process, and disclose EGSEE sustainability performance.
7. Perform audit procedures to gather sufficient and appropriate evidence on reported sustainability information.

8. Interview the board of directors, management, and other personnel charged with the preparation of EGSEE sustainability reports.
9. Confirm certain sustainability information with outside parties where applicable (donations, environmental initiatives).
10. Review important documents relevant to business sustainability mission, objectives, strategies, policies, and procedures.
11. Decide on the type and level of assurance that can be given on each dimension of EGSEE sustainability performance.

A summary of the existing assurance standards is summarized in Exhibit 11.1 and some key observations:

■ Assurance standards on different dimensions of sustainability performance vary in terms of vigorousness and general acceptability; however, the accounting profession has standards and a history in assurance.
■ Auditing standards, either AICPA (for audit of private companies) or PCAOB (for audit of public companies) in the United States as well as International Auditing and Assurance Standards (IAAS) primarily govern reporting and assurance on economic activities; however, they can be applied to sustainability information.
■ Assurance standards on other dimensions of sustainability including governance, ethics, social, and environmental standards are yet to be harmonized on a global basis and there are very significant variances between standards applied. There is a marked difference between those applied by the accounting profession and those applied by others currently providing assurance.
■ The International Standard on Assurance Engagements (ISAE) 3000, issued by the IAAS Board in 2004, provides guidance for assurance on nonfinancial dimensions of sustainability.
■ The American Institute of Certified Public Accountants (AICPA) AT 101 provides assurance standards on nonfinancial information.
■ The Canadian Institute of Charted Accountants (CICA) Handbook, Section 5025, offers assurance guidance on nonfinancial information relevant sustainability reports.
■ AA1000 Assurance Standards (AS), issued in 2008 by AccountAbility (AA), is applicable to management, reporting, and assurance services on nonfinancial dimensions of sustainability performance and is the standard most often used by non-accountants.

Reasonable versus Limited Assurance Engagements

In general, the extent of test procedures performed differs between levels of assurance. Depending on the standards applied, these levels of assurance are described differently but represent the same thing. The highest level of assurance is described as *reasonable* (ISAE 3000), *examination* (AT 101), or *audit* (CICA 5025) levels of assurance but, for simplicity, will be referred to in the following discussion as *reasonable assurance*. The lower level of assurance can be described as *limited* (ISAE 3000), *moderate* (AT 101), or *review* (CICA 5025) level assurance. A reasonable assurance engagement provides a positive opinion on whether the subject matter is, in all material respects, appropriately stated and the work performed is, of course, greater than under a limited assurance engagement. A limited assurance engagement provides what is called a negative opinion—nothing has come to our attention to cause us to believe that the subject matter is not, in all material respects, appropriately stated. A limited assurance engagement requires a lower level of work and consists primarily of enquiry and analysis supplemented by substantive work in those areas of the highest risk only.

The proposed ISAE 3000 provides additional guidance about:

■ Factors that are relevant to the practitioner's consideration, judgment, and conclusion.
■ Criteria designed to help readers better understand the differences between reasonable and limited assurance.
■ The determination of a threshold level of assurance for limited assurance engagements for the intended users.
■ The materiality concept that is determined based on professional judgments that are not affected by the level of assurance, but made in light of surrounding circumstances.

Aspects of test procedures in a limited assurance engagement including timing, nature, and extent are determined based on the practitioner's understanding of the engagement's circumstances, underlying subject matters, critical events, risk of significant misstatement of information, the materiality of information presented, the level of meaningful and relevant assurance for intended users, and professional judgment. The common understanding is that applied evidence-gathering procedures in a limited assurance engagement include an understanding of the client's subject matters (social, governance, ethics, environmental performance); inquiries of management, board of directors, and personnel; and analytical procedures. The assessment of the effectiveness of internal controls concerning subject matter information is recommended but not required. Additional test procedures may be performed if the practitioner becomes aware of matters that cause the him or her to believe the information may be materially misstated. Evidence gathered by performing additional procedures should assist the practitioners in either concluding that the area of concern is not likely to cause the subject matter information to be materially misstated, or determining that the issue causes information to be materially misstated. Appropriate working papers should be prepared for both reasonable assurance and limited assurance engagements. Working papers should document the type of engagement, considered subject matters and related information, engagement standards applied, test procedures performed, evidence gathered, and conclusions reached.

The primary objective of providing assurance on sustainability reports is so the practitioner can conclude on the assurance—reasonable or limited—presented by EGSEE sustainability performance. The assurance offered on sustainability reports by practitioners is intended to enhance the users' confidence level on sustainability performance information based on the evidence gathered by comparing and measuring sustainability subject matters with established criteria. The practitioner may present reasonable assurance on sustainability information where the gathered evidence supports the conclusion that the risk of material misstatement on the underlying subject matter is low. An unmodified conclusion (often referred to as "clean") can be offered in the case of the reasonable assurance engagement, where the gathered evidence supports the practitioner's conclusion that the subject matter information is prepared, in all material respects, in accordance with the applicable criteria. An unmodified conclusion can be offered in the case of a limited assurance engagement, where nothing comes to the attention of the practitioner that causes the practitioner to believe that the subject matter information is not prepared, in all material respects, in accordance with the applicable criteria. A modified conclusion should be expressed where the practitioner either cannot gather sufficient competent evidence to reach a conclusion or the practitioner decides that reported underlying subject matter information is materially misstated. In these cases, the practitioner expresses either a qualified, adverse, or disclaimer conclusion worded in terms of the underlying subject matter and the criteria.

Sustainability assurance on EGSEE performance reports based on the degree of assurance and content can be classified into three distinct sections or reports as follow:

1. Positive assurance on financial statements reflecting economic performance.
2. Positive assurance on internal control over financial reporting (ICFR).
3. Positive/negative assurance on sustainability reports pertaining to governance, social, ethical, and environmental performance.

The opinion paragraph on financial statements should read as follows:

In our opinion, the financial statements referred to above present fairly, in all material respects, the financial position of Any Company as of December 31, 2012 and 2011, and the results of its operations and its cash flows for the years then ended in conformity with generally accepted accounting principles.

The opinion paragraph on ICFR should read as follows:

In our opinion, Any Company maintained, in all material respects, effective internal control over financial reporting as of December 31, 2012, based on [*Identify control criteria, for example, criteria established in Internal Control - Integrated Framework issued by the Committee of Sponsoring Organizations of the Treadway Commission (COSO)*].

The opinion paragraph on the other four dimensions (governance, ethics, environmental, and social performance) can be as follows:

To the best of our knowledge, we have found that Any Company satisfactorily and effectively applied the Global Reporting Initiative (GRI) Sustainability Reporting Framework Version 4.1 and meets the content requirements pertaining to governance, social, ethics, and environmental dimensions of sustainability performance as of December 31, 2012.

Alternatively, offer a positive assurance on the entity's governance, ethics, social, and environmental performance by stating in the opinion paragraph that:

In our opinion, Any Company satisfactorily and effectively applied the Global Reporting Initiative (GRI) Sustainability Reporting Framework Version 4.1 and meets the content requirements pertaining to governance, social, ethics and environmental dimensions of sustainability performance as of December 31, 2012.

Attestation and Direct Engagements

An assurance engagement according to the Proposed ISAE 3000 can be either an attestation engagement or a direct engagement. Attestation engagements are also known as audits and reviews, where a party other than the practitioner measures or evaluates the underlying subject matter against the established and predetermined criteria and the practitioner expresses an opinion regarding the extent of compliance with the criteria. Direct engagements often referred to as *performance* or *value-for-money* audits, where the practitioner measures or evaluates the underlying subject matter against the criteria and then presents the resulting subject matter information as part of, or accompanying, the assurance report. In a direct engagement, the practitioner is not independent of the subject matter information because the practitioner develops the information, measures, or evaluates the underlying subject matter and applies assurance skills and techniques to gather sufficient evidence in order to express a conclusion regarding whether the subject matter information is materially misstated. However, the practitioner should be independent from the engaging party presenting the subject matters and the intended users of the assurance report.

Content and Format of Sustainability Assurance Reports

The credibility of sustainability reports can be improved by obtaining assurance on those reports. The main structure and content of sustainability assurance are similar to those of conventional independent assurance statements. The suggested four-paragraph sustainability assurance report should consist of the following elements:

1. **The addressee of the assurance report:** The assurance report should be addressed to either the entity's board of directors, management, or intended users.
2. **Reference to sustainability information:** The opening paragraph of the report should identify all the sustainability performance dimensions that are being reported on EGSEE. These sustainability performance

dimensions are typically presented by management in the sustainability reports.

3. **Criteria used in sustainability reports:** Management should identify in the sustainability reports guidelines and criteria used in the preparation of the report. The assurance provider should use the criteria as a benchmark in assessing the effectiveness, efficiency, completeness, reliability, and transparency of sustainability EGSEE performance.

4. **Responsibilities of management and assurance provider:** The responsibility of management and assurance provider should be clearly defined with regards to the sustainability report. Management is primarily responsible for the preparation, content, completeness, and reliability of information presented in sustainability reports. The assurance provider is responsible for the assurance conclusions provided on the reports.

5. **Discussion of scope of the work done by the assurance provider:** The scope of work done by the assurance provider should include the criteria used, analytical procedures, inquiries, and other evidence-gathering procedures performed to test for assessing the risk of material misstatements in sustainability reports. Evidence gathered should be documented and used as a basis in reaching sustainability conclusions.

6. **Description of the type and level of assurance provided:** The opinion paragraph should describe the type of the assurance on the integrated EGSEE sustainability performance or separate dimensions of the report. The assurance level (positive or negative) on the integrated report of each separate EGSEE dimensions should be clearly described.

7. **Date of the assurance report:** The date of completion of the assurance report should be specified.

8. **Signature of the assurance provider:** The assurance report should be signed by the assurance provider.

Sustainability Risk Assessment

The practitioner (audit firm) should properly assess all five sustainability-related risks (strategic, operations, compliance, reputation, and finance), as discussed in Chapter 2. Every sustainability assurance engagement presents a different set of challenges to audit firms and other service providers, as no two companies are the same and thus require different assurance considerations based on the identified risks. These sustainability risks should be incorporated into the overall audit risk model of inherent risk, control risk, and detection risk. Regardless of the type of sustainability assurance engagement—either reasonable or limited—the practitioner should assess the risk of material misstatement in sustainability information by:

1. Obtaining an understanding of the client's business sustainability, industry, and environment.
2. Inquiring of management and personnel regarding possibilities of misstatements in sustainability information.
3. Performance of analytical procedures.
4. Study and evaluation of internal controls.

SUSTAINABILITY ASSURANCE AND INTERNAL CONTROL

Internal controls are relevant to all five EGSEE dimensions of sustainability performance in the same manner that they are for financial information. The quality, integrity, and reliability of sustainability information depend on the effectiveness of the design and operation of the processes and internal controls that produces such information. Two factors that should be considered in the assessment of particular internal controls are (1) whether internal controls reduce risk of material misstatements in sustainability reports to an acceptable level; and (2) whether internal controls are cost-effective in preventing, detecting, and correcting material errors, irregularities, and fraud in sustainability reports. The Committee of Sponsoring Organizations (COSO), in 2011, released its improved Internal Control - Integrated Framework, which is useful and effective in assessing internal controls in achieving sustainable performance and increased focus on its application for internal control over external financial reporting.[25] The revised framework is designed to assist the board of directors, management, auditors, and other stakeholders in assessing internal controls. The new framework defines 5 components of internal controls and 17 principles associated with these components. These 5 components and the related 17 principles of internal controls are applicable to all five EGSEE dimensions of sustainability performance.

EMERGING TRENDS IN SUSTAINABILITY REPORTING

The 2012 joint study of Ernst & Young and GreenBiz Forum based on a survey of about 270 respondents at leading companies in 24 sectors worldwide identifies the following seven emerging trends in sustainability reporting.[26]

1. **A rise in sustainability reporting:** The survey indicates that 76 percent of respondents are now issuing sustainability reports, and 93 percent of those that are not issuing such reports are expected to do so in the next five years. Despite this emerging trend in sustainability reporting, while very encouraging, improvements need to be made to enhance reliability, credibility, and assurance on both quantitative and qualitative KPIs for all five EGSEE sustainability dimensions. Some dimensions of sustainability (financial, governance, and environmental) are more standardized and quantitatively measurable and reportable, whereas other dimensions (social and ethics) are currently reported in qualitative terms.

2. **An increase in the CFO's sustainability role:** The survey shows that one out of six CFOs are currently actively involved with the sustainability reporting process and about half are somewhat engaged. As the demand for and interest in sustainability information increases, more CFOs will be involved in preparing financial and nonfinancial KPIs on all EGSEE dimensions of sustainability performance.

3. **Employee as stakeholder:** The survey shows that employees are the second most important stakeholders after customers, who are actively engaged in sustainability programs and reporting. It is expected that more effective communication between management and employees encourages more employees to get involved with sustainability initiatives, and employees will be the main force behind future sustainability programs.

4. **GHG reporting:** The survey suggests significant growth in reporting on greenhouse gas and water use despite regulatory uncertainty.

5. **Risk of strategic materials:** The survey indicates growing concern about access to strategic raw materials (conflict minerals) as a business supply-chain issue in manufacturing products.

6. **Ratings and rankings:** The survey suggests a growing attention to outside rankings on sustainability lists and ratings in sustainability indices on the part of corporate executives.

7. **Sustainability assurance:** The survey underscores the importance of a third-party assurance (accounting firm) on sustainability information in lending more credibility to sustainability information.

SUSTAINABILITY ASSURANCE IN ACTION

A large number of sustainability assurance service providers, including audit firms, have provided sustainability assurance on sustainability information.

Exhibit 10.6 presents a sample of sustainability reports and assurance and content of such reports. Audit firms are well qualified and equipped to perform sustainability assurance services for their clients. Before accepting a sustainability engagement, the auditor should gather information about:

1. The extent, nature, and type of the client's sustainability activities and performance.
2. The complexity of the client's business sustainability.
3. The reputation, commitment, and qualifications of senior management and the board of directors.
4. The necessary expertise to effectively complete the sustainability engagement.
5. The preliminary assessment of the potential risks associated with the proposed sustainability engagement.

SUSTAINABILITY DATABASE

As more companies worldwide are issuing sustainability reports on all or many EGSEE dimensions of sustainability performance, there is an urgent need to establish a uniform, standardized, and globally useful sustainability database. This global database can be utilized by companies as a benchmark to compare their own sustainability performance. Credit agencies can use the database in developing sustainability indexes in ranking companies' sustainability performance and in establishing sustainability scorecards and best practices. Policymakers and regulators can use sustainability databases in their future sustainability rulemaking process. Investors and other stakeholders can use a sustainability database in comparing their company's sustainability performance to that of other companies in the industry, industry average performance, or globally. In 1991, RiskMetrics Groups created a sustainability database, known as KLD STATS. KLD STATS provides ratings for approximately 650 companies that comprise the FTSE KLD 400 Social Index and S&P 500. The database was significantly expanded in 2001 and 2003 and now it is covering more than the 3,000 largest U.S. companies by market capitalization. The KLD STATS sustainability database has been used by researchers working on a number of sustainability-related studies. The Thomson Reuters ASSET4 database and Bloomberg Terminals (approximately 300,000+) can also be used to get information on social, environmental, and governance (SEG) sustainability performance.

SUSTAINABILITY EDUCATION

In the aftermath of 2007-2009 global financial crisis and resulting economic downturn,companies worldwide are focusing on business sustainability as a strategic imperative to achieve not only quarterly financial results but also long-term EGSEE performance. Despite the importance of business sustainability and sustainability practices and disclosures to corporations and investors, sustainability education yet to be properly integrated into business curriculum. Business and accounting curricula should be reassessed worldwide in light of evolving business sustainability.

The public, regulators, the accounting profession, and the academic community are also taking a closer look at colleges and universities in order to find ways to hold these institutions more accountable for achieving their mission of providing higher education with relevant curriculum. A recent study of 1700 public and privet institutions of higher education indicates that about one-third of colleges and universities have been on an unsustainable financial path and another 28 percent are at the risk of become unsustainable.[27] Long-term sustainability of colleges and universities is vital to the economic growth and prosperity of our nation in preparing the next generation of human capital. The next generations of business leaders must understand the importance of ethical conduct, business sustainability and corporate governance, social responsibility and environmental matters. Thus, business curriculum must reflect promotion of ethical behavior, professional accountability, and personal integrity taught to business students. Corporate governance, business sustainability, ethics including accountability, integrity, and transparency must be integrated throughout the business curriculum.

CONCLUSION

The concept of business sustainability and corporate accountability has become an overriding factor in successful strategic planning for many organizations worldwide. It is driven by the idea that an organization must extend its focus beyond making profit by considering the impact of its operation on the community, society, and the environment. This concept of the triple bottom line is often used to assess an organization's success from three perspectives— profit, people, and the planet. This expansion of determining an organization's sustainable performance and long-term value-adding strategies has driven a need for new reporting and assurance processes, which extend beyond financial statements into disclosing financial and nonfinancial KPIs on EGSEE activities. Currently, more than 3,000 organizations worldwide including many Fortune 500 companies have adopted GRI for sustainable performance reporting and more companies are expected to follow suits. Many public companies now voluntarily manage, measure, recognize, and disclose sustainability information. Mandatory reporting of sustainability performance information and assurance of the same can bring more uniformity and consistency in sustainability reports.

ACTION**ITEMS**

1. Be ready and prepare to address emerging sustainability challenges and opportunities.
2. Consider recent initiatives by regulators are designed to strengthen auditors' independence, objectivity, and professional skepticism.
3. Transform the concept of sustainability into business strategies, decisions, activities, and performance.
4. Obtain external assurance on your sustainability reports from independent assurance providers.
5. Obtain formal/informal and/or positive/negative assurance on your sustainability reports.
6. Make sure your non-audit client brochure promotes your expertise and capability to provide external assurance services on sustainability reports.
7. Ensure overall sustainability issues are addressed, sustainability performance dimensions are measured, and relevant sustainability information is disclosed.
8. Make sure sustainability developments address entire sphere of risks, challenges, and opportunities, including risks relevant to strategic, financial, operations, compliance, and reputation.
9. Ensure your sustainability strategies reflect key successes and shortcomings as well as challenges and opportunities.
10. Ensure your sustainability development is a holistic process that enables stakeholders to understand how your organization is really performing in achieving its social, economic, and environmental value and in showing the link between an organization's strategy, governance, and business model.

11. Make sure sustainability reporting reflects analysis of the impacts of material financial and nonfinancial opportunities, risks, and performance across the value chain, and their interconnections in achieving the organization's overall performance.

12. Provide your stakeholders with early signals of material risks and uncertainties threatening your operations and performance.

13. Assess the reasonableness, quality, and reliability of assumptions and estimates used in the preparation of sustainability reports including financial statements.

NOTES

1. Kruschwitz, N., and K. Haanaes. 2011. "First Look: Highlights from the Third Annual Sustainability Global Executive Survey," *MIT Sloan Management Review* 53(1).

2. International Integrated Reporting Committee (IIRC). 2010. "Integrated Reporting Academic Network Response to IR Discussion Paper December 2011." Available at: http://www.theiirc.org/wp-content/uploads/2012/02/Global-Integrated-Reporting-Academic-Network-United-Kingdom.pdf.

3. United Nations (UN) Global Compact and Accenture. 2010. "A New Era of Sustainability." Available at: https://microsite.accenture.com/sustainability/research_and_insights/Pages/A-New-Era-of-Sustainability.aspx.

4. Ioannou, I., and G. Serafeim. 2010. "The impact of corporate social responsibility on investment recommendations." Harvard Business School working paper, No. 11-017; Ioannou, I., and G. Serafeim. 2010. "What drives corporate social performance? International evidence from social, environmental, and governance scores." Harvard Business School working paper, No. 11-016; Ioannou, I., and G. Serafeim. 2010. "The impact of national institutions and corporate sustainability on investment recommendations." Harvard Business School working paper.

5. Deloitte. 2011. "Sustainability strategy 2.0: Next-generation driver of innovation." Available at: http://www.deloitte.com/view/en_US/us/Services/additional-services/sustainability-climate-change/by-issue/79377f8055c40310VgnVCM2000001b56f00aRCRD.htm.

6. Ibid.

7. International Federation of Accountants (IFAC). 2009. "Sustainability Framework." Available at: http://viewer.zmags.com/publication/052263e2#/052263e2/1 - could only find "IFAC Sustainability Framework 2.0"

8. Ibid. 5.

9. International Integrated Reporting Committee (IIRC). 2010. "Integrated Reporting Academic Network Response to IR Discussion Paper December 2011." Available at: www.theiirc.org/wp-content/uploads/2012/02/Global-Integrated-Reporting-Academic-Network-United-Kingdom.pdf.

10. Singapore Stock Exchange (SGX). 2011. "SGX Guide to Sustainability Reporting for Listed Companies." Available at: rulebook.sgx.com/net_file_store/new_rulebooks/s/g/SGX_Sustainability_Reporting_Guide_and_Policy_Statement_2011.pdf.

11. For a complete listing of organizations currently providing sustainability reports see: Global Reporting Initiative (GRI). 2011. Available at: http://database.globalreporting.org.

12. Soyka, P.A., and M.E. Bateman. 2012. "Finding Common Ground on the Metrics that Matter." Investor Responsibility Research Center (IRRC) Institute. Available at: www.irrcinstitute.org/pdf/IRRC-Metrics-that-Matter-Report_Feb-2012.pdf.

13. Ibid.

14. Global Reporting Initiative (GRI). 2011. "G3 Sustainability Reporting Guidelines." Available at https://www.globalreporting.org/reporting/latest-guidelines/g3-guidelines/Pages/default.aspx.

15. International Integrated Reporting Committee (IIRC). 2011. "Towards Integrated Reporting: Communicating Value in the 21st Century." Available at: http://www.theiirc.org/the-integrated-reporting-discussion-paper/.

16. Ibid.

17. Securities Exchange Commission (SEC). 2010. "Commission Guidance Regarding Disclosure Related to Climate Change," Release Nos. 33-9106; 34-61469; FR-82. Available at: http://www.sec.gov/rules/interp/2010/33-9106.pdf.

18. International Financial Reporting Standards (IFRS). 2012. "Exposure Draft of the IFRS Taxonomy 2012," press release, January 18, 2012. Available at: http://www.ifrs.org/Alerts/XBRL/Exposure+Draft++IFRS+Taxonomy+2012.htm.

19. Ibid.

20. For a complete listing of organizations currently providing sustainability reports see: Global Reporting Initiative (GRI). 2011. Available at: http://database.globalreporting.org/.

21. Tonello. M., and M. Aguilar. 2012. "Shareholder proposals: Trends from Proxy Seasons (2007-2011)." The Conference Board. Available at: http://ssrn.com/abstract=1998378.

22. Public Company Accounting Oversight Board (PCAOB). 2010. "Auditing Standards Related to the Auditor's Assessment of and Response to Risk and Related Amendments to PCAOB Standards," Release No. 2010-004. Available

at: http://pcaobus.org/Rules/Rulemaking/Docket%20026/Release_2010-004_Risk_Assessment.pdf.

23. International Federation of Accountants (IFAC). 2011. "Revised International Standard on Assurance Engagements Other Than Audits or Reviews of Historical Financial Information 3000 (ISAE 3000)." Available at: http://www.ifac.org/auditing-assurance/.

24. IFAC. 2011. "ISAE 3410, Assurance Engagements on Greenhouse Gas Statements, Exposure Draft." Available at: http://www.ifac.org/sites/default/files/publications/exposure-drafts/20110111-ISAE_3410_GHG_Exposure_Draft-V1-final.pdf.

25. Committee of Sponsoring Organizations (COSO). 2011."Internal Control: Integrated Framework, Exposure Draft." Available at: www.ic.coso.org.

26. Goodman. Ann. 2012. The 6 Biggest Trends in Sustainability Reporting. Ernst & Young and GreenBIz. Available at http://www.greenbiz.com/blog/2012/01/30/6-biggest-trends-sustainability-reporting

27. Blumenstyk. G. 2012. One-Third of Colleges Are on Financially "Unsustainable" Path, Bain Study Finds. The Chronicle of Higher Education (July 23). Available at http://chronicle.com/article/One-Third-of-Colleges-Are-on/133095/?cid=at&utm_source=at&utm_medium=en#top

About the Authors

Ann Brockett, CA, Partner, Americas Climate Change and Sustainability assurance leader, leads the Climate Change and Sustainability Services assurance practice in the Americas. Ann serves a broad range of clients and has 18 years of professional experience working with public and private clients both globally and in the Americas. In that role, Ann helps clients to identify and develop alternatives to address emerging risk areas both operationally and from a reporting perspective and also provides financial and non-financial assurance services.

- Subject matter professional with many years of experience serving clients across a range of industries on climate change, carbon management, and sustainability.
- Extensive experience serving large, global organizations
- Ann has familiarity with the North American greenhouse gas regulatory and market schemes, with particular knowledge of the implementation challenges of regulatory programs.

Ann has a Bachelor of Commerce (honours) degree from Memorial University of Newfoundland and is a Canadian Chartered Accountant.

Zabihollah Rezaee is the Thompson-Hill Chair of Excellence and Professor of Accountancy at the University of Memphis and has served a two-year term on the Standing Advisory Group (SAG) of the Public Company Accounting Oversight Board (PCAOB). He received his B.S. degree from the Iranian Institute of Advanced Accounting, his M.B.A. from Tarleton State University in Texas, and his Ph.D. from the University of Mississippi. Professor Rezaee holds ten certifications, including Certified Public Accountant (CPA), Certified Fraud Examiner (CFE), Certified Management Accountant (CMA), Certified Internal Auditor (CIA), Certified Government Financial Manager (CGFM),

Certified Sarbanes-Oxley Professional (CSOXP), Certified Corporate Governance Professional (CGOVP), Certified Governance Risk Compliance Professional (CGRCP), Chartered Global Management Accountant (CGMA), and Certified Risk Management Assurance (CRMA). He has also been a finalist for the SOX Institute's SOX MVP 2007, 2009, and 2010 Award.

Professor Rezaee has published over 200 articles in a variety of accounting and business journals and made more than 210 presentations at national and international conferences. He has also published six books: *Financial Institutions, Valuations, Mergers, and Acquisitions: The Fair Value Approach*; *Financial Statement Fraud: Prevention and Detection*; *U.S. Master Auditing Guide*, 3rd edition; *Audit Committee Oversight Effectiveness Post-Sarbanes-Oxley Act*; *Corporate Governance Post-Sarbanes-Oxley: Regulations, Requirements, and Integrated Processes*; *Corporate Governance and Business Ethics and Financial Services Firms: Governance, Regulations, Valuations, Mergers and Acquisitions*, and contributed to several other books. Three of these books are translated into other languages including Chinese, South Korean, Spanish, and Iranian.

Index